PRAISE FC

SESSION

"A veteran of low-ABV 'session' brewing, Jen Talley brings an enormous amount of practical and technical information to this subject. It's obvious her time at Squatters Pub Brewery in Utah fostered respect for the art and soul of brewing beers under 4.0% ABV. **As someone who has been at this business of brewing for over 20 years, I can honestly say this book provided some keen insights into the thought processes and execution behind these fickle beer styles.** I for one cannot wait to share this information with my brewers."

—TOMME ARTHUR, Co-Founder and Brewmaster, Lost Abbey and Port Brewing Co.

"I was so thrilled to hear Jen Talley was writing this book. Jen always struck me as someone who could create anything despite whatever barriers were in her way. Way back in the early days of craft brewing, instead of seeing brewing in a low-alcohol state as a constraint, Jen found creativity and flavor. **This book contains an immense breadth of knowledge, history, and brewing recipes.** It is clear from this lovingly crafted book that every brewer should embrace the art of brewing session beers, if not for the challenge, then for the reward of being able to drink more than one and still enjoy oneself. Thanks Jen—I will have another!"

—MARY PELLETTIERI, Co-Founder and President, La Pavia Beverages, Inc.
and author of *Quality Management: Essential Planning For Breweries*

"After growing ever bolder with high-alcohol beers in the US, session beers have brought back beers for us to drink and enjoy. *Session Beers* **looks back to those authentic and exciting lower-alcohol beers that were there before the term** 'session beer' existed."

—PETER BOUCKAERT, Founder and Brewmaster, Purpose Brewing and Cellars,
and co-author of *Wood and Beer: A Brewer's Guide*

SESSION

brewing for flavor and balance

BEERS

By Jennifer Talley

BREWERS
PUBLICATIONS™

Brewers Publications™
A Division of the Brewers Association
PO Box 1679, Boulder, Colorado 80306-1679
BrewersAssociation.org
BrewersPublications.com

Proudly printed in the United States of America.

10 9 8 7 6 5 4 3 2 1
ISBN-13: 978-1-938469-41-1
Library of Congress Cataloging-in-Publication Data

Names: Talley, Jennifer, 1969- author.
Title: Session beers : brewing for flavor and balance / by Jennifer Talley.
Description: Boulder, Colorado : Brewers Publications, a Division of the
  Brewers Association, [2017] | Includes bibliographical references and
  index.
Identifiers: LCCN 2017021710 | ISBN 9781938469411 (pbk.)
Subjects: LCSH: Flavored alcoholic beverages--United States. | Beer--History.
  | Brewing--History.
Classification: LCC TP577 .T35 2018 | DDC 663/.42--dc23 LC record available at
https://lccn.loc.gov/2017021710

Publisher: Kristi Switzer
Technical Editor: Dan Burick
Copyediting: Iain Cox
Indexing: Doug Easton
Production and Design Management: Stephanie Johnson Martin and Jason Smith
Cover Design: Kerry Fannon
Production and Interior Design: Justin Petersen
Interior Images: Jennifer Talley unless otherwise noted
Cover Photo: Aaron Colussi

For my mother, Jane Talley, theatre director and teacher; and my father, Rick Talley, sportswriter, broadcaster, and author. They taught me that the most important lesson in life is to believe in myself and to never stop dreaming.

Table of Contents

Foreword

We had already drunk a lot of beer that day. We were not drunk as such, but the convivial spirit was strongly evident. Good friends, learning much, laughing easily; no one would have chosen for it to be any different on that day. What day it was, I cannot recall, for there have been many like it, a pool of brewing friends subtly shifting across time and space. In historic Bamberg, sunny San Diego, urban Chicago, and rural Belgium we enjoyed the company, the conversation, and the beer. Drinking beer that was fashioned creatively from carefully chosen ingredients and with attention to detail, not to mention and brewed with a moderate alcohol content, afforded us the chance to take full advantage of our incredibly fortuitous circumstances. By the end of the evening, each of us eagerly looked forward to repeating the experience again. When stringing together perfect days like these, moderation is crucial. Session beers are an important component of the agenda for this group. Across the table paraded a selection of tasty beers: Pilsner, wit, summer ale, lambic, dry stout, and, often to end the evening, a Sierra Nevada Pale Ale.

With this book in your possession, you hold the insightful thoughts of a gifted brewer and regular participant in these adventures. Jen is a good friend, who, from my perspective, is uniquely qualified to take on the subtleties of session beer for a few reasons.

I first met Jen through Dan Burick. Dan and I were part of the small handful of craft brewers mixed into the 1990 diploma class at the Siebel Institute of Technology. Each of us was constrained in our brewing approach at our respective breweries. I was making traditional English ales in Boston, while Dan was focused on American brews then evolving in (mainly) the western US states. Both of us made low alcohol, flavorful beers that stood in stark contrast to the industrial light lager that dominated the shelves and taps throughout the 1970s and 80s. For me, the "low gravity" approach was driven by tradition, for Dan, it was legally mandated by the state of Utah. Over the years, our close friendship remained consistently strong and included trips to visit each other. It was through Dan that I soon met Jen, his passionate and intelligent assistant brewer at Squatters. After a few years, the brewery business expanded, and in 1995, as Dan moved to build and helm the new ventures, Jen took charge at the pub. It was here that Jen focused on incrementally developing the new brands that would drive the portfolio across the entire business. A milestone on her path of learning included winning a scholarship to attend the Siebel Institute early in her career.

Brewing while constrained by tough alcohol limits presents all brewers with a flavor quandry that necessitates creative solutions, and this challenge fed Jen's curiosity. Jen is both extremely practical and intellectually gifted. I can count on the thumbs of one hand the number of people who raced mountain bikes and put themselves through a masters degree in social work while working as a professional brewer. (That one would be Jenny.) Inevitably, the conversation would drift to, and stick on, some detail of brewing. Beer pH, lautering technique, hopping schedule, sour microbes, everything seemed to be fair game and pursued until understood.

A particularly vivid example occurred on a memorable trip a group of us took to Orval. When invited to sit down with Jean-Marie Rock in his brewmaster's office, pleasantries were exchanged, beer was served, and the line of questioning by Jen began. After going over brewhouse technique, Jen next began to explore the correlation between dry hopping and microbial action in secondary fermentation.

"And how much hops do you add for the dry hop addition?" asked Jen.

Jean-Marie, in his excellent but strongly accented English, replied, "The perfect amount!"

After further probing by Jenny that somehow failed to discern any definitive quantity, she finally stated, "I'm sorry, but I don't understand."

"You are correct!" was the enthusiastic response from the veteran brewmaster. Clearly, we were in the presence of a Jedi master.[1] Over the years that followed, Jenny capitalized the numerous opportunities to further the friendship with Jean-Marie and thus avail herself of his considerable technical knowledge.

It was this tenacious focus and accumulated knowledge, plus multiple brewing trials, that facilitated Jen's entry into the world of beer competition. She was drawn to these competitions for a number of reasons. The chance to meet and converse with extraordinary brewers, sample and analyze exceptional examples of brewing styles, and put her beers to the rigors of independent and blind judging, all seem to factor into it. She is both passionate and well-informed in the judging salon and a frequent visitor to the awards stage. The medal record for her and the team that supports her is awesome. Between 2000 and 2012, I counted more than 20 medals won at the Great American Beer Festival® and the World Beer Cup[SM], spread across a diverse group of beer styles. This is all the more remarkable because of the alcohol constraints imposed on brewers in Utah.

Nobody cheers louder than Jen for their brewing buddies at an awards ceremony when they acquire hard-won hardware. Jen cares deeply for the greater community of her brewing peers. When you talk to accomplished brewery veterans like John Harris of Ecliptic brewing in Portland, who met Jen during his long tenure at Full Sail, you get a sense that that respect goes both ways. Harris remarked that Jen is a "very solid brewer," and her technical prowess was rightfully recognized when she won the Russell Schehrer Award for Brewing Innovation. This honor is administered by the Brewer's Association and annually granted by prior recipients to a brewer who has demonstrated technical acumen transformed into extraordinary beer and brewing practice.

In addition to passionately exploring, questioning, and judging beer and brewing techniques, Jen also has the ability to home in on flavor. Most professional beer tasting is a skill learned through training and focus. There is a physiological aspect to the ability to taste and describe beer, but practice is critical. I know that Jenny does this diligently and well, and I believe it allows her to successfully

---

[1] I have a sense that Jean-Marie could have just as easily waved his hand and stated, "This is not the dry hop rate you were looking for," followed up with an Obi-Wan styled, "Move along now."

incorporate feedback, completing the cycle of beer development whereby a recipe is "massaged" into its final form through multiple iterations. These are the small details that build into a greater whole—no magic bullet, just lots of little steps along the road to extraordinary beer. The elements that build to what Mark Dorber, the venerable and respected English publican, would phrase as "beauty in beer" are hidden in these small details.

So, what will you find as you read this book? First off, the answer to the question, "What are session beers?" For Jenny, they are identified as highly drinkable, well balanced, flavorful beers below 5% alcohol by volume (ABV). Although the ABV benchmark is somewhat arbitrary, definitions are needed. Ya gotta draw the line somewhere.

Next it is on to exploring the great history and tradition of session beers. The decidedly quaffable English examples cover the full range from light ales, bitters, and milds, to approachable porters and stouts. For me, the pleasures of sitting with friends in a cozy English pub are fully interwoven with the soft flavors that flow so readily within the constraints of moderate alcohol.

Belgian specialties and the wide range of traditional beers of Germany are the next subjects to be covered. The brewers who came to the New World used these beers as a springboard to develop new and uniquely American styles. Throughout the book, Jen tells the background story about how American adjunct lager evolved.

We all know making an overhopped malt bomb is relatively easy; there are lots of places to hide off flavors. Finesse and balance are absolutely necessary for delectable lighter beers. Jen's insightful lessons in the second chapter are interwoven with a personal brewing philosophy born out of long experience. Jen highlights time and again how finesse and balance are central to brewing these delicate beers. As our mutual friend James "Otto" Ottolini, Chief of Brewing Operations at Brew Hub, points out "While a Session Beer may be simpler than many styles, there is an elegance in simplicity making it ultimately sophisticated when done well. Yet doing things well and even simple can be a rather complex matter."

As you will find, sensory evaluation plays a very important role for Jen. The training that she has received and continues to develop is the next subject to be covered. Although safety and sanitation are not the sexiest parts of brewing, they are crucial underpinnings for success, and Jen makes sure to address this.

Drinkability and fostering the culture of responsible drinking are big reasons why hop-forward pale ales and session IPAs have grown in popularity in recent years. This important subject and its attendant commercial considerations, often overlooked in works like this, are clearly explained with good coverage. Developing these commercial and financial considerations further, Jen rounds off the first half of this book with an instructive look at the cost of doing business for brewpubs and microbreweries.

For me, the great collection of beer recipes in the second half, generously peppered with the personal stories of the brewers who make them, stands as the shining heart of this book. The raw brewing talent that is represented in this compendium is stunning and a testament to Jen's ability to connect with other brewers.

In conversation with Dan Burick about Jen, his friend and longtime workmate, he readily paints a picture of a driven and passionate brewer. When Jen wanted to make a new beer, step one was to understand the style. Recalls Dan, "She would organize these ridiculous tastings—organized by style—and pull together lots of people. She has a gift for bringing people together." The community Jen attracted was expansive and engaged. The opportunity to communicate about beer flavor morphed into a successful mug club at the brewery that grew into a huge following. Dan goes on to say that the more Jen would learn, the deeper her passion for beer and brewing grew: "She started high and went further. Awesome formulation technique, good brewing and cellaring practices, and attention to detail."

Through it all, Jen has a sensibility of personal style. Dan relates that during the workday Jen was wholly committed, always in white brewing coveralls and boots, but that she was equally committed at the Christmas party and other social events; she would consistently "knock it out of the park" in all aspects of brewery life. As Jen herself explains in this book, it is partially the love of spending time at good parties that drives her to focus on session beers. Immoderation just doesn't work well when matching beers with someone carrying twice your mass and duties to attend to at the brewery the following day.

I don't think that it could be said better than Dan Burick has, so we will close with his thoughts: "Jen is a good friend, and a good brewer."

John Mallett
Director of Operations, Bell's Brewery, Inc.

Acknowledgments

One of the greatest lessons I have learned in life is that I don't know everything. Thank goodness my mother raised me well and taught me the power of humbleness and open-mindedness. When I returned from my first trip to Belgium, I knew I wanted to create a barrel-aged sour beer. Despite years of being a professional brewer, I had a lot to learn about making barrel-aged sours, so I took a huge bite of humble pie and got to studying. After a year of discussion, conversing, and (mostly) listening to all my brewing friends I was successful in releasing my first sour beer. In writing this book, I took the same mindset. Of course, I had a lot to say in regards to designing, brewing, and drinking session beer, but without the brewing community and my family to help this book would never have come to fruition.

The first person I must thank is my mother, Jane Talley. If anyone in the world can remind me that I can do whatever I set my mind to, it is my mom.

She often reminds me of her favorite saying taken from Ray Bradbury, "You've got to jump off the cliff all the time and build your wings on the way down."[1] My mother is a true inspiration for me in every area of my life, from family to brewery to love. She is my guiding light and I do not thank her enough. This book could not have been written without her. In addition, thank you to my children, Dylan and Vienna Knab, who had to tolerate Mom's time at the computer (not an easy thing to do at ages ten and seven). The weekend would come and they had to give up our usual family time together to allow me the opportunity to write. Thank you, D and V, you are my life.

One of the most amazing elements about being a brewer, aside from the free beer, is being part of the greater brewing community. I do not know any other industry quite like ours. The sense of comradery and fellowship we share is extraordinary, it binds us together and makes us stronger. I would like to thank Randy Mosher and Ray Daniels, both great authors who have inspired and encouraged me in my writing, as well as deliberated beer history and styles with me. Both Randy and Ray provided wonderful insight into the historical perspectives chapter. I also have the joy of working with Ray at the Cicerone® Program. Randy and Ray's depth of understanding about beer is unparalleled and their willingness to share their knowledge is truly inspirational.

When it came to writing about hops I instantly thought of speaking to Val Peacock. Val has an incredible wealth of knowledge and experience about all things hops, and he has a true passion for exploring all possibilities when it comes to increasing quality hop bitterness, flavor, and aroma. Val believes in the value of questioning, and was happy to help me explore and increase my understanding of our mutually beloved and favorite plant. I would like to thank both John Mallett and Scott Heisel for the great insight they provided regarding all things malt. Both John and Scott are experts in the field of malts and malting, and they also provided great insight into the adjunct side of brewing. Additional appreciation goes out to Ron Ryan, formerly of the Cargill Malting Group, who spent significant time discussing the subject of protein in malted barley and the role it plays in brewing.

Squatters Pub and the Salt Lake Brewing Company will always have a special place in my heart. They were my family for two decades and the relationships I built there I will cherish forever. I could not have written this book without the opportunity they gave me in the brewery to develop my skills

---

[1] N.Y. Times News Service, Luaine Lee, "Learning is solitary pursuit for Bradbury," *Herald-Journal* (Spartanburg, SC), October 14, 1990, C1.

and learn how to brew session beer. Dan Burick, former brewmaster at Utah Brewers Cooperative and original brewmaster at Squatters, was and continues to be a mentor and dear friend of mine. He is always there to help review my ideas about brewing and especially discuss session beers. He provides me support and continued learning along the way. Other pivotal people from my Squatters family I want to especially thank are Peter and Debra Cole, Jeff and Suzy Polychronis, Joe and Lori Lambert, Jon and Heather Lee, and Jason Stock. I would also like to give huge appreciation and and a big thank you to my current brewery owners, Brian and Lisa Ford at the Auburn Alehouse, for allowing me the time and energy to write this book and keep my love for session beers alive at their brewery.

It was such a joy for me to be able to connect and reconnect with so many of my friends and fellow brewing associates while writing this book. Thank you to Mitch Steele, Garrett Oliver, Ron Jeffries, Deborah and Dan Carey, Dave Colt, Clay Robinson, Greg Schirf, Larry Bell, Florian Kuplent, Andrés Araya, Eric Dunlap, Kevin Templin, Brock Wagner, Kevin Bartol, Eric Rose, Marshall Rose, Ken Grossman, Rob Todd, Jason Perkins, Steve Hindy, Tom Kehoe, Mary Pellettieri, Christopher Bird, Fal Allen, Matt Brynildson, Jim Helmke, Tom Schellhammer, Finn Knudson, Yvan De Baets, Vinnie Cilurzo, Stan Hieronymus, Gary Spedding, Nick Funnel, Steve Parkes, Greg Casey, Carl Heron, Keith Lemke, Peter Hoey, Jan Adriaensens, Jean-Marie Rock, and Guido Waldecker for their knowledge and generosity. A large thank you goes out to all the breweries and brewers continuing to produce great session beers across America and who generously contributed their recipes for this book. Thank you to the Brewers Association staff for their help with this book, especially Chris Swersey, Julia Herz, Dave Carpenter, and Bart Watson. I want to thank the Brewers Association for having the faith in me to write this book and incredible support it provided along the way. Kristi Switzer, my publisher, encouraged me every step of the way and made the daunting process of writing a book digestible, piece by piece. The Brewers Association is an important organization to craft beer in America and its team is fundamental to our continued growth and success.

Introduction

Quality was probably not at the forefront of my Grandfather Herr's mind when he was brewing up his illegal bathtub beer during Prohibition. Grandpa Herr was a hard-working farmer and handy man in rural central Illinois. Black work pants, a black work shirt, and a black baseball cap were his only clothes. He hunted deer for the family table, churned his own butter and ice cream, brewed his own beer, and had hands that felt like sandpaper. He smelled of Camel cigarettes and sweat; I loved him dearly. Grandpa Herr, son of German immigrants, represents the working class of America that grew up on session American premium lager. It is from this stock that I was born as a brewer.

In my late teens I fell in love with both music and beer; this is no surprise as the two go very well together. I toured the countryside endlessly following many bands, but especially the Grateful Dead. When the live music ended for the night, the parking lot came alive. Veggie burritos, tie-dye t-shirts, and beer were just a few of the favorite offerings found on Shakedown Street. Time and time again I found myself reaching for a Samuel Smith's Oatmeal Stout, a 5% alcohol by volume (ABV) oatmeal stout. The rich molasses flavor, moderate alcohol, and unique bottle shape kept me coming back for more. I learned very early on in life that I didn't just love drinking flavorful beer, I loved drinking flavorful beer all evening. I am 5'8" and 125 lb.; this means drinking a lower-alcohol beer allows me to enjoy a longer evening out with friends without ill effects the next morning.

In my early twenties I did not know what a beer style was, what it took to make a great beer, or that such amazing history existed behind beer. All I knew was what I liked. At 21 years of age, I was lucky enough to attain my first brewing job and find my calling. Brewing is my passion. For the past 25 years, I have been honing my skills in constant search of how to create the most flavorful and diverse craft beer for my local community. Twenty of those years have been spent specifically brewing session beers.

My brewing career started at Squatters Pub Brewery in Salt Lake City, Utah in 1991. The state law, which still exists today, dictates that any beer served on draught in Utah must be no higher than 4% ABV. Session beer was all we brewed. Funny thing was, we didn't call it session beer at the time. We simply called it beer. To me and my fellow Utah brewers that was what beer was, high quality, great tasting, and highly drinkable. For the next two decades, all my time and energy was focused on improving 4% ABV beer. I will continue to reinforce throughout this book that, first and foremost, beer has to be made with an adherence to standards of the highest quality—session beer demands this devotion at the highest level.

In the early 1990s when I first started sampling beer from around Utah, a certain reoccurring sensory experience resonated: many low-alcohol beers, served side by side, had variable color but tasted very similar. Differentiating all fourteen taps at Squatters while maintaining the same low alcohol became one of my major goals. Through careful manipulation of ingredients and processes, a tap lineup of session beer can take on unique attributes and individual characteristics. For me, session brewing started out as a restriction, some would even consider it a handicap, but I soon discovered it to be an exciting challenge.

Around the start of the twenty-first century, the American craft market became inundated with highly alcoholic and, at many times, massively bitter "extreme" beers. Don't get me wrong, many beer styles demand a high amount of alcohol and hops, and can taste extremely delicious as a result. It seemed, however, in the early 2000s, if a beer was not over 7% ABV and 75 international bittering units (IBU), many self-proclaimed beer experts did not deem it worthy of brewing or purchasing.

The annual Beer Business Daily Summit held on January 30th, 2017 presented current trends in craft beers. As reported by Justin Kendall from the popular online brewing magazine *Brewbound*, analysts from Nielson, CGA Strategy, and CM Profit Group assessed that consumers are increasingly looking for beers that contain lower alcohol.[1] Session beer has deep roots in America and has been a part of the American craft brewing scene from the beginning, but for quite some time beer magazines, social media, and the craft beer buzz has centered on high-alcohol, highly hopped beer and crowned that king of craft.

I have been lucky enough to travel with friends to various countries around the globe, tasting all the world has to offer, visiting breweries, talking with fellow brewers, and listening to those at the bar describe their favorite local beers of the region. After multiple pints and banter, I am confident that culture plays a major role in the decisions we make in life, from selecting the city we live in or travel to, the career we should pursue, or the beer we drink at the end of the day. As a brewer or brewery owner, it is extremely important to watch cultural trends and examine the changing tide of the consumer's decision-making habits in the taproom.

About This Book

In chapter 1 we will briefly explore the beginnings and the history of low-alcohol beers that have been brewed with lots of flavor. Because this covers many different beer styles, we will journey around the world to the various locales where these balanced and flavorful beers are part of the cultural fabric and enjoyed for a variety of reasons. The United States has a fertile history in this regard, with a tradition of hard work going hand in hand with enjoying a session beer, and this book will explore both the origins of our European brethren, as well as the love for session beer in nineteenth-century America.

Presented in chapter 2 will be how to source and handle ingredients to produce a variety of session beer styles; in addition, how using creative brewing

---

[1]   Justin Kendall, "Session Beer, On-Premise Trends Highlighted by Nielsen at Beer Summit Conference," *Brewhound,* January 30, 2017, http://www.brewbound.com/news/session-beer-premise-trends -highlighted-nielsen-beer-summit-conference. .

processes can highlight and celebrate each beer's inner beauty. In chapter 3 we will discuss the many modern interpretations of session beer, and look toward the future of session beers, which have earned their seat at the craft beer table.

Chapter 4 examines the cultural milieu surrounding session beer drinking in America and Europe, as well as a look at the ever-shifting trends in regard to how session beer is approached by the consumer. Chapter 5 wraps up the first section with a detailed review of the typical cost considerations for a commercial craft brewery and brewpub.

The second section follows up with some stellar recipes from some of the finest brewers around the United States, and a few internationally as well. In each of chapters 6, 7, and 8 there is a large recipe section that will highlight for homebrewers and professional brewers the specific components that help create some of our favorite session beers in the marketplace.

Highlighted in this book will be how session beer has a distinctive place in craft brewing, can be widely diverse, and hold its own at brewpubs and in the taproom. I believe the fundamental principle of the craft brewing industry is the authentic education of the American people about the beauty and diversity that exists in beer; session beer unequivocally holds a seat at the table.

SECTION I

What Is a Session Beer?

The term "session beer" is a modern term that has only been in circulation in America since 1982 in its current iteration. Session beers themselves, however, have been produced globally for hundreds of years. Defining what a session beer is can be challenging when the term can represent so many different beer styles. Many session beers taste dramatically different from one another, and it tends to confuse and evade the craft beer consumer's palate.

For the purpose of this book with consideration to alcohol range, we will generally adhere to the definition used by the Great American Beer Festival® 2016 beer style guidelines:

Session beers are the color of the classic beer style being made to lower strength. Appearance may vary from brilliant to hazy to cloudy with style of beer being made to lower strength. Aroma depends on the style of beer being made to lower strength. Any style of beer can be made lower in strength than described in the classic style guidelines. The goal should be to reach a balance between the style's character and the lower alcohol content. Drinkability is a character in the overall balance of these beers. Beers in this category must not exceed 4.0% alcohol by weight (5.0% alcohol by volume). (2016 Great American Beer Festival: Competition Style List, Descriptions and Specifications, *s.v.* "16. Session Beer.")

Throughout my travels and interactions with brewers and multi-tap house owners alike, I often pose the question, what is a session beer to you? I usually hear various words to describe the same thing: it is an easy to drink beer, one that authentically represents a style, but without all the alcohol and is highly drinkable. Some of the greatest beer styles from around the world, such as *helles* and Vienna lager, fall in the session beer alcohol range. Trying to explain what a session beer is to German beer drinkers can be trying to say the least; to them, session beer is simply beer. Many folks will continue to argue the exact amount of alcohol that can exist in a beer termed a session beer. What is indisputably not up for debate is that session beer must be enjoyable to drink multiple pints of in a single sitting and be relatively low in alcohol. In addition, it must be unequivocally made of high-quality ingredients; low alcohol alone does not make a session beer.

The revered English writer, journalist, and beloved beer aficionado Michael Jackson had a beautiful vision about beer culture that was raw, simplistic, and incredibly insightful. Jackson addressed the judges during the Great American Beer Festival orientation and spoke to us about all the positive attributes beers possessed that would be judged over the next three days. He inspired us to look for the good and beauty in each beer, not just focus on perceived defects and negativity. This idea is important when thinking about session beers. The lower alcohol content is often dismissed by extreme beer lovers, but there are so many positive attributes of session beers to appreciate!

1

A Short History
of Session Beers

Defining a historical style of beer is customarily a straightforward process. Research the period in which it was first brewed, what breweries were producing beers in that style, and what was occurring in brewing culture at that time, and there you have it, a definition of a beer style. Session beer is not that straightforward. First, it is not just one style. Session beer encompasses many different styles that vary radically. While a German-style *leichtes weizen* and an English-style mild ale are both session beers, they are extremely different from each other. The term "session" is an adjective, an expression, a descriptor of certain beers rather than a style in and of itself. Defining session beer can feel like defining the undefinable.

There is much debate about what a session beer truly is. The discussion is tiresome for the most part and hinges on the question, how much alcohol can a beer have in it and still be a session beer? Lew Bryson has been writing about beer and spirits for over twenty years and has been a longtime contributor to *Whisky Advocate*. Bryson is an outspoken crusader and blogger for session beer and creator of a "non-profit, unorganized, unofficial effort to popularize and support the brewing and enjoyment of session beer", called The Session Beer Project™. Bryson defines session beer as a beer containing 4.5% alcohol by volume (ABV) or less, flavorful enough to be interesting, balanced enough for multiple pints, and conducive to conversation (Bryson 2017).

Conversely, the BeerAdvocate® website came out with their explanation of a session beer in 2005:

> *Any beer that contains no higher than 5 percent ABV, featuring a balance between malt and hop characters (ingredients) and, typically, a clean finish – a combination of which creates a beer with high drinkability. The purpose of a session beer is to allow a beer drinker to have multiple beers, within a reasonable time period or session, without overwhelming the senses or reaching inappropriate levels of intoxication. ("Session Beers, Defined," BeerAdvocate, October 12, 2005, http://www.beeradvocate.com/articles/653/)*

The term "session" in reference to beer has existed in conversation among brewers, writers, and most beer enthusiasts for decades. Although not specifically defined, beer lovers all seem intrinsically to know what a session beer is. Martyn Cornell, renowned and award-winning beer writer and expert on all things beer, has the most popular beer blog in Britain, *Zythophile*. On May 20th, 2011, Cornell dedicated an entire blog discussion to how old the term session beer is. Throughout the discussion no definitive resolution came to fruition; however, in the comments one reader presented a case for what is most likely the first use, in print, of the term "session beer." This *Zythophile* commenter cites the 1982 (first edition) *Pocket Guide to Beer* by Michael Jackson.

Jackson uses the term "session" in describing an evening where friends may meet at a pub, taking turns buying a round of "ordinary bitter" rather than a higher-alcohol bitter (Jackson 1982a, 73). Cornell responded to the commenter, ascertaining this very well might be the first use, in printed English, of the term session beer. Cornell personally advocates the term session beer being applied to beers at the lower end of the alcohol spectrum, as illustrated earlier in his blog post. I believe that session beers have a broad spectrum when it comes to their alcohol range, and can go as high as the just-tipping-over 5% ABV mark. In any case, the camaraderie for enjoying a session of beers together is not new and the level of alcohol may vary by drinker or event.

The Original Session Beers of the British Isles

Ales of England

One of the classic session beer styles was born in eighteenth-century England. Long before the development of the hand pump, the most commonly quaffed beer at local pubs was English bitter. Conditioned through secondary fermentation, providing for naturally low carbonation, and served at cellar temperature, bitters were drawn directly from the cask for the patron. The average draught bitter is near a starting gravity of 1.036 (9°P) and lies between 3%–5% ABV (Jackson 1982b, 146). When Michael Jackson was searching for the best way to describe England's bitters, he referred to Alan Brien of London's *Sunday Times*. Brien described the infamous English bitter romantically,

> *There were nights when six or seven pints coursed down as if served in magic thimbles. . . nothing can equal a good local brew after a long walk. . . faintly cloudy, just on the cool side of tepid. . . it wraps around you like a sticky horse blanket and cuddles you to sleep. (Alan Brien,* Sunday Times, *quoted in Michael Jackson,* The World Guide to Beer *[London: New Burlington Books, 1982], 166)*

Although Brien's poetic description paints a wonderful picture of how your evening is spent, it does little for describing the flavors associated with the traditional bitters of eighteenth-century England. Brewed in a range of colors, bitters ranged traditionally from golden to ocher brown. Since a true bitter undergoes a secondary fermentation in the cask, providing a lower carbonation level, it is not a gassy beer and provides a more calming and soothing experience for the palate. For the publican in the late eighteenth century, a desire to keep the beer slightly cooler, and to free up space behind the bar, meant casks were kept in the cellar when in use. Therefore, by the late eighteenth century the cask behind the bar had given way to the beer engine, a hand pump that manually draws a beer out, in its natural state, approximately half a pint per stroke (Jackson 1982, 163–64).

Within the catalog of English bitters exists three sub-styles: ordinary, best, and special bitter. While ordinary and best bitter categories are both the epitome of classic session beers, falling between 3% and 4.2% ABV for ordinary and 4.2%–4.8% ABV for best, the special bitter category pushes the alcohol content boundary, ranging as it does from 4.8% to as high as 5.8% ABV. Although the bitter style name implies high hopping rates, this is not the case; the hopping range is 20–35 IBUs for an ordinary bitter and 28–40 IBUs for best bitter.

THE CAMPAIGN FOR REAL ALE (CAMRA)

It is difficult to discuss the historical significance of traditional English bitter without mentioning the Campaign for Real Ale (CAMRA). CAMRA was started in the early 1970s by a group of beer drinkers in revolt against the move by large breweries to pasteurize and keg beer. At the time, much of the beer distributed in England under national brands was served from kegs, artificially carbonated and too cold, and lacked complexity and subtlety of flavor (Jackson 1982, 165).

With over 185,000 members, CAMRA continues to campaign for consumers' rights to traditional real ale. As loosely described by CAMRA, real ale is brewed using traditional ingredients, such as malted barley, water, hops and yeast, and undergoes a secondary fermentation in the container it will be dispensed from; furthermore, when tapped, no extraneous carbon dioxide will be used. If a beer-drinking trip to England is in your future and you want to discover old-style bitters, you certainly want to grab the newest copy of *CAMRA's Good Beer Guide* to help find your way into the finest pubs serving real ale and overflowing with customary pub culture. Bitters are the quintessential real ale and truly benefit from the subtle complexity developed during the secondary fermentation in the cask and the subsequent low levels of carbonation.

In the public houses of eighteenth and nineteenth-century England, mild ale was also quite common to find alongside the ordinary and best bitters. Mild ales were generally slightly lower in both alcohol and bitterness, darker in color, and with a malty, sweet taste. Fresh from the brewery, brewers used mild ale to blend with the stale beer in the market. This blend eventually transformed in what we now know as porter. Hence, the alcohol content of mild ales sometimes crept up as high as 6% ABV.

The mild ales produced today accurately represent the traditional style and no longer reach high ABV levels. The pale mild ale of England, as the name indicates, is the paler version of the classic dark mild, but it is equally as calming to drink; the classic English brown ale is the bottled version of the dark mild ale (Jackson 1982, 167). Due to its maltier profile and reduced price, mild ale was considered a worker's drink, certainly not that of an aristocrat. Jackson said it best when he referred to the classic mild as ". . . a delightful change from

PORTERS: NOT A SESSION, BUT A START

As the "real ales" of the eighteenth century were being swigged in watering holes throughout England, the darker side of session beer was soon to be born in Dublin, Ireland. To truly wrap one's head around the origin of the celebrated Guinness® dry Irish stout, it is necessary to walk back in time with its older brother, porter. The origin of how the porter style came into being is quite elusive; the general consensus is that its earliest form came from a blend of old and fresh ale created by the publican at the bar. This blended ale was consumed by workers after long hours carrying produce, vegetables, and dry goods from storehouses to markets (Oliver 2012, 661).

The original porters often had a brown or reddish color and sometimes expressed a slightly smoky, phenolic character derived from the open fire used in the toasting process of the malt. Brewers caught on to the rising popularity of blended ale and began brewing porter as a style. The initial alcohol range came in at around 4%–5% ABV, but some porters were brewed at a higher strength to nourish the strong men. Pub patrons could be heard at the bar boisterously requesting this "stout" porter from the publican. The alcohol range for these heavier stout porters came in at around 6%–7% ABV. While it is perhaps true that the early versions of porter had an alcohol range equivalent to that of a session ale today, it is extremely important to note that low alcohol alone does not make a session beer.

The first blended porters, prior to brewing porter to style by the breweries, consisted of aged ale from wooden casks, which was often vinous, stale, and slightly sour. Beer left undrunk in a wooden cask would become infected by various bacteria, such as *Lactobacillus* and *Pediococcus,* along with wild yeast, such as *Brettanomyces* (Foster 1992, 15). Although the original porters typically had a lower alcohol content, their often unplanned wild and slightly acidic flavor profile meant they were not deemed an acceptable example of a session beer. This is not to say that sour beers cannot be session beers by any means; rather, it is the crude and unpredictable way in which early porters soured that makes them unworthy as an example of a good sour session beer. As technology advancements in brewing improved, so too did the character of many London porters.

One of the largest brewers of porter, Barclay Perkins, hit the 300,000 barrel mark by 1827 before the porter craze started to level off. Changing consumer tastes, the resurgence of gin, and the growth of mild ale were just a few reasons why porter production started to diminish (Foster 1992, 38–39). By the late 1800s the porter style had fallen by the wayside and all that remained was its bold big brother, stout.

the bitter. Mild has pulled its cap down tight, tied its muffler round its collar, and confronted the cold winds of time and tide" (Jackson 1982, 167). Both the bitter and mild styles typify what a classic session beer is—just try to sit down with an old friend and only have one.

Emerging alongside the pale and dark mild ales of the eighteenth century were the first porters, first brewed under that name in 1722 (Jackson 1982, 156). The original gravity of modern porter is not what one would deem a session beer; however, it is important to pay tribute to the porter style because it gave birth to one of the most consumed session beers throughout the world today, Guinness® Draught dry Irish stout.

My Goodness, My Guinness

Arthur Guinness opened the famed St. James' Gate brewery in Dublin in 1759. The original stout brewed by Guinness was born out of the London porters and coined Foreign Extra Stout. It still possessed the phenolic characteristics from the blown malt used in the original porters, but also incorporated the new black "patent" malt produced in the roasting machine invented by Daniel Wheeler in 1817 (Alworth 2016). The next big flavor profile shift came after the passage of the Free Mash-Tun Act of 1880, which is discussed later in this chapter (see sidebar, "Taxation and Pricing"). The act allowed for the use of ingredients other than malted barley in brewing. As a result, English brewers started incorporating sugar, and Irish brewers took to using unmalted roast barley. Guinness' Foreign Extra Stout was a strong bottled beer aged in vats for a long period prior to packaging. After bottling with no priming sugar, wild yeasts carried over from the prolonged aging period worked away at the remaining sugars, changing its flavor profile and increasing the alcohol (Alworth 2016).

Alongside its bottled Foreign Extra Stout, Guinness produced a draught version of their stout that combined both vat-aged and young stout. Both alcohol and acidity were diminished in the draught stout due to this blending. The first draught version of Guinness stout was introduced in 1954 and served nitrogenized, which enhanced the already smooth character and created the most famous dark session beer in the world. The dry, yet intense, roast, coffee-like character of Guinness stout has never wavered and remains its primary defining taste today. Guinness Original (Extra Stout) is approximately 5% ABV, while Guinness Draught comes in at 4.2% ABV. Guinness stout remains popular worldwide, being brewed in 48 countries and served in over 100; it has been estimated approximately 10 million pints are enjoyed throughout the world daily (Oliver 2012, 66).

Beer lovers rarely forget their first night they spent wrapped up in pints of Guinness Draught. My first evening occurred in 1995, while attending a brewing course at the Siebel Institute for Technology. Friends and I walked to a neighborhood Irish pub. We threw darts and downed pints of Guinness Draught and I fell in love. I gained a sincere gratefulness for the trustworthy and refreshing Guinness Draught stout, and we have had a strong, honest relationship since.

Ales of Ireland

Guinness Draught stout is not the only session beer Ireland is known for. Long before the birth of porters and stouts in the eighteenth century, Franciscan monks brewed ales that fall into the session category. Smithwick's, the oldest working brewery in Ireland, first began brewing its famous Smithwick's Red Ale in 1710 in Kilkenny. Interestingly enough, it was not the people or even the breweries of Ireland that coined the term Irish red ale, it was brewing giant Coors Brewing in the early 1980s with the production of its very popular Killian's Irish Red. The recipe for this beer was originally brewed at the Lett's Brewery in Enniscorthy, Ireland in 1864 by the Killian family. Coors Brewing purchased the brand in the early 1980s and popularized it throughout America.

Traditional Irish ales are red in color, derived primarily from roasted barley, and driven by a caramel malt profile. These red beers have a mild hop bitterness and character and are extremely sessionable. Although the name implies that ale yeast is fermenting this American and Irish favorite, sometimes lager yeast is used. Irish red ales average between 4% and 4.6% ABV and although they often display a caramel and/or toffee-like malt profile they tend to finish dryer than the Scottish ales, giving them a more session-beer appeal (Oliver 2012, 495).

The city of Cork, Ireland was the birthplace of two very famous Irish breweries, Beamish and Crawford, and Murphy's. Established over 150 years ago, both breweries supplied the people of Ireland with classic, quaffable Irish red ales. Since the acquisition of these breweries by Heineken International, production of Beamish Red has stopped, while Murphy's Irish Red is still produced and exported throughout the world.

Dublin's brewing water is very high in bicarbonate, which creates a challenge for the breweries to keep the mash pH between the desired range of 5.2–5.5 (Kunze 2004, 219). It is no surprise that both traditional dry Irish stout and Irish red ale recipes call for the use, in varying degrees, of roasted barley, roast malt, and/or other caramel and crystal malts. Roasted specialty malts bring acidity to the mash, keeping the pH in the optimum range for wort extraction (Palmer 2017, 245). Dublin's water is also known for high levels of calcium. At low levels, both calcium and carbonate are considered flavorless

TAXATION AND PRICING

Taxation has always played a significant role in the operation of breweries, from what type of ingredients they use to how they price their beers in the market. In late seventeenth-century London beer outpriced gin, resulting in drunkenness throughout the streets and in the gin houses. Subsequently, Parliament answered by raising taxes on spirits and once again beer was back in the hands of the people (Moen 2003). In 1830 the Beerhouse Act was passed, allowing anyone to sell beer on his or her premises without obtaining a justice's license; therefore, it became very inexpensive and easy to open up an alehouse in England. The goal of the act's implementation was an attempt to dissuade the public from spending long periods of drunken debauchery in the popular gin houses, a move that proved to be quite successful. For the next decade, over 40,000 "beerhouses" opened and spread throughout all of England, making it very convenient for even rural folk to easily walk to their nearest beerhouse and drink copious amounts of real ale (Hornsey 2003, 492). The original Old World session beers of England were easily available, comforting to drink by the pub's fireside, and low enough in alcohol to promote long hours of drinking among fellow patrons.

In 1880, Prime Minister Gladstone put forth the Free Mash-Tun Act, which abolished the tax on malt, giving more leeway to brewers and their use of various raw materials. The Free Mash-Tun Act also shifted the levy from raw materials to a tax based on wort volume and strength (Hornsey 2003, 492). Prior to 1900 most bitters and pale ales in England had an original gravity of 15°P. Brewers soon realized the lower their original gravity prior to starting fermentation, the lower their taxes would be.

By the end of World War II, the average original gravity had dropped to 10°P. There was a clear shift by many breweries to get more from their extract and fully attenuate their beers, making for a dryer finish and a more sessionable and lower-taxed beer (Moen 2003). The English were not the only European politicians using the mash tun when writing beer taxation law. In Belgium during the nineteenth century authorities based taxation on the size of the mash tun. This also favored the brewing of lower alcohol beers (Markowski 2004, 115-116).

Therefore, not only did brewing lower-alcohol beer support the popular pub culture of drinking for extended hours, but also made it more lucrative for the brewery owners' bottom line. Taxation based on alcohol content was not a new concept for England. In the eighteenth century, a taxation system existed in England and Scotland that classified beer as "strong," "table," or "small" depending on alcohol content, and levied the highest tax for the highest alcoholic strength.

(Palmer and Kaminski 2013, 147), but when elevated above 200 ppm they can bring a "minerally" flavor profile to the final beer. Thus, the combination of a mineral flavor and caramel malt sweetness has become one of the prominent, defining characteristics of the classic Irish red ale.

Another feature that is very conducive to having a wonderful session drinking either a dry Irish stout or Irish red ale is the way it is dispensed. Both Guinness Draught and many Irish red ales served in America, as well as in Ireland, are dispensed through a nitrogen faucet. Using nitrogen to serve beer on tap enhances the rich specialty malts, because it keeps the carbon dioxide at bay and allows the full malt profile to come rushing up to greet the palate. Richness and complexity, body and balance, softness and flavor, all these can be found intermingling in a quality brewed dry Irish stout or Irish red ale, which makes for wonderful Irish-born session beers.

Ales of Scotland

The shilling system, most commonly associated with beers of Scotland, is just one example of how the countries of the British Isles structured pricing based on differing alcohol strengths. The lowest ABV beer, 60 shilling (60/-), had an original gravity of approximately 7.5–10°P, whereas the highest ABV ale, 160/-. strong ale, started roughly between 25°P and 31°P. The strong ale averaged 9% ABV while the 60/- was generally around 3.5% ABV. The brewing of strong ale and 60/- was done using a parti-gyle system (see sidebar), with the weakest wort from the final runnings yielding the 60/- ale. However, this low-alcohol ale did not necessarily make for a high-quality session beer.

In the case of the parti-gyle system, the mash sugars were not the only thing leached from the grain bed as the gravity drastically dropped between runnings. The wort lessened in strength and became increasingly alkaline, and greater amounts of phenols were brought over to the 60/- kettle. This created a harsh and astringent finish. To make matters worse, the Scottish brewers used a higher than average sparge water temperature of 190°F (88°C), which only increased the level of phenol extraction (Noonan 1993). Today's modern American craft session beers are brewed from a single mash that is thoughtfully constructed. The quickly rising pH is watched closely by those brewers making quality session beers, and the malt phenols are left behind in the mash tun where they belong. Modern breweries throughout Scotland continue to brew small beers such as the 60/-, 70/-, and 80/- Scottish ales.

They are now brewed using a single mash and tend to finish cloyingly sweet and slightly underattenuated, and while to style, it doesn't place them in the session beer class.

PARTI-GYLE

The parti-gyle system was a process in which wort from a single mash was diverted into two or more kettles to create different beers of varying strength and flavor (Oliver 2012, 641; s.v. "parti-gyle"). When wort is first drawn from the mash it is called the "first runnings." Once the initial mash water is depleted, additional water is typically added by sparging the grains, enabling the brewer to continue collecting wort. The first runnings had the highest sugar content, sometimes reaching as high as 31°P, and were typically used to create beers like strong Scotch ales or barleywine. The higher the starting original gravity, the greater the amount of alcohol produced in fermentation. Subsequent runnings drawn off over the same mash produced lower original gravity wort, resulting in a decline in final alcohol production. These additional runnings were diverted to other kettles to produce beers of lower alcohol strength, such as English bitters and Scottish ales (Oliver 2012, 720; s.v. "Scotch ale").

The goal of the brewery was to use one mash to produce two or more beers differing in strength. When the parti-gyle system was employed a single mash would be used to produce two or three different types of beer. The Belgians originally used the parti-gyle system to produce their high-alcohol *tripel*, then the *dubbel*, and a third pass through the same mash produced the "single" (Mosher 1994). In Scotland the weakest wort (the final runnings) yielded 60/- ale.

A Little Country Called Belgium

Some of the most sought-after beers produced in the world come from Belgium, which is about the size of the state of Massachusetts. Belgium has a rich history steeped in brewing, but what may come as a surprise to some is that session beers are a part of that history. *Tafelbier* (table beer) has been brewed and enjoyed since the Middle Ages. The alcohol level of tafelbier ranges between 1.5% and 3.5% ABV, and the color and malts used run the gamut from light blonde to intensely dark. Although the alcohol level is in the very low range, the flavor profile is not conducive to session beer drinking, often finishing cloyingly sweet with little bitterness. Tafelbier was brewed for nourishment, refreshment, and to be consumed by the whole family. The primary place for tafelbier was at meals, believed to be safer to drink than potentially contaminated well water and cer-tainly tasting better. In addition, monks believed that the nourishment served them well during the time of Lenten and other fasts (Lodahl 1994).

Tafelbier consumption has declined throughout Belgium, but 30 Belgian breweries continue to brew a table beer offering (Oliver 2012, 782). In 2002 I began hearing discussions with both craft beer enthusiasts and brewers that included tafelbier as one of the original session beers of the world. However, upon further research, the traditional tafelbiers do not resemble a session beer, but are instead akin to a glass of water or soft drink with your meal. Tafelbiers are not brewed for drinking many of in one sitting, but more for appealing to the youth as a better choice than sugary soda.[1] In the early part of the twenty-first century, the beer group De Limburgse Biervrienden, whose goal is to support and recognize Belgian beer culture and tradition, petitioned 30 schools in the Limburg province to replace schools' sugary soft drink choices with tafelbier. They cited the ill effects that often coincide with heavy consumption of highly sugary drinks, such as the risk for childhood obesity and even cancer. They also promoted the nourishing qualities of low alcohol beer for youth. The target pilot group of school-aged children were between three and fifteen years of age, and De Limburgse Biervrienden was not concerned about sleepiness because of the small size of the tafelbier bottles on offer.[2]

What's in a Name?

Within the fast-expanding modern landscape of the craft beer world, there is an increasing emphasis on beer styles. Some brewers feel forced to exist within the confines of style parameters that border on obsessional and be strictly obedient to beer style nomenclature. Countries with a long-history of openness with style names and categories, including Belgium, don't have the same obsession. Boxing a beer into a specific style goes against the true spirit of the classic, traditional Belgian brewers. Traveling through Belgium, I fell in love with one particular beer that exemplifies an artfully crafted session beer. That beer is Taras Boulba, brewed by Yvan De Baets at Brasserie De La Senne. While some have tried to box it into a specific style, calling it a pale ale of sorts, Taras Boulba defies such categorization.

My first experience with De Baets' passion for brewing was when I read *Farmhouse Ales: Culture and Craftsmanship in the Belgian Tradition* by Phil Markowski (2004). De Baets wrote the historical section on *saison*; I highly suggest giving *Farmhouse Ales* a read if you are contemplating brewing a saison or *bière de garde*. I soon discovered just how infectious De Baets' passion for

---

[1] "Style Studies," *Beer Connoisseur*, May/June 2016. http://beerconnoisseur.com/articles/style-studies-issue-24.

[2] Andrew Osborn, "School dinner? Mine's a lager, please," *Guardian*, June 21, 2001, http://www.theguardian.com/world/2001/jun/21/schools.education.

Figure 1.1. Taras Boulba from Brasserie De La Senne has been described many ways, but it's difficult to put it under one category. One category it does neatly fit into is "delicious."

brewing truly is. Brasserie De La Senne's website has a philosophy section that, to me, brilliantly captures the essence of a session beer when it says the brewery's light beers "further allow prolonging the pleasure—and therein lies the reason for the beer's existence."[3] Taras Boulba is 4.5% ABV, blonde, with ample bitterness and hop aroma. Its unique flavors developed through fermentation intermingle with the citrus hop character, inviting you to keep ordering more as the day, or night, progresses.

Per Diem

Sister Joan Chittister writes in *Wisdom Distilled from the Daily* that in the Rule of St. Benedict, "All must be given its due, but only its due. There should be something of everything and not too much of anything."[4] This remains true today for

---

[3]   "Philosophy," under "Beers light in alcohol," Brasserie De La Senne, accessed April 7, 2017, http://brasseriedelasenne.be/philosophy/?lang=en.

[4]   Joan Chittister, *Wisdom Distilled from the Daily: Living the Rule of St Benedict Today* (San Francisco: HarperCollins, 1991).

Figure 1.2. Yvan De Baets pouring Taras Boulba at Brasserie De La Senne.

the ordained monks residing in the six Trappist monasteries of Belgium. Finding Belgian session beer is not an easy task for those looking for something they can drink all day while wandering the beautiful countryside in search of their next brewery visit, even though *enkel* (Dutch word for single) or *patersbier* (father's beer) has been being brewed for hundreds of years in Belgium.

Joining a monastic order requires strict observance to prayer and daily work. As noted in *Brew Like a Monk* by Stan Hieronymus, the Rule of St. Benedict, written around AD 530, called on monks to be self-sufficient and to provide hospitality for the community around them. Therefore, since water was often riddled with bacteria and unhealthy to drink, beer was the beverage of choice to brew (Hieronymus 2005, 29). Prayer and work days can be very long and difficult, therefore, the monks need to be healthy in mind and spirit to give their full attention to the tasks at hand. Patersbier is brewed for the monks to enjoy a single glass of after the day's work is finished. It is unavailable outside the monasteries and brewed strictly for the monk's reward.

Visiting Westmalle with a group of fellow brewers, we were fortunate enough to be invited to the small taproom within the monastery. We were served a beautiful beer described as a single, otherwise known as Extra. The Westmalle Extra was the first beer brewed by the Westmalle monks in 1836; it was not until 1934 that the Dubbel and Tripel would be first produced. The Extra is blonde in color and only uses malted barley in the brewing process. Whole-flower hops are added for aromatics and the ABV ranges between 4.7% and 4.8%. It is blonde, delicate, and refreshingly dry. The ester development coalesced with extremely low phenolic notes stemming from the unique Belgian yeast used during fermentation. This is the beer brewed for the monks and served in a single 10 oz. pour after their day's work is complete.

Unfortunately, Westmalle Extra is not normally available to the public; it was very difficult to leave the taproom knowing I would no longer be able to drink this true nectar of the gods once I was beyond the abbey gate. Replication of Westmalle Extra would be virtually impossible given the nature of the distinctive yeast profile and brewing practices, which are well protected.

The development of patersbier came into being when monastic breweries employed the parti-gyle system and utilized the remaining sugar still available in the mash from a stronger batch. Running a second, or even third, sparge yields a low-gravity wort that is fermented separately and provides a lower-alcohol beer to quench the thirst of the monks. The parti-gyle system is no longer used and patersbier, like the Westmalle Extra, is currently produced from a single mash, resulting in a higher-quality, low-alcohol beer; unfortunately, examples of patersbier are very hard to find and sample (AHA 2017).

As our group continued its pilgrimage through Belgium, we found ourselves relaxing at the In de Vrede café associated with St. Sixtus Abbey in Westvleteren. Although we were unable to visit the brewery itself, we spent a long, magnificently indulgent afternoon sipping some of the finest Trappist beers ever made. When the café was remodeled in 1999, production ceased of the Westvleteren 4 and Westvleteren 6. It was at this time that Brother Filip introduced the Westvleteren Blonde to celebrate the opening of the refurbished café (Hieronymus 2005, 80). The Blonde is now the beer for a monastic brewer to have with their lunch when there is still work to be completed, or to reward themselves for a good day's work done. The character is slightly bitter, very refreshing, and the beer comes in at 5.6% ABV, showcasing a splendid fruitiness derived from the incomparable Belgian yeast used. For a complete in-depth look at monastic brewing and the traditions and history behind some of the world's finest and most humble beers, Hieronymus' *Brew Like a Monk* is a must-read.

> *Although the Westvleteren Blonde has an ABV of 5.6%, most American craft brewers who depend on definitions and boundaries would not deem it a session beer. My personal experience was very different. I sat alongside my closest friends on the patio at the café, taking in the view of the beautifully peaceful countryside; I enjoyed many goblets of Blonde that day in a long session of beer drinking and conversation.*

Saison, a Beer for All Seasons

Brewers are often asked what their favorite beer is. I believe this an impossible question to answer; however, I do believe that there are certain beers that we, as beer enthusiasts, revisit repeatedly. Saison is that beer for me. My fascination and love for the elusive family of beers known as saison began after reading Phil Markowski's *Farmhouse Ales.*

There are distinct parameters around the saison style, although these can vary markedly from brewery to brewery. As noted by Yvan De Baets' historical account in *Farmhouse Ales*, saisons originally developed in the farming areas of the Wallonia region of Belgium, and were brewed in the winter to satisfy the thirst of farmworkers during the summer months. Therefore, one of the longstanding characteristics of saison was to be thirst-quenching and pleasing to drink a lot of during warm days of fieldwork. Water was poor quality, so it made sense that a low-alcohol, well-hopped or spiced ale with a dry finish was served as a quality replacement for hydration (Markowski 2004, 98).

Prior to the 1900s, the original gravity hovered between 7–9°P, and most of these original saisons had an ample bitterness and lactic sourness from mixed fermentation. Intense hop bitterness due to hop alpha acids does tend to stave off the growth of certain lactobacilli because of the alpha acids' natural bactericidal properties; this is not to say that some hop alpha-acids can't be present during the production of lactic acid, but they do slow *Lactobacillus* growth and development (Sparrow 2005, 112). Historically, other grains (and pseudograins), such as wheat, spelt, rye, oats, and buckwheat, were used in place of or in conjunction with malted barley. After World War II higher-gravity beers containing more alcohol were in favor and the trend of brewing "super saisons" started to take hold (Markowski 2004, 118). It is extremely difficult to find a traditional saison, but if you find one of high quality be prepared to stay awhile because they are very hard to stop ordering.

> *Bam Biére by Jolly Pumpkin Artisan Ales happens to be a fine example of a traditional farmhouse ale and is certainly one that I have enjoyed on multiple occasions.*

Figure 1.3. Saison brewery with a view to the tanks.

White Beers of Belgium

White beers, also known as *witbier* in Flemish, are unfiltered wheat beers, opaque in color and served cloudy with a brilliant, frothy white head on top. Once you wrap your lips around them, you know you will be comforted until the last delicious sip or until the bartender decides to go home. Witbiers were first brewed during the Middle Ages but decreased in popularity during the rise of the lager beer revolution (Oliver 2012, 842). Traditionally, witbiers were made using both malted and unmalted grains, usually some combination of malted and unmalted wheat and barley, spelt, oats, or whatever else could be acquired at the local farms of the Flemish Brabant province. Hopping rates are kept low and spices, such as orange peel, coriander, and grains of paradise, are artfully layered in to provide a delicate character, which can be perceived but is difficult to specifically define. The alcohol range of witbier is 4.5%–5% ABV and the hops and spices are kept at an incredibly soft level to keep inviting you back for another.

> *After spending hours touring through the Pajottenland region of Belgium, drinking some of the most amazing sour beers ever made, it was time to settle down at a local pub and reflect on the day with my friends. When reviewing what the beer menu had to offer, all I could think about was thirst-quenching, dry, and simply refreshing, so I ordered a Hoegaarden (and then another).*

The two towns most well-known for the production of witbier are Leuven and Hoegaarden. As continental Pilsner took a foothold throughout most of Europe, the production of Hoegaarden Wit fell out of favor and the brewery doors finally closed in 1950. Thankfully, a man by the name of Pierre Celis had a love and admiration for traditional witbier and decided to start brewing his favorite beer. . . again. In his younger years, Celis worked in the Tomsin Brewery in Hoegaarden before it stopped production; he then went on to become a milkman (Oliver 2012, 231). Celis gathered all his resources and in 1966 built the de Kluis brewery, producing a traditional witbier that was reminiscent of the historically unrefined, cloudy wheat beers of the nineteenth century. In 1992, he brought his expertise to Austin, Texas and started the Celis Brewery, generating a movement of Belgian witbier brewing throughout the United States (Klemp 2007). Anheuser-Busch InBev currently owns and produces Hoegaarden Wit in the town of Hoegaarden.

Blanche De Chambly, brewed by Unibroue, and Allagash White, brewed by Allagash Brewing Company, are two amazing witbiers currently sold in the United States. Witbier continues to refresh and impress beer enthusiasts throughout the world, and is still one of the greatest session beer styles produced.

A WORD ON PREFERENCE

It is important to acknowledge that not all palates are built the same. There is a wonderfully elusive character to the human palate, described as "preference." As we travel through the different stages of life, we are exposed or not exposed to various tastes and smells. All of this plays a part in the development of what we prefer regarding flavor. Humans begin their development of taste even before they are born. In fact, taste buds begin to develop in the embryo in the first eight weeks of gestation (Dr. Rainer Wild Foundation 2008). At birth, taste is the most developed of the senses, and most taste preferences continue to mature through learned behavior and exposure. For instance, a taste for sweet is shown to be favored by newborns but sour is rejected. Sweet triggers a signal to say that it is a source of energy and a safe food to eat, whereas acidic (sour) warns of a possible source of toxicity from spoiled food. Family and cultural upbringing also have a great influence on what foods and tastes we are exposed to and develop an affinity for. Learned behavior kicks in, and how we understand taste and connect those familiarities with positive and negative experiences plays a significant role in what we deem is good tasting and bad tasting (Dr. Rainer Wild Foundation 2008).

At this point, you are probably wondering what all this has to do with session beer. Everything. What one person deems sessionable might not be sessionable to another. There are basic characteristics that most people agree should be part of a beer's make up to qualify it as a session beer, such as low-medium hop rate, 4%–5%(-ish) ABV, and ability to drink several pints in one sitting. The last point is probably the most important. If one cannot drink multiple pints of a given beer in one sitting, it is simply not a session beer... to that person. One sitting differs for everyone and can often depend on many variables. Generally speaking, one sitting could mean anywhere from two to six pints. This is where preference plays a major part.

The Session Beers of Germany and Central Europe

Taste preference can play a major part in what a person considers sessionable (see sidebar, "A Word on Preference"). I have an extreme affinity for the taste of sour. This has not always been the case, but as my palate has developed sour beers have played a greater and greater role in my life. Therefore, as this book continues to uncover the origin of session beer throughout the world, we find ourselves in Berlin.

Where Is My Berliner Weisse?

In 2013, I had the opportunity to speak to a group of students at VLB Berlin, the Research and Teaching Institute for Brewing in Berlin. Prior to that, I had grown up in the American craft beer movement hearing about the historic and mysterious style of Berliner *weisse*. My primary goal when arriving in Berlin was to run to the first brasserie and order an authentic Berliner weisse. Sadly, this became a daunting task. Eric Warner, author of *German Wheat Beer*, predicted in 1992 that the style of Berliner weisse would soon see a reinvigoration by a bolstering tourist economy; unfortunately, as much as I had hoped this would be true, my efforts to find this elusive beer style proved sadly unfruitful. Regardless of scarcity, a properly crafted Berliner weisse is a wonderfully sour session beer, highly difficult to master but worth its weight in gold when done right. The birth of the Berliner weisse dates back to 1680, and was coined the "Champagne of the North" in the early nineteenth century by Napoleon's soldiers (Warner 1992, 33). The defining temperament of a Berliner weisse is a low starting gravity (7–9°P), extremely low IBUs (4–6), and a high degree of attenuation through a mixed fermentation of *Lactobacillus delbrueckii* and *Saccharomyces cerevisiae* (Warner 1992, 33). The ABV range is usually 2.5%–4% and the degree of attenuation can be as high as 98%. The pH should vary between 3.2 and 3.4 depending on the success of the lactic fermentation. It has also been suggested that *Brettanomyces* is often artfully employed when creating a beautiful Berliner weisse. When properly made, all these components coalesce to form a proper Berliner weisse that is tart, refreshingly dry, and slightly fruity.

The trend in Berlin is to serve a Berliner weisse with a small shot of raspberry or woodruff to help cut the acidity for those who have not yet developed an affinity for highly sour beer. As my quest for this historic beer was being blocked at every turn, I surrendered to the fashion of sweetening and ordered a Berliner weisse made with woodruff—it was at this time the barkeep asked if I would like a straw. Fortunately, my wonderful hosts were able to provide me with a beautiful Berliner weisse brewed at the VLB pilot plant. When the wheels of my plane lifted off, I was able to say I had drunk a fabulous Berliner weisse in Berlin, but what I really wanted was more.

Wheat Beers of Bavaria

Although Berliner weisse comes from the northern part of Germany, wheat beer production is more commonly associated with Bavaria in the south. However, unlike Berliner weisse, the wheat beers of Bavaria are not sour. Located in southeast Germany, the region of Bavaria has been producing *weissbier* since the seventeenth century. Over 20% of all beer produced in Bavaria is made from wheat and many different sub-styles of weissbier make up these sales in increasing numbers (Warner 1992, 5). Weissbier, made of high quality ingredients and having a restrained alcohol level, can be a wonderful session beer. The German beer tax structure is organized by starting wort extract. There are four categories of extract strength, beginning with the weakest: *einfachbier* (simple beer) at 0.5%–1.5% ABV; *schankbier* (draught beer) at 1.5%–2.6% ABV; *vollbier* (whole beer) 3.5%–5.5% ABV; and, lastly, *starkbier* (strong beer), which starts at 6.5% ABV, not 5.5% as one might assume. Ninety-nine percent of all beer sold in Germany is vollbier (Dornbusch 1997, 100). That would mean that most all beer sold in Germany is session beer, if we simply defined session beer as having under 5% ABV. Some weissbiers do exceed the 5% ABV value, which style zealots seem to insist on, but to say that a quality weissbier is not a session beer just because the ABV exceeds 5% would simply be wicked.

Hefeweizen is the most popular and widely produced of all the weissbier in Bavaria. Golden in color and turbid from the yeast still in suspension, a beautiful hefeweizen is an excellent choice for the morning after the night before. Many Bavarians believe that weissbier eases digestive problems and helps maintain a healthy stomach. When traveling in Bavaria it is very common to observe the locals waiting for a train and quaffing a hefeweizen from a kiosk. Once again, the concept of preference plays a major role in defining whether a weissbier will prove to be a session beer for you. The unique character derived from the yeast used in traditional weissbier brewing creates phenolic and ester notes that are not welcomed by some beer drinkers.

A typical pale hefeweizen starts between 11.7°P and 13.8°P and finishes at 2.1–4.1°P, ending somewhere in the 5%–5.6% ABV range, which would carry it out of the "boxed" description of a session beer, if you wanted to be that strict. The hops are low, 10–18 IBUs, and the beer highly carbonated, presenting with a white, frothy head due to the large percentage of wheat used. The amount of wheat malt that was historically used in Bavaria was much lower than today's standard, being around 35%. With technological advances in both malting and brewing equipment, modern Bavarian weissbier falls between 50% and 70% wheat. The characteristic phenolic flavors, mainly 4-vinylguaiacol, are derived primarily from the specific mash procedures employed. The most often used descriptor for this dominant flavor is clovelike.

I personally believe that what makes a great weissbier is the relationship the brewer has with the weissbier yeast strain, which leads to the artful manipulation of 4-vinylguaiacol levels and that of other phenols and esters. Isoamyl acetate is one of the primary ester compounds that also develop during fermentation, and it has a rich banana flavor. A beer drinker's love or dislike for the spicy character derived from 4-vinylguaiacol is what will either keep them ordering weissbier or go reaching for a helles instead. Weissbier is by no means one-dimensional. The interplay between ester and phenolic compounds, a healthy fermentation yielding a well-attenuated beer, and the high carbonation all make for a great experience. To dive further into the exact process of making a weissbier, I highly encourage you to pick up Eric Warner's book, *German Wheat Beer*.

There are many wonderful weissbiers produced throughout Bavaria, but, sadly, weissbier enthusiasm has not taken hold with the American populace. Dancing Man Wheat from New Glarus is probably the best example of great American-made weissbier . The wheat beer trend in America began in the mid-1980s, but the wonderful weissbier yeast strains traditionally used in Germany were not selected and ale yeast became the popular choice for fermentation. It is my belief that the decision to use a low-ester and low-phenol producing yeast came out of early American craft brewers' fear that the American palate was not ready for the unique flavor profile of a classic weissbier. In addition, the specialty yeast used by Bavarian brewers is top cropping and has a lower generation threshold than standard American ale yeast, making it much more cumbersome to manage in the modern American craft brewery. What's more, classic Bavarian weissbier is usually bottle conditioned, which also requires the brewer to take special steps during the final preparation to ensure high carbonation. Creating a great weissbier is not for the faint of heart, but if done correctly it is well worth the effort and the result is an exemplary session beer.

Some Bavarian and Austrian brewers produce a filtered version of the traditional weissbier called a *kristallweizen*. Kristallweizen is similar to hefeweizen in its flavor characteristics, except it is devoid of yeast and served brilliantly clear. A properly made kristallweizen is tightly filtered and naturally or forced carbonated as opposed to bottle conditioned. This presents a brilliantly clear final beer, which changes its final personality entirely. However, the classic ester and phenol profile developed by the weissbier yeast remains. Another version of the classic hefeweizen is one that is lighter in alcohol, called a *leichtes weizen*. The Bavarians still employ artful handling of their brewing procedure and ingredients to create this lighter version of weissbier (Warner 1992). Leichtes weizen is brewed in the traditional way of a hefeweizen, but with an alcohol level that does not exceed 4% ABV. The bitterness is on the low side, between 10–12 IBUs, so as not to dominate the other flavors. Dextrin malts are part of the grist to help lift the body up.

The Birth of Lager Beer

The history is controversial about just where and when the first pale European lager was born; was it the smooth gold Pilsner of Bohemia, the hoppy German Pilsener, or the Bavarian helles of Munich? With new discoveries and innovation occurring in the European breweries of the mid-nineteenth century, brewers scrambled to jump onto new trends. This story is beginning to sound very similar to the craft beer wagons boarded today. Who's on first?

One thing we can depend on in the brewing industry is friendship and collaboration. It is widely accepted that the friendship between Anton Dreher and Gabriel Sedlmayr helped launch the revolution of German lager brewing. After an eye-opening trip to Britain in 1833 with his friend Dreher, Sedlmayr was impressed by the paler malts employed, and his family run Spaten brewery in Munich turned their focus to producing lager beer lighter in color using higher-quality malt (Dornbusch 2000, 35).

Later, in 1841, Dreher and Sedlmayr discovered lager yeast used by a Bavarian monastery, and both brewers went to their family run breweries and brewed the first commercially recognized lager beers. At the same time that Dreher and Sedlmayr were developing their own versions of lager, the mission to produce a high-quality pale lager was also underway in the town of Pilsen, located in Bohemia (now in the modern Czech Republic). In 1842, a Bavarian monk brought lager yeast to Pilsen and Josef Groll, an immigrant from Bavaria, began brewing pale lagers. Bohemian Pilsner was born.

Dreher, from the city of Vienna, Austria, began development at his Schwechat Brewery of what would one day become the reddish, slightly toasty-malty Vienna lager style. In Munich, Sedlmayr took the lager yeast to his family's Spaten brewery and hotly pursued a more straw-to-golden version; however, prior to improvements made in malting, the lager beer Sedlmayr brewed was rather dark in color and considered a Munich *dunkel* (Fix and Fix 1991, 8). Unfortunately, the pale malts used in the city of Munich were inferior and Sedlmayr's first pale lager trials yielded poor results. In Vienna, Dreher was having more success by using Moravian barley that had a deeper color and lower acidity, which helped control the pH of the mash. Although the Vienna-style beer Dreher created was not hopped as much as the pale beers of Pilsen, they still carried a noble hop flavor.

By 1874, operation of the Sedlmayr family brewery had passed to Gabriel's three sons. Eventually, the early Spaten Munich dunkel would give way to helles. Spaten brewery sold the first helles in 1894, three years after

Gabriel Sedlmayr passed away (Dornbusch 2000, 39). Although the Spaten brewery continued to brew the dunkel, sales fell as the popularity of its helles soared. The flavor profile of the classic helles is one of high quality malt with little to no hop nose or forward bitterness. Well-attenuated and finishing dry, a true helles will offer up a wonderful malt experience, complemented perfectly by noble hops that never take a front seat. Helles soon became the most popular beer in Bavaria, selling almost one out of every two beers drank (Dornbusch 2000, 39).

The driving force behind the transition of Bavarian beers from dark to light in color was the technological advancements made to kilning during the industrial revolution. Another advancement came while Dreher and Sedlmayr were refining their lager brewing, when German engineer Carl von Linde invented the "cold machine," now called the refrigerator, in 1873 (Dornbusch 2000, 40). Prior to refrigeration, Dreher was brewing his beer in March and storing it with ice in the brewery's cellar to keep cold. Once refrigeration was developed, the traditional Vienna lager became a year-round beer with a lower starting gravity and less alcohol than its big brother, Märzen, which was now brewed especially for the festivals in October (Fix and Fix 1991, 12). Filtration, another fantastic result of the industrial revolution, was developed by Bavarian inventor Lorenz Enzinger in 1878; it transformed the earlier dark, slightly turbid lagers of Germany into the renowned straw-to-golden brilliant lagers of today (Dornbusch 2000, 84).

Bavarians have a culture drenched in beer consumption and the development of the subtle helles is quite conducive to long hours spent in Bavarian beer gardens. Although the traditional Oktoberfest celebration carries the name of the Märzen/Oktoberfest style, the majority of beer consumed at the festival is helles. For helles, the ABV generally falls between 4.7% and 5.4%, with a range of 18–25 IBUs. There are three classifications of helles: *urhell*, meaning original; *spezial*, usually designated a seasonal helles; and *edel* (noble) helles, emphasizing the noble hops used. The term export helles is also used, signifying alcohol above 5% ABV and referring to helles shipped outside of Bavaria (Dornbusch 2000, 21). Helles has a high protein level, creating a medium-to-full body and rich creamy head. Since the attenuation dips the final gravity under 3°P, helles is light enough to drink multiple liters of over a period of time. That is just what the Bavarians continue to do— even though German Pilsener dominates throughout the country, helles still reigns supreme in Bavaria.

Bohemian Pilsner finishes with a more assertive hop note compared to Bavarian helles, but is considered more malt forward than German Pilsener. It is common to experience a light malt biscuit note in an authentic Bohemian Pilsner, which attenuates slightly higher than German Pilsener, making Bohemian Pilsner the blood sister to Bavarian helles . The largest flavor difference between these siblings is the malt finish of the helles compared to the slight hop finish of the Bohemian Pilsner (Dornbusch 1997, 117). Two of the best-known Bohemian Pilsners that originated in the former Czech Republic are Budweiser Budvar and Pilsner Urquell (*urquell* means "the ancient source" in German).

As far as the German Pilsener style goes, Spaten, Warsteiner, and Bitburger all produce excellent examples that are readily available throughout the United States; however, their quality of character will greatly depend on how fresh one finds them. The pale lager made in the Bohemian region is spelled "pilsner," while the German lager adds an extra "e" to the spelling. However, the spelling is not the only difference between these two beautiful session lagers. The German Pilsener is more hop forward in aroma, straw in color, finishing dry, and emphasizing a snappy hop bitterness. The Bohemian Pilsner has a bready malt front nose, golden hue, and lower attenuation. Although there are subtle differences between these two great European lagers, they are more alike than not. Both beers are high in carbonation, creating a beautiful effervescent synergy between the hops and high-quality malt employed (Miller 1990).

At the Schwechat Brewery in Vienna, Dreher remained a staunch advocate for the use of high-quality ingredients. His unwavering commitment to the finest malted barley and hops made for a wonderful beer and laid the foundations for his creation of the classic Vienna style. With the advent of refrigeration and modern kilning methods, Vienna lager was transformed into a true masterpiece. In a Vienna lager, the complexity in the malts used should not overpower the noble hop aroma and medium bitterness. Amber in color, it should be filtered bright and finish soft with no astringency. Adherence to quality ingredients, as well as procedure, should be steadfast and will ultimately result in a fabulous session lager.

The best way to describe the flavors in Dreher's traditional Vienna beer is to compare them to my daughter, Vienna MaryJane. She is complex, yet soft in nature; the balance of her true beauty rests in the quality of her character. This is also true of a classic Vienna lager.

The modern day *schwarzbier* first emerged around the same time as Vienna lager, in Kulmbach, a district of northern Bavaria, and also just east of Kulmbach in the state of Thuringia. The Köstritzer brewery, founded in 1543 in the town of Bad Köstritz in Thuringia, is one of the oldest breweries in Germany and continues to brew the world famous black lager, Köstritzer Schwarzbier. Kloster Mönchshof Schwarzbier, originating in the Franconian city of Kulmbach (capital of the Kulmbach district), is another celebrated black lager still widely available today (Klemp 2010). Dark monastic beers were in existence for centuries prior, but the change to lager yeast refined the primitive dark ales as it did so many beers throughout Europe. Kloster Mönchshof Schwarzbier literally translates to "black beer from the monk's courtyard cloister" (BYO 2002).

Schwarzbier, often referred to as "black Pilsener," presents with roast malt complexity, finishing dry, with medium body and an alcohol level that falls between 4% and 5% ABV. Never harsh in flavor, the roast malts should not bring heavy astringency as the noble hops balance the malt backbone. The dark color of schwarzbier can be intimidating to a novice beer drinker, but the medium body and artful use of roast malt and noble hops bring you back repeatedly for another sip. Up until the industrial revolution of the mid-nineteenth century, crude kilning procedures kept the brewers malt on the dark side. Prior to the invention of the iron drum in 1817, kilning was carried out over open fires, which yielded unpredictable enzymatic quality, phenolic smokiness, and darker colors. It is most likely that the early schwarzbier had a smoky phenol character to it.

Ales of Germany

The two German cities that decided to forego the lager uprising were the city of Köln (Cologne) and, just over 20 miles to the north, Düsseldorf. To this day, they both celebrate and are well known for their individual and classic session ales.

Kölsch is mostly found in the city of Cologne and within about a 60-mile circumference of the city. The culture that surrounds Kölsch in Cologne is infectious and so is the drinking of a perfect Kölsch.

> *I met my friend Guido Waldecker while judging at the 2002 World Beer Cup in San Diego. Guido works for one of the most successful and largest Kölsch breweries in Germany. When I asked Guido about the Kölsch style for this book, his response was, "Excuse me, but what is session beer?" I had to explain what the term session beer meant in America. Apparently, the term session beer has not made it to Germany yet.*

Guido Waldecker, a brewer of Kölsch, explains that Kölsch is served in small, 0.2 L Kölsch glasses (*Kölner Stange*) and are consumed fast and always fresh. The waiters in Cologne are called *Köbes*, guys you'd better not start arguing with. Immediately, they bring you a new beer without asking for it, unless you put the *Bierdeckel* (coaster) on your glass. They also like to get invited for a glass of Kölsch too. Though these beers are consumed quickly, you also can enjoy them slowly, or in company with any food. Kölsch is clean, dry, and very drinkable. Not too hoppy, not too malty, but much better than just water, of course. The remaining unfermented sugars left in solution usually amount to a final gravity below 2°P, with an original gravity between 11°P and 12°P, resulting in an alcohol level of around 4.5%–4.8% ABV. Guido shared,

> [T]here is nothing better to drink after a long-distance bicycle race, a run, or a session at the gym, than two bottles of Kölsch at home. I would not call that a session, but I prefer having such a beer after those physical activities rather than any other style!

Many people enjoy these styles of beer following sport activities: they quench your thirst, relax your muscles, but do not knock you out like a higher-alcohol beer might do. In the Eifel, a low mountain range in western Germany, session beers are very important to the local social life. (There are, of course, similar traditions all over Germany.) Several times a year, for example, during the celebration of the town's patron saint, village people gather to celebrate and enjoy session beers. Guido related how, one time in 2015, he saw people in the town of Weibern start drinking beer on Friday at 7:30 p.m. and stop the next morning at 5:00 a.m. They continued the party on Saturday at 7:00 p.m., or even a bit earlier, and again ended early in the morning the next day. On Sunday afternoon the party restarted, and went till the late evening. Traditionally, many people also had vacation on Monday, and so kept going, drinking from the early afternoon till late at night. Guido is quite sure that things like that would not be possible with stronger beers!

Düsseldorf is the state capital of North Rhine-Westphalia, where the legendary *altbier* originated and still quenches the thirst of residents and tourists today. It is one of the oldest styles in Germany—production of ale in the region dates back to AD 873 when the town of Gerresheim (now a borough of Düsseldorf) was given license to brew (Dornbusch 1997, 108). Altbier remains very popular in the town of Düsseldorf, as well as in the *Niederrhein*, or the Lower Rhine region of Germany. Many German *Feste* (fiestas, parties, festivals), like Carnival, local *Kirmes* in small towns, Oktoberfest, and so on, are hard to imagine without a session beer like one of these. Tell me of any other beer of which you can have a couple of in a few hours, quickly consumed, without regretting it during the session or the next day. Altbier does not intoxicate you too quickly, there is no heavy hopping drying your throat, and no strong malt body filling up your stomach.

The early ales of the Rhineland were wild and unrefined, as were most ales prior to the industrial revolution. The scientific advancement that helped drive European ale and lager quality was the ability to cultivate pure yeast cultures. It was the Danish botanist, Emil Christian Hansen, from the Carlsberg Brewing Company of Copenhagen, who in 1881 classified the bottom fermenting (*Saccharomyces pastorianus*) and top fermenting (*Saccharomyces cerevisiae*) yeasts (Dornbusch 1997, 82). Combined with the invention of refrigeration in 1873, German brewing launched into a lager revolution. However, the region of the Rhineland did not toss their beloved ales to the side for the newly isolated bottom fermenting yeast. In fact, they did just the opposite by decreeing ordinances that protected ale brewing throughout the centuries and controlled the importation of lager beer into the region.

The literal translation of *alt* is old, referencing the extended time altbier ages in the secondary fermentation cellar. At Zum Ueriege, established in 1862 and one of the most famous pub breweries in Düsseldorf, the young Alt, called "yummy droplet," is aged in the cellars for a minimum of three weeks.[5] One of the most inspiring parts of a tour when visiting Zum Ueriege is the coolship room. The hot wort is delivered to the copper coolship, where it chills to 122°F (50°C) before going through the drip cooler and eventually on to primary fermentation.

Altbier, fermented with an ale-lager hybrid yeast, enjoys a cooler primary fermentation than standard ale yeast strains. Perhaps this is why altbier makes for such a stellar session ale. The bittering profile of altbier ranges quite a bit and can fall anywhere from 25 to 50 IBUs depending on the brewmaster's inclination. The alcohol also ranges between 4.5% and 5.2% ABV. Ueriege Alt is hop forward, utilizing the finest German-grown hops, and contains 4.7% ABV. As you stroll down the cobblestone streets of the Altstadt ("old town") district of Düsseldorf, tasting different altbier along the way, you begin to appreciate the relationship between caramel and roast malts; perhaps also, you appreciate the long, cold maturation

[5] "»Dat leckere Dröppke« – so wird es gebraut," Uerige website [in German], under "Lagerkeller," accessed April 8, 2017, http://www.uerige.de/brauerei-brauprozess.html.

period when altbier yeast cleans up any potential off flavors. The resulting clean finish and malt complexity surely invite one back repeatedly to the wooden casks filled with altbier, which is what makes it such a great session ale.

German culture has a long-proven relationship with quality when it comes to beer. They have advocated, and at times legislated, for a commitment to quality brewing and the use of quality ingredients. This is evidenced most famously by the *Reinheitsgebot*, the 500-year-old Bavarian purity law of 1516. It specified all beer must only contain barley, hops, and water. Yeast had yet to be isolated in 1516 and the contemporary understanding of fermentation was very rudimentary. During the time before modern refrigeration, early ales brewed in the summer months were infected by either wild yeast and/or bacteria, making them very unpalatable for the Bavarians. The Reinheitsgebot most likely was an attempt to help refine these crude ales. In the Rhineland region, around the year 1540, there is record of a local duke, Wilhelm III, issuing a police ordinance regulating both quality of beer and price. In 1603, the Cologne city council announced only top fermenting beers were allowed to be produced (Dornbusch 1997, 107). These are just a few of the early laws and regulations originating from the German political sphere that affected beer quality and maintained a high standard in brewing.

The enduring popularity of session beer is a feature of German beer culture. This is how Guido Waldecker explained it to me:

> In addition to local parties and celebrations, Germans also enjoy an after-work beer, or Feierabendbier. *Well balanced and tasty, they refresh and make your day, even if you do take heed of your doctor's advice and just have two glasses. The German craft beer scene is slowly rising, with local and international specialty beers growing in popularity. I really do appreciate that—no doubt about it—but, nevertheless, I firmly believe that the majority of German beer drinkers will keep on drinking session beers. It is like I said about German Feste: any beer needs its occasion! Prost! (Cheers!).*

New World, New Beer

It was originally believed that the Native American tribes had no alcohol prior to the arrival of Europeans, but this was debunked in the twenty-first century.[6]

6   Heather Whipps, "Beer Brewed Long Ago by Native Americans," *Live Science*, December 28, 2007, http://www.livescience.com/4770-beer-brewed-long-native-americans.html.

Native Americans had been brewing a crude sort of ale prior to the arrival of the Europeans. Archeologists discovered that over 800 years ago the Pueblo Indians of Mexico were brewing up a weak beer, called *tiswin*, with the use of corn. European colonists brought with them the know-how to brew the ales of England and soon began to do so once settled in their new land. These rough versions of what the colonists drank in their homeland were fashioned very similarly to the early ales of Europe, with the exception of introducing a new brewing material, corn (maize). The Wampanoag tribe introduced corn to the settlers in Plymouth, Massachusetts in the mid-sixteenth century; the settlers readily used it in brewing their crude ales, which often rose to 6% ABV, were dark and turbid, and most likely contaminated (Smith 1998, 14). Corn grew easily in the New World and was used for survival anywhere it could be found, so naturally it made sense to use it in the brewing process.

As German immigration steadily rose in the mid-nineteenth century, hundreds of breweries opened throughout the major cities of America, such as St. Louis, Milwaukee, New York, and Chicago. Credit for the first lager brewed in the New World goes to John Klein and Alexander Stausz, who began brewing in the small town of Alexandria, Virginia in 1838 (Ogle 2006, 14). They brought with them the know-how to brew lager beer and the love of doing so. Soon, the affection for lager spread throughout the land and it quickly became the most popular choice of beer. The light body and color of lager was very appealing when compared to the usual dark and muddled ales.

In German culture, steeped in brewing beer, had long been a central part of celebration and life; therefore, it was quite natural for German immigrants to bring beer and their love for it to the New World. However, many settlers moved toward consuming whiskey instead of beer. Early American life focused on survival, as one can imagine, and the growing of barley and hops to produce beer seemed tiresome compared to the distillation of whiskey. Whiskey soon took the front seat, and by 1820 the average American was consuming seven to eight gallons of whiskey a year (Ogle 2006, 23). With this type of consumption, it did not take long for the first uprising against the evils of alcohol to set in.

The first American temperance movement began in 1820, and folks gathered in hordes to crusade against drunkenness and dicuss the need for morality in the developing world. The temperance movement clashed with German immigrants' love for beer and soon immigrants were seen as the cause of morality's demise in America. All this crusading led to the first prohibition law enacted by Neal Dow, Mayor of Portland, Maine. The Maine law banned the manufacturing, sale, and consumption of alcohol. This sent a ripple effect throughout America and 11 out of 31 states followed suit with prohibition laws of their own (Ogle 2006, 26). Thankfully, where there is a ban there is an uprising. Temperance and anti-immigration went hand in hand and soon folks pushed back. In the 1850s, violence erupted in the streets of several major cities with prohibition laws, as happened with the Lager Beer Riot in Chicago. The German immigrants had power in numbers, and it was not violence that served them but their vote. They quickly threatened to vote against any pro-prohibition, pro-slavery politician, and so the first fire of the temperance movement was smothered. . . for the time being. The emotional state that developed during the early temperance movement planted the seed that alcohol and immorality were intertwined. Where one was, the other soon followed.

With prohibition laws squelched for the time being, lager flourished. Lager breweries popped up all over America and beer flowed throughout the land. The early American lager was different from the Pilsener and helles of Germany and Bohemia. Six-row barley became the choice for most brewers, as opposed to the two-row Chevalier variety used in Germany and Austria. Specifically, the Manchuria six-row variety grown in Wisconsin and Minnesota proved far superior in enzymatic strength and better adapted for use in conjunction with unmalted cereal grains than the two-row varieties grown in the Montana region (Wahl and Henius 1908, 450). One other factor that contributed to the success of the Manchuria barley was its ability to handle the rapid changes in weather.

Combining the popular American six-row malted barley with 25%–40% corn and/or rice in the total grain bill yielded a very different flavor profile than the two-row, malt-forward pale lagers of Europe. The body of a pre-Prohibition lager is light, with medium malt mouthfeel. The hops were aggressive compared to the mass produced light lagers of today. Although the use of adjuncts has continued in modern lagers, the hop bitterness has gradually declined over the last hundred years. It has often been discussed, in an urban legend-like way, that as August Busch III grew older in his life, his affection for hop bitterness declined and so did the bitterness of his beers. In any case, pre-Prohibition lager, which demonstrated a medium-to-high amount of noble hop flavor, aroma, and bitterness, greatly decreased in hop character due to decades of recipe adjustments. Despite the flavor differences between pre-Prohibition lager and the premium American lager of today, they both demonstrate the archetype of a session beer for beer drinkers partial to an adjunct-forward pale lager.

2

Brewing Session Beer: Nothing to Hide Behind

In session beer brewing there is nothing to hide behind. There are hundreds of flavor compounds in beer: esters, phenols, acids, aldehydes, bittering compounds. . . and the list continues. Some compounds are more intense than others and can dominate or mask other compounds. Alcohol is a major flavor constituent and as the alcohol level in the beer lessens, other flavors become amplified.

Imagine cooking a basic spaghetti sauce. As you increase your garlic suddenly your pepper notes are lost; or perhaps, when your back is turned, your five-year-old daughter thinks it is funny to pour a cup of sugar in the sauce, and so it becomes unbearably sweet. Although this is a very simple analogy, it is an attempt to demonstrate the interplay between flavors and the effect this has throughout a beer's profile. One of the traditional ways to define a quality beer is that it is "free from defect"; the oldest example of a codified attempt

Figure 2.1. Yin and yang. The beauty of a session beer is a fine balance of flavor and lower alcohol.

to achieve quality is seen in the *Reinheitsgebot* purity law of 1516 (Pellettieri 2015, 6). Throughout the entire brewing process there are multiple opportunities to create or avoid defects in the final beer.

The "free from defect" definition of quality, as outlined by Mary Pellettieri in her recent book, *Quality Management*, has shifted and changed over the last 200 years to stay current with modern brewing trends. A sour beer, once defined as a potentially defective spoiling beer during the light lager craze following Prohibition, may now be held in high regard by today's sour beer enthusiast. What beer consumers believe to be a good quality beer one decade might shift the next, and the biggest challenge for brewers and publicans is the ongoing proper education about beer style variance to the consumer (ibid.).

When a brewer considers cutting a major flavor constituent like alcohol down to the level of 4% ABV, envision how the brewer's attention to detail must increase. Everything a brewer does is vitally important to the flavor profile of the final beer; from sourcing the freshest hops and finest malted barley, to slow and accurate carbonation.

I will never forget the time when my bar manager accidentally tapped a keg of the first sour beer made at the pub. I had prepared to introduce the beer to the staff during an educational session the following week, but instead it was tapped in place of our regular amber ale. The taste was found to be unpleasant because the pub guests and bartenders thought they were being served a freshly hopped amber ale, when in fact they were tasting a Flemish red. Does this mean the Flemish red was not a quality beer? Not at all. Education is key in the discussion of quality and essential when discussing how to make a quality session beer.

Yin and Yang: Balance Is Key

When talking about balance, I find the following description helpful:

> *In Western society, Yin-Yang is often referred to as "Yin and Yang" and brings to mind simple contrasts such as dark and light, male and female, logic and emotion. But Yin-Yang is much more than mere opposites. Rather, it represents the idea that the interaction of contradictory forces not only creates harmony, but also makes for a greater, more complete "whole." (Rebecca Shambaugh,* Huffington Post, *December 19, 2012, http://www.huffingtonpost.com/rebecca -shambaugh/integrated-leadership_b_2330535.html)*

A session brewer must be extremely tough on maintaining a quality process and, on the other hand, be delicate in their use of ingredients. This is the yin and yang of making a great session beer. Care must be taken in every aspect to protect the beer from being dominated by one flavor. Not only can an off flavor overpower a delicate session beer, but intense malt flavor or hops can also ruin a defect-free session beer. Quality measures a brewer should take when brewing a session beer are the same for brewing any beer of stronger ABV. However, if these measures are not attended to with strict obedience and managed correctly, the session beer will suffer to a greater extent due to its delicate nature. This concept is also true when manipulating anything in the process of brewing session beers.

From Grain to Glass

The phrase "grain to glass" is often used in the brewing world on tours, articles, and in conversation. When embarking on any given endeavor one usually

Figure 2.2. Malted barley is known affectionately as the "soul" of beer. Photo © Getty Images/LICreate.

considers the first steps they must take to reach their goal. However, when producing great session beer I would encourage both the homebrewer and professional to design their beer from glass to grain—begin with the end in mind. Imagine what the final beer will taste like in your glass. Whether emulating a certain style or giving birth to a new type of beer, beginning with the end in mind will guide the process before the ship leaves the harbor. Before grains are selected for the malt bill, consider what malt flavors you want in the final beer and how these malt flavors will interact with the hop profile. What yeast will be selected for fermentation and how will the flavors of fermentation comingle? Beginning with the end in mind when building a session beer recipe helps any brewer yield the flavor results desired. It's like reading a map and knowing where you are going before you start your car, it makes the whole trip much more successful.

Grain Selection

After the final beer has been fully envisioned in your mind, it is time to select the grain. As previously mentioned, a session beer is a very delicate and naked beer. All decisions a session brewer makes regarding their beer are exposed, there is simply nowhere to hide. Therefore, when selecting for the grain bill, it is helpful to pay particular attention to the base malt. If a German-style beer is being formulated, using German malt for the base is recommended to bring forth the unique nuances specific to that region. This in no way means that a quality American or Canadian base malt can't be substituted to produce an English or German-style session beer, but if the resources are available to the brewer, using the base malt that reflects the beer's region is the best option. If higher color and caramel flavors are desired, using a mid-range caramel (also known as crystal) malt in conjunction with a lower-color caramel malt is a good technique. The higher-color rated caramel malt will add significant flavor; using that malt with a light touch will prevent it from overpowering all other flavors.

One of my favorite session beer brewing techniques to drive color without heavy flavor is the use of dehusked black malt. There are many in the market to choose from, but my preference is Weyermann Carafa® Special III, which has the ability to contribute beautiful color without the harsh astringency usually associated with a traditional black malt that still has its husk. If you are looking for the blood-red color that black malt can offer, a great technique is not to add your dehusked black malt to the mash upon mill in. Instead, mash all your other grains and then mill in the black malt so it falls on top of the mash bed. Do not stir it into the mash, simply sparge over it and it will give you beautiful color.

Adding a malt backbone to a session beer is very important, especially if you are planning on hopping it up or adding any specialty ingredients. Several malts can enhance mouthfeel and aid body. When building your grain bill for a session beer, you have to keep in mind the low original gravity and you may want to consider using 1%–5% of dextrin malt. Ale yeast only has the ability to consume mono- and disaccharides, while lager yeast can also consume maltotriose. Dextrins are oligosaccharides, which are larger carbohydrates that cannot be digested by ale or lager yeast (Mallett 2014, 96). This means, as a brewer, you can add dextrin malt without contributing to the fermentable extract of the beer. Since 1945, Briess Malt & Ingredients Co. has produced a popular dextrin malt called Carapils®. Carapils adds mouthfeel, increases foam stability, and improves head retention, all without contributing flavor or color. Carapils has the full glassiness of a caramel malt but without the color, being only 1.5 degrees Lovibond (°L). The opposite of glassiness is known as mealy. Kilned base malts and Munich malts are known for being mealy. A malt that has both characters is known as "half."

Another way to build body and increase mouthfeel, as well as up the overall maltiness of a session beer, is through the use of Munich malt. Many of my personal session beer recipes include 5%–10% of light (10°L) Munich malt. Lighter colored Munich malts do have fermentable and enzymatic qualities, albeit lower than typical base malts. They can be used as a larger portion of the grist to produce nice malty characteristics. Munich malt is sold by nearly every malt supplier in the United States and Germany and is offered in a range of color strengths (Mallett 2014, 118).

Milling

Setting the grind of the mill is an important step in producing any style of quality beer. This remains true for session beers. Although a session beer starts at a lower original gravity than a higher-alcohol beer, the goal of obtaining a properly constructed grist is still the same. The grind should be set in a way that preserves the husk for mash filtration in lautering, but at the same time correctly crushing the grain to obtain the most extract available. By setting the rollers of the mill to the appropriate size gap, the brewer attains the most value from their purchased grain while also guaranteeing a successful lautering experience.

Going into the different types of mills and milling systems is beyond the scope of this book on session beers. However, session beers are delicate beers that can be negatively affected by an improper grind. The result can be cloudy wort and too many polyphenols being sent to the kettle, giving a bitter, husky, and astringent character in the finished beer. Since the majority of craft brewers employ dry milling, doing a sieve analysis (see sidebar, "Sieve Pans") will allow you to put numbers to your grist and help you track, evaluate, and better understand the results you get from it.

Water Preparation

Wait, don't pull the slide gate yet! Having good potable water free from contaminants is required for brewing any quality beer and equally critical for a session beer. Smell and taste the brewing water regularly. Also helpful is acquiring a local water report regarding the make-up of the water supply you use. The flavors you experience in the brewing water directly correlate with the flavors in your final beer. In addition, it's important to know the alkalinity of the mash and sparge water, as well as the desired pH of the mash. When brewing a quality beer containing a high percentage of pale malts, acidification of the mash water should be done to achieve the desired

SIEVE PANS

Every brewer's milling operation is slightly different, and the differences can become more pronounced over time. The easiest analysis of your own milling operation is a simple visual examination, making sure there are not any whole, uncracked kernels, and only a limited amount of flour. It is recommended for anyone who is milling grain to purchase a set of sieve pans. Sieve pans allow you to measure and analyze the grind profile with a repeatable method. The cost of the pans is relatively cheap when you consider how much extract can be left behind, or how much time a proper grind can save you with the lauter tun.

In the US, Seedburo Equipment is a supplier of sieve pans. When looking to purchase pans, you will also need a lid/cover and a catch pan. Sieve pan tests can be run mechanically or by hand. Mechanical tests use a Ro-Tap® machine. The American Society of Brewing Chemists (ASBC) has a procedure for doing it by hand.

BASIC GRIND SPECS

Pan #	Pan size[a]	Min %	Ideal %	Max %
14	1.40 mm	55	75	80
30	0.60 mm	5	15	30
60	0.25 mm	0	5	10
Thru	–	0	5	5

[a] Note 0.1 mm equals 100 microns, so 0.25 and 0.60 mm are 250 and 600 microns, respectively.

mash pH of 5.2 (Kunze 2004, 219). It is particularly important for the brewer to correctly prepare their mash and sparge water to prevent harsh-tasting, astringent polyphenols from being extracted due to rising pH (Sanchez 1999, 41). This is most important toward the end of the sparging process where high-alkaline water will raise the pH of the mash and aggressively pull the harsh-tasting polyphenols into the kettle. These polyphenols will greatly distract the consumer from enjoying the finer flavor attributes present, especially in a session beer.

Water varies from region to region, making it very important to test the alkalinity of the local water before embarking on your brew day. Affordable and easy-to-use alkalinity kits are available from many lab supply stores. For the homebrewer, a brief telephone call to your water department can help to determine your water's alkalinity. If your region has high-alkaline water, simply adding 1%–3% acidified malt, available at most homebrew supply shops, can help bring a high-pH pale malt mash down to within the correct pH range. Dark malts also assist in lowering the pH of the mash and buffering against rising pH throughout the sparging process; therefore, acidification of the mash is rarely necessary when brewing a session brown ale or dry Irish stout.

A very simple measure in the brewhouse to enable proper pH control is to have an accurate and well cared for pH meter. They are simple to use and should be calibrated weekly using, at least, two-point calibration. The technical department available at most laboratory equipment supply houses are very helpful when it comes to using brewery instrumentation, so do not hesitate to seek their advice. Knowing how to take a sample, calibrate, store, and properly use the brewhouse laboratory equipment is extremely important in yielding honest and accurate results that help guide both decision making and trouble shooting. *Water* by John Palmer and Colin Kaminski is a fantastic book to help you gain more in-depth knowledge regarding the preparation and use of water throughout the brewery. For the homebrewer on a limited budget, color-coded pH strips are obtainable for a reasonable cost and are extremely easy to use.

It is common practice to add calcium in some form to the mash to help buffer against rising pH, protect certain malt enzymes from heat, and enhance starch conversion (Sanchez 1999, 43). Since only about 40% of the calcium added to the mash carries over to the kettle, a kettle addition may also be warranted depending on the regional water and beer style being created. Session beer styles come in many forms, from light to dark, malty to hoppy, phenolic to ester-forward, and everything in between. Therefore, recommending just one type of salt addition for session brewing would be extremely short-sighted. However, when producing many varying styles of session ales and lagers, I have found it more beneficial to use calcium chloride over calcium sulfate. Calcium chloride provides a palate fullness and rounds out a lower-alcohol beer, whereas calcium sulfate is helpful when looking to increase and enhance a dry finish to the beer (Sanchez 1999, 43). There are many great resources offered by the Master Brewers Association of the Americas (MBAA) and Brewers Association (BA) that explain how to calculate calcium additions necessary for the mash and boil.

Mashing

Once your brew water has been properly prepared, it is time to decide what the proper rest temperature should be for the session beer and if a step mash should occur. The amount of fermentable sugar needed for a session beer is less than that for a higher-alcohol beer. It is also favorable to carry over unfermentable dextrins to help develop palate fullness and body for the beer (Fahy and Spencer 1999, 114).

The alpha-amylase enzyme, which breaks down long starch chains into smaller dextrins, performs best at 149–153°F (65–67°C). The beta-amylase enzyme produces maltose by randomly chomping off maltose groups from the end of starch chains, also producing glucose and maltotriose (Kunze 2004, 217). The ideal temperature for beta-amylase performance is between 126°F and 144°F (52–62°C; Fahy and Spencer 1999, 114). Since the requirement for fermentable sugar in the wort is less for a lower-alcohol beer and the desire for dextrin is greater, the optimum mash rest temperature for conversion is 155–157°F (68–69°C). The highly modified malt of today needs little to no protein rest when brewing a standard session ale; however, session beers containing a high percentage of wheat or under-modified barley must be treated differently due to the elevated amount of protein.

When a brewer is provided with a malt analysis, both the total and soluble protein percentages are listed. Typically, the soluble-to-total protein (S/T) ratio is between 40% and 44%, which should allow for an easy lauter in a single infusion mash. Ron Ryan, who has held a number of positions in the craft brewing and malting industries, has a great deal of knowledge and experience when it comes to malt and malting in North America. Ryan helped greatly to shed light on the subject of protein in regard to wort production.

The free amino nitrogen (FAN) level is an important malt measure relevant to protein level, says Ryan. Initially, all barley protein is insoluble and must be broken down. Historically, malt was very under-modified and long protein rests were therefore needed to help further break down soluble protein into FAN, which helps provide enough nutrients for yeast metabolism. The well-modified malt of today has more than enough FAN for the yeast. In fact, a beer entirely made with well-modified barley malt sometimes provides too much FAN, driving up the pH and making the beer more susceptible to bacterial infection. If a beer has a high amount of residual FAN and is also low in alcohol, the risk of bacterial infection becomes even greater. An average FAN level for today's highly modified two-row will hover around 180 parts per million (ppm).

A protein rest is unnecessary today when there is such easy access to well-modified malts. There are exceptions, however, such as when a particular season's barley has an exceptionally high beta-glucan content. Another reason to use under-modified malt requiring a protein rest would be if the brewer wanted to emulate a historic session beer style, such as an extremely light-colored Czech Pilsner. Ryan explains that you cannot modify malt without producing some color, therefore, if an extremely light color is desired, the amount the malt is modified will have to be considered.

Residual soluble protein in the finished beer is known to contribute to palate fullness and head retention. It is theorized that this results from residual soluble protein lowering surface tension, increasing viscosity, and forming a film on the gas bubbles that helps stabilize foam (Briggs et al. 1981, 270). Although the session beer brewer definitely needs to ensure the malt they are purchasing has enough soluble protein for body, yeast metabolism, and head retention, too much low-molecular-weight protein can cause haze in the finished beer and should be monitored.

The behavioral traits of the particular yeast strain being used in fermentation must also be given attention when determining the best mash rest temperature. For the purposes of fermenting wort made with highly modified malt and using a standard American ale yeast, resting between 155°F and 157°F (68–69°C) creates enough fermentable sugar for a healthy attenuation while also producing dextrins to build body. The goal is to not attenuate the beer to such a dry point that it falls off the palate with no remembrance. A session beer must be one that you keep coming back to, time and time again.

Figure 2.3. With a lighter backdrop of alcohol in a session beer, hop bitterness during the boil requires a delicate balance. Photo © Brewers Association.

Boiling and Hop Bitterness

As mentioned previously in the Water Preparation section, only approximately 40% of dissolved calcium from the mash is carried forward to the boil, making it often necessary for another calcium addition in the kettle, if the style of session beer justifies it. Your salt addition goals to achieve the desired result should be worked out prior to the beginning of the brew day, and will vary with the session beer style being produced. Calcium is not the only mineral to consider by far, but is the most important due to its many favorable benefits throughout the entire brewing process. There are no special considerations regarding boil time for a session beer as compared to a higher-gravity wort; 60–90 minutes should be sufficient. The objectives of the boil are much the same for low and high-alcohol beers: wort sterilization and concentration, extraction and isomerization of alpha acids, color formation, and protein denaturation (Rehberger and Luther 1999, 165). If added caramelization is desired through Maillard reactions, a lengthier boil time may be needed, but you will need to consider wort concentration in regard to original gravity. Since wort concentration is usually not necessary due to the typical low starting gravity of a session beer, it takes a back seat in boil priorities.

More often than not, the need to reduce the original gravity becomes apparent during the boil. Watering down your wort to hit your target gravity is best done, if necessary, toward the beginning of the boil. I believe extracting and isomerizing alpha acids from the boil hops while the wort is close to the target original gravity helps to create a well-constructed and uniform taste profile in the final session beer. (Most of my research regarding this conjecture is trial and error over 20 years brewing session beers in Utah.) Therefore, it is necessary to take a gravity reading when the kettle is full. The specific kettle evaporation rate and the degrees Plato the beer needs to drop to hit target original gravity will dictate the appropriate water addition. A typical evaporation rate for a 60-minute boil is 6%–10%, but this will vary with elevation, wort viscosity, and type of kettle. Therefore, wort gravity should be measured throughout the boil. For the homebrewer, simply brewing consecutive batches and taking multiple gravity readings will help you develop a rhythm for determining and hitting the desired original gravity.

Special care and attention must be given when calculating hop bitterness and building the flavor profile for the final session beer. Unfortunately, there has been little research conducted on hop placement in the boil and how it relates to the quality of bitterness experienced. Choosing the best hop variety to express the type of bitterness and aroma desired while taking staling features and cost into consideration are all important aspects of selection. In chapter 3 I will review the importance of developing quality hop character in session India pale ale (IPA), along with the most recent research regarding theory and technique.

Since the alcohol level usually falls below 5% ABV, the amount of bitterness a session beer can handle is limited. This helps explain why most session beer styles, such as British ordinary bitters and milds, German helles and Kölsch, and dry Irish stouts, all have lower IBU specifications in the relevant style guidelines. What you can infer from this is that maintaining an appropriate bitterness level that compliments and completes a session beer is crucial. The primary defining characteristic of a session beer is that it must be extremely enjoyable and repeatable; keeping the customer coming back for additional pints is essential. No one flavor component can strongly overpower another. Balance is one of the most important aspects of brewing session beer, especially with regard to IBU calculations and how hop bitterness will interact with maltiness, ester and phenol development, and yeast load. We will revisit the importance of balance when developing bitterness throughout the boil in chapter 3.

Many session beer styles have a rating of 12–47 IBUs. Because of how sensitive people's perception of bitterness is between different IBU values at the lower end of the IBU spectrum, this 35 IBU range is vast. Figuring out where to drop the IBU pin is a fundamental decision when constructing a session beer. I often use the word "delicate" when discussing session beers. Merriam-Webster's dictionary has been helping us understand the English language since 1828; here is its abbreviated definition of the word *delicate*:

> *[1b] pleasing to the senses of taste or smell especially in a mild or subtle way. . . .[2a] marked by keen sensitivity or fine discrimination. . . .[3b] easily torn or damaged. . . .[4a] requiring careful handling. . . .[5] marked by great precision or sensitivity.* (Merriam-Webster OnLine, *s.v.* "delicate," accessed April 9, 2017, http://www .merriam-webster.com/dictionary/delicate)

To say that session beer is delicate is an understatement. Trial and error to find the right bittering hops and the exact IBU level that compliments your beer's overall profile is the best technique for brewing great session beer.

Yeast and Fermentation

Highly drinkable session beer is neither too bitter nor too malty, neither too sweet nor too dry. Balance is key for drinkability. Hundreds of flavor constituents are developed through fermentation that aid or detract from the overall impression of a session beer. Therefore, creating the best environment possible for the yeast to complete the fermentation cycle will produce the highest quality session beer possible.

The technique of starting the fermentation for a session beer at a high original gravity (e.g., 14–16°P) and arresting fermentation through cooling to halt alcohol production is highly discouraged. The thinking behind this process is that the cooling causes the yeast, which is actively fermenting, to prematurely flocculate and sink to the bottom, so producing less alcohol. What is left in the final beer is residual sugar created during the mash. High residual sweetness does not equal high drinkability and it also puts the beer at greater risk of bacterial infection. Generally speaking, a more appropriate original gravity for creating a highly quaffable session beer is between 9°P and 12.5°P. Furthermore, arresting fermentation prior to completion by cooling the beer is abusive to the yeast and the beer. Diacetyl, a vicinal diketone (VDK) responsible for the buttery flavor that can be very offensive in many beers, is easily expressed at inappropriate levels when fermentation and maturation are mishandled. During the initial stages of fermentation the yeast forms the diacetyl precursor, acetohydroxy acid. Through oxidation, acetohydroxy acid is converted to diacetyl and 2,3-pentanedione, another VDK. Many factors, such as pH, temperature, and oxygen levels affect the rate of this conversion.

The formation of VDKs via oxidation is part of the natural process for both ale and lager yeast fermentations. Once the diacetyl has developed in the fermentor, it must be reduced by the yeast to prevent its manifestation in the final beer. If provided with the correct environment, healthy yeast has a strong capacity to metabolize diacetyl to 2,3-butanediol, which has a very high flavor threshold. The yeast must be given adequate contact time with the beer to remove diacetyl; therefore, chilling the fermentor and causing premature flocculation will leave high amounts of residual diacetyl unmetabolized (Kunze 2004, 377). The stress of premature cooling can also create problems down the line when harvesting and pitching the next batch of yeast.

One of the most important quality measures a brewer can perform is to count their yeast prior to pitching. This is especially true for the session beer brewer. Being accurate with the amount of yeast is crucial for healthy fermentation and keeping off flavors, such as acetaldehyde, at bay. A very simple procedure to determine you are using the appropriate amount of yeast when pitching is through the use of a hemocytometer. Detailed information on the process of counting yeast is outlined in Pellettieri's *Quality Management* (pp.76–77), and detailed practices are listed by the American Society for Brewing Chemists (ASBC). I cannot emphasize enough the importance of having the correct amount of viable yeast for a healthy fermentation. The general rule of thumb for a healthy pitching rate is 1 million cells per degree Plato (Knudsen 1999, 240). For the homebrewer this rate equates to 0.95 billion cells per gallon of wort per point (1.001) of gravity (Palmer 2017, 111). However, many homebrewers do not have a microscope or cell counting chamber available, but I bet they have a brewpub nearby. Many brewers, especially in small breweries, are happy to half-fill a clean growler with fresh house yeast. In the small batch brewing I conducted at Squatters in Utah, I found that half a pint (8 fl. oz., or about 250 mL) of fresh yeast was a healthy amount of yeast to ferment five gallons (19 L) of a low-gravity beer.

Having the correct amount of yeast is just one factor in producing great fermentations. Knowing the yeast strain—its attributes and behavioral characteristics as they relate to flavor production—is also imperative. One of the best ways to develop "true to style" session beer, such as a traditional altbier or pale weissbier, is to pitch the proper yeast strain. The unique flavors developed by individual strains are an important factor when constructing the complexity and beauty inherent in a session beer and should not be overlooked. Once you have selected a particular yeast strain, a key component to investigate is its optimal temperature range for fermentation. For example, White Labs performed a gas chromatography trial using two different beers fermented at slightly different temperatures with California ale yeast. One beer was fermented at 66°F (19°C) and the other at 75°F (24°C). The levels of many flavor compounds, such as ethyl acetate, diacetyl, and acetaldehyde, to name a few, were all elevated in the warmer fermented beer (White and Zainasheff 2010, 109). Certain expressive yeast strains, such as saison yeast, will also produce varying phenolic characteristics depending on the temperature at which they are fermented. Unlike hop aroma, once phenolic flavors are produced they do not dissipate with time. Knowing the selected yeast's ability to produce various flavor compounds and controlling the fermentation temperature according to the flavor profile you desire in the final beer is crucial.

Most modern fermentation vessels have temperature controllers that make it easy to control temperature. For the homebrewer, controlling fermentation temperature can be one of the most challenging things about producing beer. If fermenting in a carboy, there are cost effective, color-coded temperature stickers available. For the more advanced homebrewer, digital temperature monitors and electric heaters are available. Cross-checking your instrumentation is always recommended for those brewers who prefer to get to sleep at night. For those using a digital temperature probe, make sure to calibrate it regularly by placing the probe in a glass full of ice water (mostly ice), where it should read 32°F (0°C).

Dissolved oxygen in wort is another major consideration when providing the perfect environment for a prosperous fermentation. When fermenting a session beer, which usually starts below 12°P, 8–10 ppm of dissolved oxygen is the suggested range (Takacs and Hackbarth 2007). Worts with a higher original gravity, especially over 17°P, require larger amounts of dissolved oxygen. If your brewery produces higher-alcohol beers, medical oxygen is often used for the oxygen supply. Once production of a session beer starts at a brewery, a keen eye should be kept on the dissolved oxygen entering the wort stream. It is easy to overoxygenate wort when using medical oxygen, as opposed to using air. Air is a mixture of gases and will not overoxygenate your wort. If the brewery is switching between high-gravity wort and low-gravity wort while using the same medical oxygen supply, then care must be taken to prevent overoxygenation. Luckily, it is a simple process to monitor the dissolved oxygen in wort through the purchase of a dissolved oxygen probe and meter. Many high-end pH meters can also change their probes out and accept a dissolved oxygen probe, which can kill two birds with one stone.

There are so many variables that can be manipulated to help yield a fruitful fermentation. I have always said that wort is made in the brewhouse and beer is made in the cellar. No matter how successfully sugars were extracted from the mash, or how vigorous the boil, nothing can change the off flavors developed from an unhealthy or mismanaged fermentation.

Maturation

Recipe design for a session beer, like any beer, does not end after you have scratched out the malt and hops you want on the back of a coaster. Yeast and water are also equally important ingredients. Production of a quality session beer is not complete until the perfect pint is poured three to four times and a smile is on the brewer's face. Management of the yeast and beer after fermentation should be handled with care to ensure any off flavors developed have been reabsorbed by the residual yeast.

A diacetyl rest should be done for at least 24 hours after fermentation is complete, indicated by a halt in gravity drop. It is good to have a hard rule of thumb on when to call the primary fermentation complete. My rule for a complete fermentation has always been if there is no more than a 0.15°P drop over a 24-hour period. The difference between the original gravity and final gravity is called attenuation. Brewer's yeast typically attenuates a beer anywhere between 65%–85% (White and Zainasheff 2010, 109). Knowing the approximate attenuation expected for a given yeast strain will assist the brewer in determining when primary fermentation has ended.

After fermentation is complete it is essential to remove the yeast from the beer to prevent off flavors due to yeast autolysis, which is the self-destruction of yeast cells as the yeast gets old or is stressed. The yeast cell wall and cell membrane are selectively permeable, which allows for the controlled transport of certain substances, like sugars and fatty acids, into the cell interior. Toxins, such as alcohol, are also excreted out of the yeast through the cell membrane and cell wall to the exterior environment, which, in this case, is the beer (Kunze 2004, 85). When a yeast cell autolyzes, however, all of its contents are released into the beer. After fermentation is complete, the rate of yeast autolysis increases during both cold and warm storage, and is a source of very unpleasant off flavors in the final beer (Patino 1999, 318). When producing session beer, everything a brewer does can significantly affect the final outcome due to the delicate nature of lower-alcohol beer. Managing the maturation temperature and yeast after primary fermentation is extremely important to keep off flavors out of the final beer, allowing the balanced malt and hop profile created in the brewhouse to captivate the drinker and keep them coming back.

Clarification and Stability

After maturation, it is time to decide how clear the session beer will be. There are a great number of yeast cells and other turbid particles still in suspension during maturation. Filtration is the main process used by breweries to remove these yeast cells and other turbid material from the beer (Kunze 2004, 453). There are many types of beer filtration methods and all require the brewer to keep a sharp eye on potential oxygen pickup throughout the process. At the end of maturation, there is very little oxygen in beer. Typical readings through a dissolved oxygen meter are in the single digits in parts per billion (ppb). Oxygen is the brewer's worst enemy. All the wonderful flavors a brewer has artfully combined into their beautiful session beer can be quickly ruined by the ingress of oxygen. Carbonyls, such as aldehydes, make up the largest group of flavor substances that can undergo oxidization when a beer ages. Aldehydes are themselves oxidation products from alcohols. The main source of carbonyls is through Maillard reactions, and through enzymatic degradation and autoxidation of unsaturated fatty acids. The presence of oxygen is what activates oxidation of carbonyls and/or their precursors, therefore, it is essential to protect the final beer from it (Kunze 2004, 504).

When deciding to filter or not, the brewer has to take many things into consideration. If the appearance and flavor profile warrant a certain amount of turbidity in the final beer, such as a weissbier, then perhaps no filtration process will be necessary. Or, possibly, the final beer is best served with running a course filtration, where most of the yeast and particles are removed but some remain for flavor and appearance purposes. When weighing all the choices of filtration, how and when the beer will be consumed is extremely important to consider. At a brewpub, where beer is consumed fresh on tap, shelf stabilization is not as high of a concern when compared to beer being shipped across the country. Meaning, if a clear filtered beer is desired and it will be shelved on a grocery store aisle, a diligent eye must watch over any potential oxygen ingress.

Diatomaceous earth (DE), the skeletal remains of microscopic plants deposited on ancient ocean and lake beds, is the media used in beer filtration. It is the porosity of DE that creates the filter cake and traps yeast and particulate matter, clarifying the beer (Patino 1999, 307). The porosity of DE is both the greatest friend and enemy of the brewer. Unfortunately, DE is very good at taking on oxygen, subsequently oxygenating the beer during filtration. Many brewers purge their DE filter bed with carbon dioxide for a designated length of time to reduce the amount of oxygen trapped in the filter and so reduce the chance of adding oxygen to the final beer.

There has always been a debate within the brewing industry regarding filtration and its "stripping" effect on beer flavor. Some brewers decide to use finings instead of filtration to clarify their beer, while some choose not to filter or clarify at all due to the fear of losing flavor and aroma. There are many great fining products on the market that can reduce yeast and protein load when added to either the fermentor, during maturation, or the bright beer tank. Typically, finings need cold temperatures to work and 24–72 hours to perform their settling.

For the homebrewer, there are safer and easier products than DE to use. Adding finings, such as gelatin, isinglass, or a silicic acid clarifier, is a great way to produce clear beer at home. They are simple and safe to use and do not require a filter. But wait, before you grab for that next exciting product that will help make your session beer clearer, keep it simple and consider the properties of the yeast used to ferment your beer. When using a highly flocculent yeast, adding a clarifying agent is often not necessary to yield crystal-clear results. Simply setting your homebrew refrigerator to 33–36°F (1–2°C) and letting the yeast settle to the bottom of the carboy before racking the clear beer off the cake can yield remarkable results.

Each brewer will have to test the flavor-stripping theory for themselves when using their specific beer and filtration technique. Conducting side-by-side tastings will help determine whether filtration serves the session beer or takes away from it. Consider whether the filtered beer has less malt and hop flavor, as well as aroma. For instance, it may be surprising during bench trials how a now brilliant dry-hopped pale ale actually displays more hop flavor and aroma due to lack of yeast load. Therefore, in bench trials, sensory tasting should be conducted with a cover around the tasting cup so the panelists are unaware of how the beer looks when deciding on taste and aroma. However, while a true blind taste and aroma test is valuable, remember that this is not how a customer will enjoy your beer. Having a slight haze to an ale often gives the consumer a perception of fullness due to the lack of clarity. This can help a session beer be perceived as having more body just by visual effect alone. People use all their senses when consuming beer and the visual effect a beer has should not be overlooked.

If all brewing processes have been watched and monitored closely, filtration should not diminish the final beer flavor. Some of the world's best session beers that I have enjoyed are brilliant and bright filtered beers. In fact, when brewers choose to leave a heavy yeast load in their session beer to retain its "full" flavor, often times the heavy bitter yeast taste dominates and can cause the beer to become very unpleasant. The great flavors built into a session beer will not be undone by filtration; if oxygen is kept away from the finished beer in the filtration or clarification process, all those wonderful flavors should remain.

Balance and Specialty Ingredients

It is important to note that more does not always mean better in brewing. Whether it's overdoing the bitterness in the boil or driving up 4-vinylguaiacol in fermentation, having a heavy hand when brewing session beer is never good. Ease up and you will reap great rewards. Remember the yin and yang of session beer brewing. Use an intense focus on quality and process, while gently manipulating the ingredients. We live in uncharted territories in the craft brewing industry. New breweries are opening daily, and everyone wants to create something new to differentiate themselves. One of the most difficult tasks an all-session beer brewer faces is differentiation between their lower-alcohol beers at the taps, especially if you have 14 taps! If session beer is what your brewery is trying to create, then driving alcohol up to make the beers different is not an option.

When confronted with this challenge, specialty ingredients are often used. Cocoa nibs, coffee beans, vanilla, or fruit might come to mind while planning your next seasonal rotation. The recurring theme of this book is balance; steadiness will always serve the unique session beer you are creating. Conduct bench trials when adding a specialty ingredient you have never brewed with before. Decide how the the specialty ingredient will be used in the brewing process. Will it be roasted, smashed pumpkins in the mash tun? Or perhaps ground fresh spice, placed into a muslin sack and hung in the kettle at the end of boil? I have always favored cold side infusion over hot side when working with specialty ingredients, and less is ALWAYS better, especially in a session beer.

When conducting a bench trial at home or on a small scale in the brewery, procure some base beer from the tank or from the local bottle shop. For example, if you are preparing to brew a vanilla stout, obtain a traditional stout to use as your base beer in the trial—then you can experiment! Slice open one vanilla bean and start by infusing it cold into a beer sample. Allow the bean to steep in your fridge for a couple of days. Sensory is the best guide in experimentation, which brings us to the next section.

Sensory Evaluation

Sensory evaluation for determining if a beer is free from defect has been an established practice for breweries throughout the world for hundreds of years. It can be as simple as tasting your beer daily as it ferments and especially prior to filtration or packaging, to developing a formal sensory analysis team and daily training on off-flavor detection. The ASBC has been dedicated to bringing uniformity and assistance to the brewing community to improve beer at the technical level since 1934 (ASBC 2017). It has conducted copious amounts of work on flavor threshold detection in beer. A flavor threshold indicates the lowest concentration at which an odor or flavor can be detected in a beer. For its members, the ASBC website lists a beer flavor database of 624 molecules in beer, with concentrations given in milligrams per liter. The base beer that was used to determine the threshold of the compounds did vary, but "with most being international lager beers."[1] Since international lager beers are typically between 4% and 5% ABV, the threshold

---

[1]   "Beer Flavor Database," ASBC Methods of Analysis, accessed April 10, 2017, http://methods.asbcnet .org/Flavors_Database.aspx.

concentrations listed by the ASBC for common off flavors will suffice for a session beer sensory evaluation.

The prevailing view from brewing industry research is alcohol level alone doesn't seem to predict flavor thresholds, but we do know the masking effects of, for example, the many different compounds found in hops, do have an impact. One study reported that the concentration level of linalool in beer affected whether it could either mask or promote off flavors like DMS (Hanke et al. 2010). The same study found similar results with the esters, ethyl acetate and isoamyl acetate.

There are hundreds of compounds in a beer's make up that interact to determine beer flavor; more research needs to be conducted on the multitude of interactions between these compounds and their effect on beer flavor. Many brewers believe that it is harder to detect certain off flavors at or just above their threshold level, because high IBUs creates palate fatigue. This makes sensory training for the session beer brewer essential. For the brewer producing session beer, a trained palate is critically important when evaluating the beer to determine it is free from defect. There are many tools and flavor dosing kits in the marketplace for developing sensory evaluation protocol in the brewery. Training the palates of the brewing company staff does not need to be difficult and elaborate, but is absolutely essential in producing high quality, flavorful session beer.

Figure 2.4. Sensory training is essential not only for competitions, but also throughout the beer-making process to assure quality in the finished product. Photo © Brewers Association.

Safety and Sanitation

The brewing of quality session beer shares the same fundamental production principles of all brewing: safety and sanitation. From grain to glass, all details of the process must be given the highest attention for every beer.

Safety First

Safety in the brewery must be attended to first and foremost. Personal protective equipment (PPE) needs to be available for all personnel on the production floor, and also for homebrewers. . . that means your kitchen! In a commercial brewery, common PPE includes proper eye protection, ear protection, steel-toed footwear, and heat- and chemical-resistant gloves. What department a brewer is working in will dictate what specific PPE is required to keep them safe. In the malt handling room, all respirators should be routinely checked for proper fit and filtration cartridges replaced. Various glove wear needs to be purchased for each specific activity the brewer is attending to. Brewing glove wear is not all built the same. Depending on whether the brewer is handling hot wort, various chemicals, or working on a bottling line the correct type of gloves should be worn. Shorts are not part of the brewer's attire and should be saved for relaxing and drinking beer after work.

In addition to basic PPE, other brewery safety measures need to be attended to prior to producing quality beer. In commercial breweries, the use of anti-static vacuums is highly recommended to reduce the chance of dust explosions. All hazardous chemicals should be clearly marked and properly designated to be compliant with the Globally Harmonized System (GHS), which provides universally agreed upon guidelines for the classification of chemical hazards and a standardized approach to label elements and safety data sheets. Map out forklift travel routes and label them for safe walking and driving. Ensure pallet racks are properly assembled and stacked according to all safety regulations, taking into account loading and offloading activities. Make certain that pressure for both air and carbon dioxide gas is regulated properly. Carbon dioxide typically comes into the brewery at 110 pounds per square inch (psi.) and needs to be regulated down upon entry to at or below 60 psi. when applicable. It is a very rare situation that brewing staff will need carbon dioxide at levels higher than 60 psi. It is also highly advisable to install carbon dioxide monitors throughout the production and packaging areas to alert any employees to hazardous levels of carbon dioxide.

By far the absolute most important safety measure any brewery can do is build a safe brewery culture. Establishing routine training sessions and having proper safety procedures demonstrated by all brewery employees, at whatever level, helps form and cement a culture of safety. Production brewery work is fast-paced and tiring. Attending to safety precautions before the work day starts will greatly help prevent injuries. Proper training of all employees regarding safe brewery procedures must be the highest priority.

Providing a safe working environment does not need to be complicated, in fact, the simpler it is the better. For the novice homebrewer it's as easy as making sure all your hazardous cleaning chemicals are stored in a cool, dry environment, inaccessible to children and pets. When wort is boiling in your garage or on the stove, family and friends need to be protected from burns; make sure you have a first-aid kit available in case of accidents. When bottle conditioning, caution needs to be used when storing bottles during re-fermentation, in case overcarbonation causes bottles to explode. Bottle explosion is a common experience for many homebrewers when first learning to bottle condition, and it can be very dangerous. For advanced homebrewers using regulated gas, all precautions should be taken handling carbon dioxide under pressure, and regulators should be accurate, correctly set, and in good working order.

Safety precautions and protocols are probably the last item any brewer wants to discuss when conversing with their fellow brewers, but it is the most essential piece. We must keep ourselves and our brewers safe, first and foremost, to be able to brew beer. Without healthy, safe brewers there is no beer. In addition to Pellettieri's *Quality Management*, the BA website has a wealth of resources outlining good manufacturing practices (GMP) and governmental regulations and requirements, as well as free online safety training. Go to the "Best Practices" section of the BA website, http://www .brewersassociation.org/best-practices/. Other free online safety resources are available from the MBAA.

Cleanliness Is Next to Godliness (No Rest for the Weary)
One thing all brewers know is that the job never ends. There is always something left to clean, yeast to be handled, or ingredients to be sourced. Next to safety, cleanliness is the most important task in the brewer's day. Hop compounds, alcohol, carbon dioxide, as well as low oxygen and low pH all inhibit the growth of microbiological contaminants (Vaughan 2005). Session beers, therefore, are

more susceptible to microbial spoilage due to their lower alcohol content and lower bitterness range. Hops protect beer from lactic acid bacteria because of the antibacterial properties of alpha acids and beta acids found in the soluble hop resins, although these only inhibit the growth of Gram-positive bacteria (Vaughan et al. 2005). Interestingly, the pH of the final beer greatly affects the protective effect of the iso-alpha acids derived from the hops. The antibacterial activity of iso-alpha acids decreases as the pH level increases. An increase in pH by as little as 0.2 can reduce the protective effect of the iso-alpha acids by as much as 50% (Vaughan et al. 2005). This demonstrates how important it is for the brewer to be aware of pH throughout the entire brewing process. The typical pH range of finished beer usually falls between 4.25 and 4.6.

When cleaning, attention to detail should be the utmost concern for a session beer brewer and should never be taken lightly. First and foremost, standard operating procedures (SOP) need to be set in place for all cleaning and sanitation actions that occur during the entire production process. A well-protected and clean brewhouse can produce very clean wort, but this can be ruined by the introduction of beer-spoiling bacteria in packaging. No stone should remain unturned. There is extensive information throughout industry publications and organizations, such as the BA and MBAA, outlining proper cleaning regimes for each area in the brewery. Another great resource when designing a specific brewery SOP program is to request one through your chemical supply company. When deciding what chemical company to purchase supplies from, it serves the brewer to review the technical resources and support provided by the supply company. It is essential for brewers of any size brewery to realize that they are not just buying chemicals, they are building a relationship, and should be getting accurate and timely support in improving their SOP program.

Making decisions about cleaning and sanitation should be given ample time and not be taken lightly. There is an entire language to assimilate when learning how best to keep your brewery clean and sanitized. A simple, but key, example is to know the difference between sanitizing and sterilizing. To sanitize is to reduce microbial contaminants to an insignificant number, while to sterilize is to kill or eliminate the microbes altogether (Palmer 2017, 29). Sanitization is usually sufficient for most brewing applications, but sometimes a brewer needs to employ sterilization to assure zero microbial contaminants exist in the process.

The need for sterilization often occurs in packaging, or when a brewery produces both clean beers and beers that include lactobacilli, where cross-contamination from uncleaned equipment becomes an extremely high concern. In addition to acid-based sanitizers, heat is also a great way to sanitize and is commonly used throughout the entire brewing process to protect beer from most beer-spoiling microbes. To destroy active bacteria, yeast, and fungi, maintain a temperature of 175°F (80°C) for 5–10 minutes (Raines 1993). Using 185°F (85°C) hot-water sanitization for 25–30 minutes is a common procedure prior to knocking the wort out from the kettle to the fermentor and in bottling equipment just prior to packaging.

Questions about whether to sanitize or sterilize, whether to use chemicals or heat, and what the duration of contact time should be, must all be reviewed for each production department, from brewhouse to packaging. Disadvantages and advantages regarding each process and chemical usage must be carefully weighed. The cleaning process does not stop once the brewer has removed the initial organic soiling with detergent. Protein build-up must be taken into consideration, usually tackled using a low-corrosive phosphoric acid cleaner or nitric-phosphoric acid blend. How often a bright tank will be de-gassed, opened up, and cleaned with caustic and/or acid must be reviewed. What type of sanitizers are to be used and when they will need to be employed? The list of questions demanding proper answers that take into account cost, efficiency, and labor are endless and could fill a book of their own. However, one aspect of the cleaning process that should not need any deliberation is inspection. Every brewer should carry a working flashlight to make daily cleanliness inspections easy.

The task is not complete once the cleaning and sanitation cycle has ended; a cleaning plan must include how the brewer will dispose of the chemicals. All food and beverage manufacturing plants have a responsibility to protect their local community and environment from effluence. When developing their cleaning and sanitation SOP, I encourage all brewers to continually ask two guiding questions: how will this affect the quality of the final beer, and how will this affect the environment? Good manufacturing practices are the minimum processing requirements, established by the Food and Drug Administration, for keeping food and beverages safe and wholesome. All breweries should adhere to GMP and establish their cleaning and sanitation SOP accordingly.

For the homebrewer making session beer, cleanliness is equally as important. There are plenty of simple techniques and chemicals in the marketplace that can be used to keep your beer clean and fresh. Bleach is inexpensive and has proven effective for sanitizing equipment at home. A homebrewer does not usually need to sterilize equipment, but certain situations warrant it—in this case, heat is always an effective method. Boiling (at 212°F/100°C, depending on elevation) homebrew equipment for 20–60 minutes is a great way to sterilize. Alternatively, an oven can provide dry heat for sterilizing. The hotter the temperature the shorter the duration needed. For example, items in an oven at 338°F (170°C) only require 60 minutes, whereas items in a 250°F (121°C) oven will require 12 hours (Palmer 2017, 37). Always exercise caution when using chemicals, boiling liquids, or placing foreign objects in the oven, so safety first and protect the family!

Properly maintaining equipment is equally as important as properly cleaning equipment. One might ask, which came first, the chicken or the egg? In the case of brewing, that question is easy to answer. Before any brewing commences, a brewery must be built and assembled. But the relationship with the maintenance department certainly does not end once building stops and brewing begins. Routine preventive maintenance is essential in running an efficient and productive brewery. At the center of a solid preventive maintenance program is accurate record keeping. It is difficult to know where you are going if you do not now where you have been. Proper records should be kept throughout the entire brewing process, and this should also be the case when it comes to maintaining the equipment. In between preventive maintenance, periodic inspections should be performed on all equipment to check for any signs of possible failure, as well as general wear and tear. As any brewer knows, it is far less disruptive to catch a problem with a piece of equipment in advance and fix it before a breakdown occurs. Nothing is worse than being in the middle of a brewing or cellaring day when a crucial piece of equipment breaks and the mash has to be discarded, or the wort or finished beer must be sent down the drain due to mechanical failure.

The Intangibles

Brewing great session beer is a marriage of art and science. For example, technical brewing knowledge is necessary to hit specific parameters when facilitating starch conversion in the brewhouse. But, Vinnie Cilurzo reminded me that mash tun dimension also influences conversion. Although specific mash temperatures were mentioned in the above section, the dimension and configuration of each brewer's mash tun is unique and this can have a specific effect on attenuation and final gravity; therefore, rest temperatures will need to be manipulated accordingly. Each brewer will have to see for themselves how their process and equipment affects the outcome of the beer and troubleshoot based on their specific system.

It is wonderful to become highly educated regarding the fundamental science of brewing, but nothing replaces actually brewing on a given system and letting it guide you through the process. As Yvan De Baets has said a hundred times to me, "Jennifer, you must listen to your beer, it is your partner, and it is a relationship." I couldn't agree more. In fact, for the first five years of my brewing career all I did was listen to my beer. I had no formal brewing education at that time, and I had just come off seeing 100 or more Grateful Dead shows. Being in tune with and listening to my beer was all I knew, and answering to produce an even better beer was how I lived my life then and still do now. Theory and application help greatly in the brewing process of a session beer. However, at the end of the day, when the brewer is drinking the fruits of their labor, they must always ask the most important question, "Do I want another?" Even if errands call and time for another is not possible, asking the question is still important. Listen to your mind but lead with your heart, and your answer should always be yes.

3

Modern Interpretations

For millions of Americans, the definition of beer is a modern American lager. This is not to say that all mass-produced American lagers taste the same. There are flavor nuances, usually in the form of certain elevated or diminished esters, and other flavor compounds that differentiate macro lager beers on the shelf. Every day across the US, people in droves enter convenience stores to buy their favorite session beer.

Modern American Lager

Modern American lager is typically easy to drink, low in alcohol, low in bitterness, and low in flavor. This brings the conversation about session beer back to the roots of people's preference. What one beer drinker prefers, another may not.

Differentiation in beer styles in the US was repressed for many decades following Prohibition. Generations were born and raised with extremely limited choices in beer. I believe it is the fundamental purpose of the craft brewing industry to properly educate the American public that beer is more than the modern American lager. Beer comes in many different colors and flavors, with varying levels of bitterness and alcohol. Having choices at the tap is an incredibly important freedom that all Americans should have a right to. At the end of the day, however, many Americans may still prefer to drink macro American lager beer by the suitcase. It is the most consumed modern session beer in America. To fully understand how we became a nation that grew up on American lager, it is important to review how we got here.

High-Gravity Brewing

Americans have proven their love for beer decade after decade. As the demand for beer rose, the large brewing companies had to respond by increasing output. One of their techniques for increasing output was through a process called high-gravity brewing. High-gravity brewing has been employed by large brewing companies in America since the 1980s to help increase capacity (Kunze 2004, 509). High-gravity brewing allows a brewery to produce higher volumes of wort with significant energy savings. The water used for dilution after fermentation does not have to be heated and boiled, saving greatly on energy costs. Reduced labor, increased capacity, and decreased energy costs can incentivize a brewery to employ high-gravity brewing. While the economic advantages of creating beer through dilution are obvious, the resulting flavor can be affected.

The best way to protect the final beer from noticeable flavor changes when producing high-gravity wort is by keeping the wort between 12°P and 16°P. If dilution occurs post fermentation, de-aerated water is used to reduce oxygen pickup. Kunze states in *Technology Brewing and Malting* that high-gravity wort above 16°P runs the risk of producing greater fermentation by-products, which can carry over to the finished beer. Therefore, staying under 16°P for the starting gravity is highly recommended (Kunze 2004, 510).

One of the biggest negatives to high-gravity brewing is that foam stability suffers due to the water dilution. Since the 1980s, many American palates have been trained on large macro-brewed American lagers produced by high-gravity brewing. Weekend after weekend coolers throughout America are loaded down with macro American lager as families and friends head to their favorite sporting events, camping spots, lakes, or rivers. As long as the beer is kept cold, many macro American lagers taste very refreshing. The low ABV and extremely low bitterness make them easy to drink throughout the day and into the evening.

> *I have fond memories of fetching "barley pops" in Paducah, Kentucky for my Grandpa Herr so he wouldn't have to get off his tractor.*

Adolphus Busch

Budweiser® has certainly proven to be king of all macro American lagers, both in sales and notoriety. Adolphus Busch came to America from Germany in 1857. He married Lilian Anheuser and began working in her father's brewery. By 1877, Adolphus started brewing a beer style that resembled the Bohemian lager he had once enjoyed back home. There has been enormous controversy surrounding the slogan "King of Beers" and the Budweiser brand name, and with good reason. In 1842, during the birth of the German lager beer revolution, a Bohemian-style Pilsner was born in the town of České Budějovice, or Budweis in German, in what is now the Czech Republic. One such Czech Budweis beer, from the Budweiser Budvar brewery, was very popular in many of the royal houses throughout Europe and coined the "Beer of Kings" (Ogle 2006, 74). The brewing of Budweis beer dates back 700 years, and the town that built the first civic brewery is steeped in rich brewing tradition. The beer produced by Budweiser Budvar has shifted over time with modernization. Budvar is still produced today and distributed in over 50 countries. However, due to trademark disputes with Anheuser-Busch, Budweiser Budvar exported to North America is sold under the name Czechvar.

Pre-Prohibition Budweiser produced by Anheuser-Busch had much higher hopping rates than the current low-bitterness Budweiser of today, which hovers around 12 IBU. Anheuser Busch has referred to this shift since the early 1980s as a trend resulting from climate changes, consumer tastes, and changes in ingredients (Hieronymus 2012, 179). Others have speculated the downward creep in hopping rate developed from the changing preference of August Busch III and his desire for a lower bitterness as his palate changed throughout his life. Regardless of the exact reasons behind the bitterness drop, Budweiser, along with many other mass-produced American lager beers, has extremely low bitterness. Rice, two-row, and six-row malted barley comprise the grist bill for Budweiser. Rice has a very dry and neutral flavor, and adds enormous amounts of starch for conversion. This starch is only made available once the rice has been modified in a cereal cooker; because rice lacks the enzymes necessary for starch conversion, it must be cooked for a certain time in order to gelatinize the starch (Wahl and Heinus 1908, 466). Budweiser incorporates about 10% malted barley in the cereal cooker to make use of the malt's alpha-amylase enzymes. Adding a portion of malted barley to the cooker helps break down the gelatinized starch and reduce the viscosity of the adjuncts prior to pumping the entire portion into the mash (Bradee et al. 1999, 76). Using a cereal cooker at home to prepare rice for an American lager mash is quite labor intensive for the average homebrewer. Substituting a portion of flaked rice to the grain bill instead is a great way to emulate Budweiser at home. Brewer's flakes are preconditioned (gelatinized) by the manufacturer by rolling preheated grain (corn or rice) between steam-heated rollers before drying. This process eliminates the need for a cereal cooker (Bradee et al. 1999, 81).

The Quality of Adjuncts

When Adolphus Busch began formulating his New World Bohemian lager, like many German-born American brewers did at the time, he incorporated adjuncts. A well-known trade journal, *American Brewer*, was widely read during the late 1800s by the new generation of American brewers. The magazine's editor was Anton Schwarz, a Bohemian-born native who had studied under Karl Balling at the Polytechnic Institute in Prague in the mid-1800s. Limited land and low crop yields drove the price of malt up during this time, and Balling had therefore focused much of his research on the use of adjuncts in brewing. Schwarz emigrated to the United States in 1868 and began writing professional articles in *American Brewer* on the benefits of adjuncts in brewing. Schwarz quickly became promoted to editor of the magazine, and became one of the first prominent advocates of adjuncts in brewing. Although the different brews containing adjuncts often cost more to make than the traditional all-malt Bavarian beers, the new generation of American brewers quickly realized that they had a wide appeal to the American drinker (Ogle 2006, 75)

For many Americans in the latter half of the nineteenth century, working hard in the hot sun is how they spent their days. The flavor of a slightly sweet, heavy-bodied Bavarian helles was not what the American palate called for during these times. Published in 1933, *History of the Brewing Industry and Brewing Science in America* outlined a description of the American beer drinker's preference for beers made using malt adjuncts, stating,

The fact remains that the American taste as a whole was for beer ... carried to its utmost refinement of vinous consistency, pale color, and a hop flavor submerging the malt flavor, necessitating a beer made partly of unmalted de-germinated cereal products. (Arnold and Penman 1933, 98)

Both Anton Schwarz and Dr. John E. Siebel were experimenting with malt adjuncts and publishing their discoveries, professing that malt adjuncts did not make an inferior beer (Arnold and Penman 1933, 122).

At around the same time that Schwarz's career in America was beginning, Busch was attempting to develop a Bohemian lager clone using just high-protein six-row malted barley and was having poor results. My discussions with Scott Heisel, Vice President and Technical Director of the American Malting Barley Association (AMBA), indicate that, most likely, during the late 1800s specific barley strains for feed and malt were not yet developed. The maltsters, usually themselves part of the brewery staff, attempted to select the finest barley to be malted. Busch's early test batches were full-bodied and dark in color in comparison to the straw-colored and effervescent Bohemian Pilsner he loved so much (Ogle 2006, 74).

With adjuncts being promoted as another useful way to lighten the high-protein six-row barley, Busch began using a percentage of rice in his grist and was extremely pleased with the results. His new American brew was now the color of straw and lighter in body. Both rice and corn were readily available, lightening both the color and flavor of American beer in a way that was welcomed in the hot climate.

In her book, Ambitious Brews, *Maureen Ogle writes elegantly about the beginning use of adjuncts, and what I find so endearing are the commonalities between the first German-American immigrant brewers of the late nineteenth century and the modern craft brewers of today. For instance, an article will be written about a local brewery producing an imperial stout in a whiskey barrel and, next thing you know, almost every microbrewery in the nation has whiskey barrels in their cellars. The beauty of our craft is the sharing of ideas with our fellow brewers, inspiring and honoring each other through emulation.*

The advantages to using adjuncts to produce a widely distributed, light-in-color and easy-to-drink lager are numerous. Nationwide demand for beer was rapidly growing and having a shelf-stable beer that could travel long distances was necessary. Adjuncts, such as corn and rice, provide a paler color, more neutral flavor, and lower nitrogenous and phenolic compounds, producing less chance for haze formation. The lower protein contribution in adjuncts dilute the barley malt's high nitrogen content, which increases both colloidal and microbiological stability (Bradee et al. 1999, 75). In addition, the beer is less prone to flavor deterioration because adjuncts have lower levels of lipids (fats), which can contribute to staling when they undergo oxidation as the beer sits on the shelf (Briggs et al. 1981, 224).

There is a common misconception among craft brewers that the inclusion of adjuncts in American brewing culture was driven purely by economic reasons. However, as noted by Thausing et al. (1882, 206), "The extract from barley malt may frequently be cheaper in places where the expense of transporting rice is high or in seasons when the price of barley is low." The price of corn, rice, and barley fluctuated greatly during the late 1800s. Weather, transportation, and market trends greatly affected pricing. Corn was the less expensive adjunct in 1890, but by 1908 pricing had shifted and leveled the playing field.

Prices of barley, corn, and rice, like any agricultural commodity, vary with seasonal weather, acreage planted, disease, and supply and demand. One year the price of barley may be higher, while the following year corn or rice might take the lead. A review of historical data on agricultural commodities of the late 1800s and early 1900s show evidence that the use of adjuncts in early American lagers was not purely price driven. Adjunct use in American lager recipe formulation was therefore more likely due to flavor preference and quality than lower prices.

As previously stated, adjuncts help maintain shelf stability due to the low soluble protein content of the wort. In addition, with light, effervescent session beers proving popular with the workforce during the middle to late 1800s, adjuncts provided a lighter and dryer body compared to the all-malt, full-bodied, Bavarian-style beers. Another advantage was that adjuncts tended to be more predictable, helping maintain consistency in the brewery as well as shelf stability. Unlike brewing with today's highly modified, two-row barley malt, barley produced during the late nineteenth century often fluctuated in quality. Not knowing the condition of an upcoming barley shipment probably caused many a brewer immense stress when trying to consistently attenuate a beer. In the late 1800s many larger breweries malted their own grain, but still depended greatly on the farmer for quality barley. The unpredictability of the malted barley's performance in fermentation due to the rudimentary growing and malting practices caused early brewing malt to be highly variable in its enzymatic potential.

While early craft brewers may have viewed adjuncts negatively, attitudes seem to be shifting. There was a time when "extreme" beer was the only thing you could find at your local pub, but now the pendulum has swung and session beers are being widely promoted throughout the craft market. There are many positive ways to use a moderate percentage of adjuncts to achieve the goal of producing high-quality, light-bodied session beers. Craft brewers seem to be warming up to the use of adjuncts as just another tool in their toolbox for making great beer.

Most craft brewers lack a cereal cooker and, due to equipment limitations, are unable to prepare raw adjuncts for conversion (flaked adjuncts are pregelatinized and mash-ready for conversion). Thus, dextrose (corn sugar) seems to be the adjunct of choice for many American craft brewers, although it is not typically used in the production of session beers. Dextrose can be added late in the boil to raise the degrees Plato and it attenuates extremely well in fermentation, providing a dry finish to double and triple IPAs. Small percentages of dextrose benefit by contributing additional sugar for conversion and the increased attenuation that results produces a more microbiologically stable beer due to the lower level of residual sugars in the final beer.

Shelf stability in the name of quality is one major reason why adjuncts were incorporated historically. It begs the question, would an IPA made with 10%–20% rice be a superior beer? Perhaps it would taste fresher after traveling across a continent, the quality surviving longer on the shelf next to the other IPA offerings. Whether the benefits of adjuncts will find greater acceptance as craft beer evolves remains to be seen, but their role in producing quality beer, especially light-bodied, session beer, is clearly long-established.

Oldest Brewery in America

As described in chapter 1, "A Short History of Session Beers," many German brewers emigrated to America in the nineteenth century looking to build their fortune, and hundreds of breweries were opened across the country. D.G. Yuengling was one of them, as was Adolphus Busch. While Anheuser-Busch became the powerhouse of the macro brewing world, D.G. Yuengling & Son remains as the oldest surviving brewery in America, having been founded in 1829 (Yenne 2003, 142). D.G Yuengling arrived in Pottsville, Philadelphia in the 1820s, bringing with him his family's recipe book, a yeast sample, and little else. There were no national brands at the time and beer was extremely regional. While Yuengling has always had a history of brewing diverse beer styles that appeal to many different tastes and nationalities, the brand line up at Yuengling has always focused on session beers, both ales and lagers. Many early Yuengling brands were traditional beer styles that D.G. Yuengling used to drink back in Germany, such as dunkel and helles. Competition among regional breweries was fierce in the New World and in order to survive he made sure to listen to his customers.

Figure 3.1. D.G. Yuengling & Son is the oldest surviving brewery in America and continues to be family-owned and operated.

Yuengling Premium is a very popular regional beer in Pennsylvania and probably best resembles what the pre-World War II beers in America tasted like. Yuengling's most popular beer is their Traditional Lager. This lager has a slight caramel note to it in comparison to the Premium, which sets it apart. Yuengling brewmaster Jim Helmke's favorite two beers are the Yuengling Lord Chesterfield Ale and Yuengling Porter.

> *When I traveled to Philadelphia I noticed that all you had to do in the local bars was order a "lager" from the bartender and they brought you Yuengling Lager. I enjoyed many of the lagers during my week's stay and can personally attest to their highly sessionable nature.*

The Lord Chesterfield Ale is one of the few examples of a very early style of beer that used to dominate in North America but was not written about much. Lord Chesterfield Ale is a well-attenuated, dry-hopped pale ale. It's fermented at warm temperatures like ale, above 60°F (16°C), but cold-conditioned like a traditional lager. The bitterness is much higher than the mass-produced American lager of today, coming in at 30 IBUs. The style was born in the region of Eastern Canada and New England; hard to describe in the context of modern existing styles, this old session favorite is something like an American pale ale meets California common beer. Unfortunately, it seems to be a style on its way out, but one never knows when history will repeat itself again and lagered pale ales will once again take center stage.

Yuengling is one of the largest porter brewers in the world, and Yuengling Porter is one of the oldest, continuously brewed porters. This very sessionable porter is not sour, unlike many of the old versions of porter brewed in the mid-1700s that often had a slight sourness. Much of Yuengling's porter production goes into the making of the popular Black and Tan brand. Yuengling continues to demonstrate a passion for producing diverse styles of craft beer, many of which are under 5% ABV and extremely sessionable. In 2015, Yuengling created a 5% ABV India Pale Lager, which exhibits their sustained commitment to session beer innovation by using the popular fruit-forward hops Bravo, Citra, Belma, and Cascade.

The Impact of the Brewers Association

The Brewers Association (BA) has helped shape and grow the modern craft brewing movement in America. From its early roots in the 1980s, it has grown into an incredibly influential resource and advocate for both small and regional-sized breweries today. One of the prominent actions the BA executed was an attempt at defining a craft brewery. Due to the ever-changing politics of the craft brewing industry, the definition has been constantly evolving, ebbing and flowing with the tide. The three tiers that the BA uses to define whether a brewer is a craft brewer are that the brewery has to be small, independent, and traditional. In February of 2014, the BA revised the "traditional" tier by recognizing that adjunct brewing is traditional. Paul

Gatza, BA Director, said, "The revisions to the craft brewer definition reflect the evolution in thinking regarding the elements of the definition. As the industry continues to rapidly advance, so must the framework that upholds and reflects it." Deschutes Brewing Company's Gary Fish, then Chair of the BA Executive Committee, concurred: "The revised definition provides room for the innovative capabilities of craft brewers to develop new beer styles and be creative within existing beer styles." He added, "Taken as a whole, these changes are about looking forward, about the BA of the future, making the association stronger and keeping staff focused on the vital work they do for all of us in the craft brewing community."[1] Under the revised definition, Yuengling is now considered a craft brewery and their numbers can be used when assessing the growth of craft. History seems to be repeating itself. When the first German immigrants entered America and began using adjuncts, it was seen as innovative. Now, over 150 years later, adjunct use is considered innovative once again.

Birth of the Craft Session Category

To date, most of my career in brewing was spent in the state of Utah, producing beer on draught that has a government restriction of 4% ABV. Despite the 4% ABV ceiling, Utah brewers continue to reproduce wonderful, historical styles of beer at lower alcohol levels. Many awards are won by Utah brewers at the Great American Beer Festival® (GABF) in style categories that fall at or below 4% ABV, but also in style categories that rise above the 4% ABV mark.

The most influential event that the BA runs is the GABF. I have been honored to be a GABF judge since 1997, and I have seen enormous changes within the competition and its impact on the craft beer culture. Chris Swersey, competition manager (and judge) for both the GABF and the World Beer Cup[SM] (WBC), noticed that brewers restricted to brewing beer at 4% ABV or below have a disadvantage in many categories. He routinely spoke to Dan Burick, former brewmaster of the Utah Brewers Cooperative, and me about creating a category for low-alcohol beers. Burick and I did not favor the idea of having a "special" category for beers made lower in alcohol, preferring to give our best among the rest and enter style categories that specified a lower alcohol range, like Schwarzbier and Ordinary Bitter, to name a few.

[1]   "Brewers Association Board Meeting Produces Strategic Changes." Brewers Association, March 3, 2014. http://www.brewersassociation.org/press-releases/brewers-association-board-meeting-produces -strategic-changes/.

Despite our lack of enthusiasm for Swersey's well-intentioned idea, the Other Low Strength Ale or Lager category did appear for a single year at the 2007 GABF competition. Burick and I appreciated Swersey's efforts immensely in trying to create a fair playing field for states with alcohol-restricted beers, but the category name was about as sexy as a banana hammock. On our way back from the 2007 GABF, we ran into Swersey in the airport and discussed whether the lower-alcohol category was going to stay and, if the number of entries supported it, would he consider renaming it to something more appealing with which to market a medal. Burick and I had been using the name "session beer," along with many other brewers in the industry, for many years, mostly in the context of describing our beers as being "sessionable." Two years prior, in May of 2005, Full Sail Brewing Company in Hood River, Oregon released Session Premium Lager, which quickly gained in popularity. So, the term session was not new to the brewing industry and it was routinely used as a descriptive word, rather than a specific style.

In 2008, the Session Beer category debuted at the GABF and the number of entries doubled from the number entered in 2007's Other Low Strength Ale or Lager category. In 2010, the Low Strength Ale or Lager category at the WBC also became the Session Beer category. Having a category at the two most prestigious beer competitions in the world gave session beer a home among craft brewers. Craft brewers have always been concerned about separating themselves from the large brewing companies, and increasing the alcohol level has been one technique that has helped them to do so. With the birth of session beer categories at national and international competitions came a greater acceptance among craft brewers that craft beer does not always have to mean high ABV.

Most modern craft session beers brewed are brewed with an all-malt formulation, but when pre-Prohibition styles are being emulated, a small percentage of adjuncts are usually employed. So, when does a beer warrant entry into the Session Beer category? Swersey explained that when a beer can be entered into another category under a given style parameter, like a Vienna lager or cream ale, then it should be entered into its appropriate category. Many of the categories at the GABF have ABV ranges that fall on or below 5%, but when a beer is made with less alcohol than its style normally calls for then it should be entered as a session beer. For example, a traditional *bock* averages 7% ABV, therefore, when brewed at 4.5% ABV it can be entered as a session beer.

Session-Style Pale Ales and IPAs

By 2014, the GABF Session Beer category grew to 94 entries. Swersey quickly noticed that a large majority of these entries were sessionable India pale ales (IPAs). Therefore, at the 2015 GABF, the Session India Pale Ale category was introduced, debuting with 161 entries, the third-largest category of the competition. Session beer encompasses a vast amount of individual styles under its umbrella, much like the general terminology of sour beer or dark beer. The most prominent session-style being brewed by craft brewers today is, by far, the session IPA. Although the phrase "session IPA" was not coined until sometime around 2011 or 2012, session-style IPAs were being brewed throughout the US many decades before. Mark Twain eloquently captures the evolution of all things in his quote,

> *There is no such thing as a new idea. It is impossible. We simply take a lot of old ideas and put them into a sort of mental kaleidoscope. We give them a turn and they make new and curious combinations. We keep on turning and making new combinations indefinitely; but they are the same old pieces of colored glass that have been in use through all the ages. (*Mark Twain, a Biography – Volume III, Part 1: 1900-1907, ed. *Albert Bigelow Paine [Project Gutenberg, 2004, 103] http://www.gutenberg.org/etext/2986)*

Session IPA is nothing new, just a new name for what is old, simply a rebranding of a great beer. At its best, a session IPA is a hoppy pale beer, light to medium in body, with dry finish, fantastic hop flavor, and pungent hop aroma.

GABF Session India Pale Ale Guidelines:[2]
Original gravity: 9.5–12.9°P
Final gravity: 3.1–4.6°P
ABV: 3.7%–5%
IBU: 40–55
SRM: 4–12

Session IPAs are gold to copper, with an allowable hop haze. Fruity ester aroma is light to medium. Hop aroma is medium to high; however, hop flavor should be strong, while malt flavor is only low to medium.

---

[2] *2016 Great American Beer Festival: Competition Style List, Descriptions and Specifications*, s.v. "17. Session India Pale Ale," accessed April 12, 2017, http://www.greatamericanbeerfestival.com/wp-content/uploads/2016/05/16_GABF_Beer_Style_Guidelines_Final.pdf.

Mitch Steele's book on IPA provides a rich and elaborate account of the story behind India pale ales and how culture, economy, and preference have affected the evolution of the IPA style worldwide over the last 200 years (Steele 2012). As one traces the ebb and flow of how classic IPA came about and then continued to develop over time, it becomes clear just how elusive the development of a beer style can be.

The birth of the American session IPA style was still new at the time Steele was writing and it is not specifically outlined in his book. The session IPA style might have been born from the ordinary bitter style. In Terry Foster's *Pale Ale* book from the *Classic Beer Styles Series* he cites that "AK bitters," a seemingly popular style of beer in nineteenth-century England, shared similar characteristics with modern bitters, having an original gravity of 11.2°P and being highly hopped and well-attenuated (Foster 1990, 67). Although the meaning of "AK" is obscure, Martyn Cornell, in his popular *Zythophile* blog (Cornell 2017), cites an advertisement showing the "AK bitter" designation dating back as far as 1846.[3] In reviewing the BA's GABF style guidelines, it is apparent that the session IPA of today resembles some of the common bitters of yesteryear. The style of bitter covers a broad range of beers produced in England. Some bitters tended to display a significant malt profile and hops took a back seat, but other bitters were dry-hopped and very hop forward. England's hoppy bitters resembled today's American session IPAs in both starting and finishing gravities, IBU range, and light-to-medium body.

The line between the English bitter and English IPA style is very blurred indeed. For example, the IPA produced by London's famous Barclay Perkins from 1928 to 1956 had a starting gravity of 7.72–11.5°P and attenuated to 1.5–3.5°P. The higher original gravities were recorded in the late 1920s and slowly dropped over time, resulting in the alcohol level falling from 4.8% ABV in 1928 to 3.01% ABV in 1956 (Steele 2012, 298–99). Many classic ordinary bitters fall in the same range. As Twain so vividly put it, these styles are "the same old pieces of colored glass."

The most significant difference between the English bitter and English IPA styles and the American session IPA style is the hop varieties used throughout the entire process. Classic English bitters and IPAs are typically brewed using English hop varieties, as opposed to the high-alpha acid American hop varieties characteristically used in today's session IPAs. English hop varieties, such

---

[3] Martyn Cornell, "Second thoughts on the mysterious origins of AK," *Zythophile* (blog), July 23, 2014, http://zythophile.co.uk/2014/07/23/second-thoughts-on-the-mysterious-origins-of-ak/.

as the widely used East Kent Goldings, display more earthy, citrus, herbal, and spicy characteristics, whereas many of the popular high-alpha acid hops used in America display a wide array of intense flavors and aromas, ranging between tropical fruit and floral aromas to garlic and onion notes, depending on harvest time and specific variety.

As we open up the kaleidoscope of beer styles and start separating the pieces of glass, a discussion of what exactly constitutes a session IPA can begin. Delineating the session IPA from the classic American pale ale is yet another blurred style boundary. Typical American pale ales have very similar specifications to session IPAs, such as IBU range, hop character, color range, and percent ABV. What sets American pale ales apart most prominently is their slight caramel malt character and the usual lack of dry hopping, the hop flavor and aroma frequently coming from the artful use of hops toward the end of boil and whirlpool. First brewed in 1980, Sierra Nevada Pale Ale is the most widely consumed American-standard pale ale. Although it falls just out of arm's reach from the session beer guidelines at 5.6% ABV, to say Sierra Nevada Pale Ale is not a session beer is just plain ludicrous. This is the perfect illustration of why it is so difficult—near impossible—to place rigid limits on styles in the ever-changing world of craft beer.

After many nights conducting research on session beer, I can personally attest to Sierra Nevada Pale Ale's sessionability. . .

In the mid 1990s a movement toward hop-forward, low-alcohol beers was beginning to bloom in Utah. In 1995 I was greatly inspired by the hop-forward beers of the Pacific Northwest. Luckily, the original founders of Squatters Pub Brewery, Peter Cole and Jeff Polychronis, gave me immense creative freedom with recipe design and tap line up. Enthused by Northwest hops but restricted by Utah alcohol laws, I created the dry-hopped, 40 IBU, Full Suspension pale ale. The vision I had at the time was an IPA-like beer, but bitterness that would not overpower the 4% ABV we were restricted to. Not surprisingly, the awards that Full Suspension ended up winning in the early 2000s were in the ordinary bitter category.

Just one year later, in 1996, a collaboration between Dick Cantwell, former owner and brewmaster of Seattle's Elysian Brewing, and Eric Dunlap, Salt Lake City's Red Rock Brewing Company's brewmaster at the time, produced and released a collaboration beer called IPA Jr., an unfiltered, dry-hopped pale ale. Cantwell, being a native Seattle brewer, brought with him an enthusiasm for hoppy

IPA. IPA Jr. is still one of Red Rock's most popular seasonal releases to date. That same year, yet another Utah brewery, Uinta Brewing Company, started producing and selling a 4% ABV version of IPA, simply called "IPA." Since the recent popularity of the word session, this beer has now been rebranded as Trader Session IPA.

It seems there was a collective, unconscious awakening among American craft brewers that led to a wave of hop-forward, lower-alcohol pale ales during the mid-1990s and beyond. Many were simply called "IPA," but not everyone used the term IPA in their branding—some stuck with the then tried and true name of pale ale, while others came up with names like "junior IPA." The year 1996 saw the release of the infamous Bridgeport IPA out of Portland, Oregon, capital of all things hoppy in the mid-1990s. Although Bridgeport IPA's 5.5% ABV means it does not officially qualify as a session IPA according to GABF style guidelines, it is one of the most well-balanced and sessionable IPAs to have come out of the western United States. Bridgeport IPA's original gravity is 13.5°P and bitterness is 50 IBUs.

Possibly the first session IPA that would qualify by today's category guidelines came from Firestone Walker Brewing Company out of Paso Robles. Firestone had been brewing session beers since 2000 when brewmaster Matt Brynildson and his team introduced Pale 31, a dry-hopped American pale ale with a fruit-forward hop flavor derived from Cascade, Centennial, and Chinook hops. Pale 31 is a blend of Firestone's Extra Pale Ale and Union Jack, and is 38 IBU, 4.8% ABV, and 7 SRM. Pale 31 carries all the components of a great session IPA except the name itself. The Extra Pale Ale itself has taken home three GABF medals and two WBC medals in the Session category.

By 2005, Full Sail had released their Session Premium Lager that was helping give a huge lift in popularity to the term session. Founder's Brewing Company took silver at the 2010 GABF in the Session Beer category with their Endurance IPA Jr., a version of their now popular session ale, All Day IPA, which was first introduced under that name in 2012. All Day IPA, a 4.7% ABV and 42 IBU session IPA, was released as Founder's first canned beer in 2013. It comprised 25% of Founder's total sales volume and surpassed their popular Centennial IPA (7.2% ABV and 65 IBU).

In 2010, Dan Carey, owner and brewmaster of New Glarus Brewing Company in New Glarus, Wisconsin, released Moon Man. In Carey's words, "If big IPAs were a reaction to bland beer, Moon Man is a reaction to extremism."[4]

---

[4] "New Brew: New Glarus Moon Man No Coast Pale Ale," *43North/89West* (blog), March 26, 2010, http://43north89west.wordpress.com/tag/moon-man/.

Bottle-conditioned, Moon Man tops out at 5% ABV, delivering amazing hop flavor and aroma using five hop varieties, but without high alcohol. Creatively described by New Glarus as a "no coast pale ale," Moon Man is a wonderful example of a session IPA. It is not surprising that session IPAs have gained rapidly in recognition among craft beer drinkers, especially after being inundated with extreme beers that were full of body, IBUs, and alcohol. Other good examples of the session IPA style on the market today are Lagunitas' Day Time IPA, Stone's Go To IPA, and Firestone Walker's Easy Jack.

My apologies if I have not mentioned all of the first-generation session IPAs born out of the 1990s and early twenty-first century. I am sure there are some I missed. All of the session IPAs I have mentioned share very similar qualities. They tend to be light to medium in body and well-attenuated, with ample hop bitterness, but avoiding over-the-top bitterness due to the lower alcohol level. The hop flavor and aroma is intense and usually created through the artful use of high-alpha acid American aroma hops, either fruity or dank in nature or some combination of both. Essential to producing a great session IPA is the delivery of clean hop bitterness, flavor, and aroma to create a highly drinkable and refreshing beer you will want to revisit over and over again.

Figure 3.2. Bitterness from hops is not one dimensional and can be created in many different ways during the brewing process. Photo © Getty Images/jeka1984

Development of Quality Hop Character

Hops are enigmatic. Session beers, with their low gravity, are easily thrown out of balance by misplaced bittering and flavor hopping. A brewer would do well to remember, "Things are not always what they seem; the first appearance deceives many; the intelligence of a few perceives what has been carefully hidden in the recesses of the mind" (Phaedrus, Book IV, Prol. 5). Many variables need to be considered when deciding how and when to incorporate hop bitterness, flavor, and aroma into a session beer, especially a session IPA.

Starting with the end in mind is always a solid technique for attaining the final results you are looking for. Envision the final session beer in front of you and virtually drink the beer using your imagination. What do you smell and taste? When do you experience the hops—as the beer first enters your mouth and moves over your tongue, or as you swallow? Eventually, it is hoped, the experience will leave the consumer wanting more! Begin charting out what variety hops provide you with the flavors you're longing for. Tropical, fruity, spicy, dank, onion, garlic, lemon, piney, orange. . . there are so many flavor choices to think about. One single hop might not realize your vision, therefore, different hops may have to be combined.

> I like to brew single hop beers to get an idea of how a certain variety will taste. If I do not want to make an entire batch of a single hop, then I make a hop tea to evaluate the aromas.

Availability is another major factor that must be considered. If this will be a one-off beer, then the world is your oyster. But if this new session IPA will be in the regular lineup and high sales are anticipated, a contract with a hop supplier may be needed. Before pen hits paper and you draw up the perfect session IPA hop profile, make sure you can access the specific hop varieties required for the entire year and that you've test-brewed an amazing batch that all your customers are raving about.

Once the varieties to be used for hop bitterness and flavor are determined, it's time to decide how the consumer will experience these hops. Brewing is an arduous task. There is often not enough time in the day to sit and eat, yet alone ponder how hops are experienced by the end consumer; however, taking the time to think about these things can help make a better beer. I do not believe it necessary to decide with certainty the dry-hop aroma at this stage. Fermentation flavors affect the final beer in numerous ways and it is best to continually revisit the fermenting beer prior to making a final decision on the dry hop and dry-hop technique.

When brewers discuss hops, it is common to hear a lot of discussion about what flavors and aromas are coming from the hops; it is much less common to hear talk concerning how the beer expresses hop bitterness. Not all bitterness is equal. There are many different ways to create bitterness in a beer. Different hop varieties are designated as either bittering or aroma hops. Many brewers are still surprised to find out that hops do not have to be boiled to contribute bitterness to the wort and, therefore, to the final beer. Alpha acids in hops are isomerized in the boil as well as while steeping in hot wort; in fact, isomerization is taking place from start to finish, right up until the wort flows through the heat exchanger for cooling. This means isomerization of alpha acids occurs with the final hop additions and in the whirlpool. The lower the temperature of the wort and the lower the contact time, the less utilization you will get for a given hop addition. All these factors must be accounted for if you are striving for a particular IBU mark.

Hop acids are grouped into two series, the alpha acids and beta acids. The alpha acids comprise humulone, cohumulone, and adhumulone; when isomerized, these become isohumulone, isocohumulone, and isoadhumulone, respectively (Kunze 2004, 55). Lloyd Rigby was the first to theorize, in 1972, that the pleasant, or softer, hop bitterness experienced from aroma hops correlated with their lower cohumulone level (Rigby 1972). Although there has been some debunking of this theory over the recent decades, many German brewers, as well as other brewers from around the globe, still believe Rigby's theory holds true (Wackerbauer and Balzer 1992).

Gaining a softer bitterness level is not the only consideration a brewer has to make when selecting a hop variety. Cohumulone has a greater utilization factor than the other alpha acids, partly due to its heightened solubility in water (De Keukeleire 2000). Val Peacock, one of the brewing industry's foremost hop researchers, shared some very interesting stories relating to bitterness quality and boil time. Peacock suggests that quality bitterness is more related to the hop variety than to boil-time additions. Peacock believes that only focusing on cohumulone levels can be short sighted and the vast differences between hop varieties should be considered when choosing the type of hops to be used (Val Peacock, pers. comm.). In addition, brewers should taste for hop flavor and aroma preferences as a major part of the hop selection process.

Researchers have only begun to scratch the surface regarding the way in which numerous hop compounds contribute to and take away from a positive hop experience in beer. Peacock notes that there is new research on the relationship between auxiliary hop bittering substances and quality of bitterness. In *Hops: Their Cultivation, Composition and Usage*, research states that 70%–80% of all bitterness in conventionally hopped beers is derived from iso-alpha acids. There are many auxiliary hop bittering compounds that can contribute to overall bitterness: uncharacterized soft or hard resins, hop polyphenols, substances derived from non-isomerized alpha acids (humulinone and humulinic acids), and substances derived from beta acids (hulupones, hulupinic acid, and hydroxytricyclolupulone). When combined in large numbers, auxiliary bittering substances contribute to overall bitterness in the final beer (Biendl et al. 2014). Spectrophotometric analysis can detect and measure iso-alpha acids in beer, as well as other auxiliary bittering substances, by extracting them using iso-octane. However, polyphenols are insoluble in iso-octane and therefore cannot be measured using spectrophotometric analysis. The ratio between total IBU and iso-alpha acids helps to measure the amount of bitterness contributed by auxiliary bitter substances (Biendl et al. 2014). Since the total IBU to iso-alpha acids ratio will increase as the proportion of alpha acids in hops decreases, this means the ratio will be higher for aroma hops versus hops used primarily for bittering, particularly so in the case of older European aroma varieties.

The above cited research suggests that the ratio of beta acids to alpha acids is still the best indicator of the level of auxiliary hop bittering substances in beer. The hypothesis is that the quality of bitterness increases with an increase in the total IBU to iso-alpha ratio, and the total IBU to iso-alpha ratio increases with increasing levels of beta acids.

Over the last 50 years a myth or theory has circulated about Frank Schweigert, who was the German-trained head brewer of Anheuser-Busch from the 1950s to the 1970s. It is said that Schweigert believed acquiring quality bitterness was best accomplished by boiling European aroma hops a long time and only adding the American cluster hops at the end. Therefore, the hypothesis that higher-beta acid hops will produce a higher quality of bitterness parallels Frank Schweigert's belief that quality bitterness is best accomplished by boiling European aroma hops a long time. The theory behind this partly rests on the fact that the auxiliary bittering compounds derived from beta acids, like hulupones, are created during the boil. As more of these compounds are created during the boil, total IBUs rise with respect to just the iso-alpha acid level alone, so increasing the total IBU to iso-alpha acid ratio.

It is important to note that exposure to oxygen will degrade hops and polymerize the hop polyphenols, producing harsh bitterness. Hops need to be kept fresh, away from air, and used in a timely fashion to gain the highest degree of quality bitterness.

Look in the coolers of most modern craft breweries and you will find high-alpha acid hops dominate. The technique of pouring copious amounts of high-alpha acid hops in the kettle at the end of boil and/or in the whirl-pool and then dry hopping has cemented itself in many American craft breweries, particularly when making any version of IPA (session, double, or triple). There is no doubt that using hops at the end of boil drives hop flavor into the finished beer, but that is not all it drives. After many sensory experiments in the Squatters brewery with 4% ABV beer, my colleague Dan Burick and I discovered we experienced a very harsh bitterness when we used a lot of hops, especially high-alpha acid hops, at the end of the boil. We described the bitterness as harsh, astringent, and drying, and like many brewers tend to do, we gave it a name: tonsil grabber (TG). Not a very scientific name, but hey, we're brewers. Most of our draught beers were built to be under 45 IBUs and, being session beers, did not have much forgiveness. We found that gaining most of our bitterness up front in the boil provided a much better quality bitterness experience. We noted less TG, and driving both hop flavor and aroma through creative dry-hopping techniques instead of copious end-of-boil hopping helped stave off harsh bitterness.

In 2016, a group from S.S. Steiner published a technical paper in the *Technical Quarterly of the MBAA* on humulinone formation in hops and hop pellets (Maye et al. 2016). Their research indicates that humulinones, which form from the oxidation of alpha acids, increase after pelletization and can add significant bitterness to the final beer through dry hopping. Humulinones contribute little bitterness when added to boiling wort, but they are extremely soluble in beer when dry-hopping rates are 1–2 lb./bbl. or more. In fact, 87% of the humulinones present after pelletization were found to have dissolved into the beer within 2–3 days after dry hopping, which can have a noticeable effect on the final bitterness of the beer.

Additional research indicated that the pH of the final beer increased about 0.14 pH units when dry hops were added at 1 lb./bbl. Sensory analysis was conducted by the Steiner team to gauge the bitterness experience from a drop or rise in final beer pH (Maye et al. 2016). The pH was lowered using sulfuric acid and the sensory results indicated that the beer lowered to pH 4.5 had increased bitterness compared to the same dry-hopped beer at pH 4.91. Another significant finding by Maye et al. (2016) was that the iso-alpha acid concentration was reduced in the beers dry-hopped with pellets, especially so in beers with high IBUs.

The most compelling outcome from Steiner group's research was the sensory results in regard to the bitterness character derived from humulinones. The article indicates that humulinones are reportedly about 66% as bitter as iso-alpha acids. The sensory team spiked a low-IBU beer with 22 ppm humulinone and spiked another sample of the same beer with 14.5 ppm iso-alpha acid. The results indicated both beers had a similar level of bitterness, but the humulinone spiked beer had a "smoother" bitter profile compared to the iso-alpha acid beer. The authors concluded that this sensory experience made sense, because humulinones are more polar than iso-alpha acids and, therefore, should not linger on the tongue as long (Maye et al. 2016).

There is still so much to learn about using hop flavor and aroma to invite the customer back for more of the same beer. Hop freshness must always be a top priority. Second to that is proper record keeping so your hop experiments are not lost. Change what you do in the brewhouse if you think your beer can be better, and don't be afraid to try new ideas, although do it on a small scale first before ramping up to full size. Remember that every brewhouse is different and what works for one brewer might not work for you. It is fascinating, as a brewer, to ponder what we have to look forward to in hop manipulation in our quest for producing great beer.

My goal in including this section here is to highlight how important having pleasant bitterness is in a session beer. Hop bitterness needs to be an essential part of any IPA, but in a session IPA this can easily be overdone due to the low-alcohol nature of a session beer. Alcohol has the tendency to mask and alter many flavors, and the higher the alcohol the less delicate the beer. If you have harsh hop bitterness, it will not be as evident in a high-IBU, 6.5% ABV IPA as it will be in a delicate 4.5% ABV session IPA.

Other Session Offerings

Session IPA is currently the most talked about and marketed session beer by far in the craft industry, but there has been a greater inclination to use the "session" label when selling a lower-alcohol pale ale as well. A recent example is Bell's Brewery's release of Oatsmobile Ale. Oatsmobile, released in June, 2016, is 4.3% ABV and uses a blend of classic and modern Pacific Northwest hops. It is described by Bell's as a "hop-forward session pale ale," highlighting the use of oats by saying that it gives Oatsmobile "a body that you don't see in most other session pale ales."

Although the name session is not always used, the theme of producing lower-alcohol beers for the national craft market is evident from other recent releases. In May 2016, Lagunitas Brewing Company released The Down Low at 3.9% ABV. A "dry and hoppy copper ale" that uses dark crystal malts and Northwestern hops, The Down Low is tagged as a "tropical, earthy, and stoooopidly slammable ale." Lagunitas also produces Daytime Ale, released in 2012, that is labelled as a fractional IPA at 4.65% ABV.

In the 2010s, craft breweries started releasing all-malt pilsners with relatively low alcohol levels. Firestone Walker released Pivo in 2013 and described this hoppy pils as a classically rendered Pilsner with a West Coast dry-hopping twist, showcasing stylistic influences from Germany, Italy, and the Czech Republic. Pivo Pils has taken home three consecutive GABF gold medals in the German-style Pilsener category in 2013, 2014, and 2015. They proclaim on their website that "lighter beer styles like pilsner have been hijacked by industrial lager beer in the United States, and it's time for craft brewers to take it back." I agree that craft brewers were once scared to make reduced-alcohol beers for fear of acting too much like the large American brewing companies. However, that time seems to have passed and the craft world is changing yet again.

Sierra Nevada Brewing Company, the leader of the craft brewing industry, released Nooner in 2014, so named because it is a "midday go-to." Tellingly, Sierra Nevada go on to describe the "easy drinking" Nooner as their take on "the classic German-style pilsner—one of the original session beers." STS Pils from Russian River also made its debut in 2014, a beautiful, classic European Pilsner from a brewing company celebrated for its high-alcohol, hoppy IPAs. Although, STS Pils, Nooner, and Pivo come in just slightly above the invisible ceiling of the session ABV so-called limit, they are all wonderful examples of session Pilsners and absolutely fall under the umbrella of session beer.

Gose Rising

"Sooner or later," writes Stephen King, "everything old is new again."[5] Craft brewers have a deep passion for taking what was once old and breathing life into the embers to reinvigorate the fire. Gose is a 1,000-year-old style that has been resurrected and is now being emulated across the country in many craft breweries, both large and small. Although originating in the town of Goslar, Germany, the popularity of Gose in the city of Leipzig led to it being commonly referred to as Leipziger Gose. It is pronounced "Gose-uh" and was originally served in tall, wine-like bottles, indicating its significant difference from other German beers and setting it apart for the consumer.

According to the German Beer Institute, Gose is a sour and saline-tasting ale fermented with both *Saccharomyces* yeast and *Lactobacillus*. Made with 50% wheat and 50% malted barley, it is blonde in color and served with a dense, white head due to the high protein content of the malted wheat. Coriander, along with small additions of hops, are often used for flavor and the IBUs are almost non-existent, falling between 10–15 IBU. Original Gose was spontaneously fermented and, therefore, some displayed slight characteristics of *Brettanomyces*, but the overriding character has always been a tart sourness resulting from the production of lactic acid, coalescing with slight salinity. Gose gets its name from the Gose River, which runs through the mining town of Goslar. One of the most abundant minerals of the area was salt, and the water that filled the aquifers and supplied the local breweries had high salinity; the saltiness became a defining characteristic of the traditional Gose (Burnsed 2011).

One of my favorite versions of the Gose style is brewed by my good friend Eric Rose, owner and brewmaster of the Hollister Brewing Company in Santa Barbara County, California. Rose, inspired by the 2008 release of Gose Speziell Weizen from Minneapolis' Herkimer Pub & Brewery, created Tiny Bubbles, a 4.5% ABV, refreshingly tart, traditional Gose brewed with wheat and Pilsner malts. First brewed in 2009, Tiny Bubbles is gently flavored with coriander and a small addition of salt. Tiny Bubbles was awarded the silver medal for German-Style Sour Ale at the 2010 GABF. One of the most wonderful components of Tiny Bubbles is the authentic multi-stage lactic fermentation, creating beautiful lactic complexity and setting Tiny Bubbles apart from the many modern interpretations of this very Old World style. The Gose style was not quick to catch on in the modern craft brewing scene in the early years of the twenty-first century, and Rose was most definitely ahead of the curve. If you

---

[5]   *The Colorado Kid* (New York: Dorchester Publishing, 2005).

are ever lucky enough to make it to Hollister Brewing Company in the spring or late summer, you just might get lucky enough to experience several glasses of Tiny Bubbles. There has been a noteworthy upswing in Gose production from breweries nationwide in the mid-2010s.

The most widely produced and distributed Gose is Otra Vez from Sierra Nevada Brewing Company, gold medal winner at the 2016 WBC in the Session Beer category. Sierra Nevada puts an interesting twist on the traditional style by combining prickly pear cactus with a hint of grapefruit to give this tart, refreshing Gose-style ale a unique flavor profile. Anderson Valley Brewing Company dove headfirst into brewing Gose through its HWY 128 Session Series, celebrating craft beers made between 4% and 4.5% ABV. Anderson Valley brewmaster, Fal Allen, uses their Gose-style ale as a jumping off point for brewing tantalizing and creative interpretations of this ancient style.

Anderson Valley has embarked on making Gose using a modern American souring technique, which is kettle souring. Anderson Valley follows the general kettle souring approach. A normal mash is doughed-in and the wort is run over to the kettle. A blanket of argon gas is released continuously over the standing wort to protect against the growth of unwanted bacteria. The optimum temperature of the wort arriving into the kettle is 110°F (43°C), and heat is applied if necessary. At this point, a propagated *Lactobacillus* culture is pitched into the kettle and begins to consume all the available sugars. It takes Anderson Valley about 7–8 hours to reach their desired pH of 3.3–3.4, at which point the wort is then slightly hopped and boiled. After boiling, the wort is cooled to the fermentor and the house ale yeast strain is pitched to finish the fermentation. Allen explained that it takes about six months to develop a new version of Gose.

The first in Anderson Valley's Gose lineup was The Kimmie, The Yink and The Holy Gose, which was released in 2014 and became a runaway success. Bright, golden in color, and presenting with a creamy head, the earthy undertones of The Kimmie, The Yink and The Holy Gose intermingle with a slight mineral and citrus aroma. The refreshing tartness, due to the kettle souring process, coalesces artfully with a myriad of tropical fruit flavors, coriander, and delicate salinity.

Second in the Anderson Valley lineup came their Blood Orange Gose. Blood Orange Gose was developed using the base recipe of The Kimmie, The Yink and The Holy Gose, but with abundant additions of blood orange puree during fermentation, which imparts tangy citrus notes and a slight sweetness to complement the salinity and tartness in this refreshing session wheat beer.

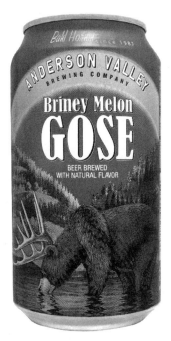

Figure 3.3. Briney Melon Gose is one of a variety of gose-style beers produced by Anderson Valley Brewing Company.

The third creation is the Briney Melon Gose, debuting in 2016. Again, the base beer of The Kimmie, The Yink and The Holy Gose was used, but this time watermelon flavors were incorporated. The fourth Gose project at Anderson Valley is the G&T Gose, a gin and tonic inspired Gose that uses traditional gin spices, cucumber, and cinchona bark for mimicking the tonic component. Each of these Gose-style ales is brewed at 4.2% ABV and kettle soured the same way.

Barrel-aging Gose is another exciting venture underway and is sure to produce some really interesting and exciting new session sours from Anderson Valley; I anxiously anticipate the next modern rendition of this historic style from Allen and his team. Allen reports that sales are extremely strong for their Gose lineup and continue to rise, indicating the shifting tastes of craft beer consumers.

Cream Ales

Cream ales are yet another session beer offering, providing a beer for the macro lager drinker who has decided to finally open the bar doors of a brewpub or uncap a different bottle from the beer cooler. One of the world's most famous cream ales, Boddington's Pub Ale, is served nitrogenized both on draught and through the use of a widget that dispenses nitrogen from the can. The Boddington's Brewery was founded in 1772 in Manchester, England. A very low bitterness level, 4.6% ABV, and creamy head due to nitrogenization makes Boddington's Pub Ale a highly drinkable session beer.

American pre-Prohibition cream ales were widely brewed in the northeast and mid-Atlantic states, offering a different choice to the lager of the day. Like lagers, adjuncts were traditionally employed in the recipe, particularly if made in large volumes. However, modern versions from craft breweries typically choose all-malt recipes (Oliver 2012, 273). The profile of an American cream ale offers up a moderate bitterness of between 12 and 30 IBU, and a low-medium ABV of 4.2%–5.6%. Although the name cream suggests the use of dairy, no dairy products should be used in the brewing of a classic cream ale.

The Genesee Brewing Company is one of America's oldest breweries, founded in 1878. While over the last few decades ownership has changed multiple times, production of Genesee Cream Ale continues. The iconic American cream ale, Genesee Cream Ale was first brewed in 1960, offering a different selection to the mass-produced American lager beers. The slogan for their renowned cream ale states "The goal was simple: a beer with the flavor of an ale and the smoothness of a lager." Since 1987, Genesee Cream Ale has garnered 10 medals at the GABF, carrying history forward to generations of new beer drinkers with every sip.

What Once Was Old Is Now New Again

In the great state of Wisconsin, most taproom servers will steer you to one of my favorite American session beers, Spotted Cow. Sometimes described as a cream ale by online rating websites, New Glarus Brewing clearly calls their beloved and widely sold Spotted Cow a farmhouse ale. It is a slightly cloudy, fruit-forward ale that defies style definition and is simply brewed to refresh.

The evolution of craft brewers offering fresh, low-alcohol beers like Spotted Cow symbolizes how history has come back around, with brewers sharing their century-old appreciation of America's roots with consumers again. It's a rite of passage, in a sense, and a desire to satisfy their consumers. A brewery must consider its patrons' needs and desires as it determines how to build a portfolio of beers. There are many crucial decisions a brewery must make when first putting their plan of producing and selling beer into action. Beer styles, yeast choices, malt selection, all meld together to determine how the American craft brewer will experiment and settle upon a family of beers. The choice to offer up an easy-drinking session beer, light in color and body, bringing both the new and experienced craft beer drinker to the table, has proven to be a successful path for many brewpubs.

Even in the early years of craft brewing, it was characteristic to have a golden or blonde ale on a tap list for this purpose. Blonde or golden ales are usually lower in both alcohol and bitterness and very sessionable by nature. This tradition has continued and sometimes breweries give them a twist by adding fruit, or another unique ingredient, but always with the goal of keeping them quaffable and inviting. Taking a historic style and changing it in some fashion is a very common technique for keeping things interesting around the local pubs and beer aisles.

American brewers have been spinning the kaleidoscope glass ever since Adolphus Busch came over from Germany and changed the classic helles, adding his own spin with rice and reducing the heaviness of the six-row barley. We are lucky enough to be living in a time of great change, growth, and experimentation in American brewing culture. So many wonderful session styles are being recreated in local breweries, either in traditional fashion or with a modern twist. It is not uncommon to find a representation of a Vienna lager, schwarzbier, Gose, Pilsner, helles, or dunkel on tap. At the end of the day, they are all great session beers meant for celebrating life with friends.

4

Drinking Session Beers

D.G. Yuengling & Son's brewmaster, Jim Helmke, remembers hearing the term "drinkability" as far back as the 1970s. In 2008, Anheuser-Busch began a massive marketing campaign pitching Bud Light as a beer with drinkability, and the use of the term in the craft arena has been on the decline ever since. Craft beer breweries have worked very hard at differentiating themselves from the macro brewing companies and language is an integral part of maintaining this separation. Just think how it would look if craft breweries started marketing their beers using the tag line "cold-filtered." It appears the term "sessionability" is starting to quickly replace drinkability in the craft beer community when describing a beer of lower alcohol that is designed so the consumer can drink multiple pints of it.

Defining Drinkability

In the early 1990s the Utah brewing scene used the term drinkability when describing lower-alcohol beers produced with light to moderate hopping profiles. The Merriam-Webster Online Dictionary defines drinkability as "suitable or safe for drinking." Clearly, this is not how brewers have been using the term drinkability, and sessionability is not even in the dictionary (yet). Regardless, both terms are used often when describing beers that are pleasant to drink and warrant repeatability if the situation allows.

Defining exactly what drinkability is in a beer is an arduous task. According to a paper published in *Brauwelt International*, drinkability "implies a special harmony and balance, as well as an incentive to drink more of the [beer]" (Gastl et al. 2008, 148). Many different components make up whether a beer is highly drinkable or not. Factors affecting drinkability range in scope, from the taster's sensory experience and cognitive influence, to the ingestion and absorption traits of the beer (Gastl et al. 2008). In the realm of sensory evaluation, quality is the most important facet of a beer. Off flavors that detract from the beer's overall harmony should not be present. For instance, high levels of dimethyl sulfide (DMS) have been associated with a negative sensory impact; in addition, diacetyl in the aroma is often perceived and interpreted as a heavier-bodied beer (Gastl et al. 2008). Other sensory components that either positively or negatively influence the taster are carbonation levels, the ratio between sugar and pH, beer style, hop bitterness and aroma, phenolic and ester compounds, protein levels, and alcohol content.

A drinker's sensory experience can be greatly influenced through several criteria. Ingredient quality, storage, and handling can help increase drinkability; yeast strain selection and proper yeast management is also crucial when producing a highly quaffable beer. In chapter 3, I dedicated a large section, "Development of Quality Hop Character," to the pursuit of quality bitterness for the very sake of drinkability. To reiterate the main point here, bitterness is not just one-dimensional. Hop variety, quality, and placement in the brewing process all greatly influence a beer's drinkability. Researchers at the Department of Brewing and Beverage Technology at the Technical University of Munich's Weihenstephan campus performed both analytical and sensory trials using a taste sensor (an "electronic tongue") alongside a human sensory panel (Gastl et al. 2008). Their goal was to further study the factors associated with drinkability and the results of the electric tongue versus those from a sensory panel. Since bitterness is such a huge component of a beer's drinkability, it was studied first.

Alcohol, pH, and dextrin composition were manipulated in conjunction with varying iso-alpha acid levels. One of the most interesting results, especially with regard to session beer, is that elevating the ethanol content leads to a weakening of the bitterness signal. The study also indicated that both pH and ethanol content have a "distinctive effect on bitterness impression (bitterness intensity) and astringency." Although this study could not possibly cover the full range of factors that influence drinkability, the results do indicate that quality bitterness and astringency in particular can be affected negatively by changes in pH and alcohol level (Gastl et al. 2008).

When discussing quality in the quest for drinkability, both ingredients and process must be considered at every level. For example, a common process misstep that negatively affects drinkability is the astringency extraction from malt tannins toward the end of runoff when the pH rises above 5.8. *The importance placed on both ingredient quality and process should never be underestimated when pursuing high drinkability in one's final beer, especially a session beer.*

So much is involved when exploring how one experiences a beer. Flavor is a major aspect, quite possibly the most important, but flavor does not tell the whole story. Japanese researchers closely studied how a beer is enjoyed in relation to the ingestive and absorptive effects of beer. They discovered that as the stomach becomes fuller, the person becomes more satiated, and the less appealing beer becomes (Nagao et al. 1998). A person's cognitive and emotional state of being also play a role in how beer is experienced. Time of day, age, culture, social status, gender, and drinking habits are all at play as the pint glass moves toward the consumer's lips, intermingling to form an opinion on drinkability. Optical aspects, such as foam and head retention, temperature, and glassware can have a big impact on whether the consumer decides a beer is highly drinkable. The brewer has their greatest influence on drinkability when focusing on quality and brewery procedure. This does not mean that breweries don't also try to influence the cognitive experience of the consumer through marketing and other means.

A Session Society

Leo Vygotsky, the Russian psychologist, founded social learning theory in the early 20th century: "Through others we become ourselves."[1] He theorized that culture plays a crucial role in human development and that society's cultural

---

[1]   L.S. Vygotsky, "History of the development of the higher mental functions," (1931): 105, quoted in H. Daniels, M. Cole, V. James, eds., *Cambridge Companion to Vygotsky* (New York: Cambridge University Press, 2007), 56.

norms have an extreme behavioral influence. In contrast to Jean Piaget, the famous Swiss clinical psychologist, whose model of cognitive development stated that development precedes learning, Vygotsky felt the opposite was true, that learning precedes development (Vygotsky 1978, 25). Therefore, life experiences and interactions are constantly shaping who we are and how we act. Throughout her book, *Ambitious Brew*, Maureen Ogle eloquently describes how culture shaped beer drinking behavior. Ogle frames American culture during the first half of the twentieth century where Americans "rejected hard labor, which had devoured women's energy, in favor of convenience: soups, vegetables, and fruits from cans; factory-made bread; store bought mayonnaise. Washing machines. Detergents in boxes" (Ogle 2006, 228). Unfortunately, the more processed foods became, the more flavor they lost, thus spawning an era of "bland America." The American lager taste turned away from discerning flavor profile and into what is now generally termed as modern American industrial lager, where malt and hop flavor take a back seat to sales. Ogle cites the president of the Wahl-Henius Institute, a leading beer institute during the mid-1900s, who warned brewmasters that they should not let their own personal taste for malt and hops interfere with the public's desire for blandness (Ogle 2006, 229).

The current IPA craze is also indicative of the symbiotic relationship between brewer and consumer. During recent years, more and more hops have been literally thrust down the throats of craft beer drinkers. The lupulin threshold, defined by Vinnie Cilurzo as a line that is crossed when a once extraordinarily hoppy beer now seems pedestrian, continues to rise and so too has the customer's desire for more hops (Hieronymus 2012, 193). As cultural shifts often show us, history repeats itself and what was once old is new again. In 2016, it became evident that yet another style of IPA is on the rise. The recently coined New England-style IPA is distinguished by a hazy appearance, diminishing hop bitterness, and a juicy, full-hop flavor and aroma (Fowle 2016). Perhaps our craft brewing culture is evolving again along its ever-shifting fault line. Perhaps extreme bitterness and alcohol will fall in the crevasse, leaving flavor and sessionability free to materialize. What goes up must come down, and the growing popularity of session beer is indicative of Americans' ever-changing palettes and drinking culture.

Celebrations have been part of human culture from the beginning. Although the way we celebrate as a nation and these rituals of revelry have changed, the fact remains, drinking typically goes hand in hand with many adult celebrations throughout American culture. As we welcome new life into the world or say goodbye to departed souls, both birthdays and funerals warrant toasting to what will soon become or who will be dearly missed. Festivities surrounding weddings, graduations, holidays, and music fill city streets and open fields every month of the year across America. Life is stressful and sometimes downright painful; to celebrate life is to live life and recognize both suffering and joy. Many celebrations are not of short duration. For instance, a typical wedding can require participation for an entire weekend, especially if you are part of the wedding party. Thanksgiving, Fourth of July, Christmas, and other holidays involve entire days or more of informal and formal festivities.

> *The quickest celebration I have ever attended is the modern five-year-old's birthday party. The small guests arrive, the games begin and end, cake is served, and presents are ripped to shreds. It usually takes about two to three hours and everyone goes home feeling like they just ran a marathon. My five-year-old's birthday parties were atypical and always involved a keg of special beer to help the adults get through it.*

Session beers heed the call when a celebration occurs, especially when extended festivities are held. It is harder to maintain composure when drinking multiple pints of higher-alcohol beer than it is when drinking session beer, for obvious reasons. Of course, taking a break from drinking alcoholic beverages and grabbing water or soda is always a great way to go to preserve your self-control. However, peer pressure and societal norms mean that sometimes consecutive alcoholic drinks are presented before us. When deciding what to drink next, choosing a session beer can help make longer hours in the saddle more enjoyable. The ultimate goal of celebration is to have a good time, get home safe, and wake the next day with fond memories. Different drinks are often associated with specific celebrations, and even with specific parts of a celebration. Champagne is a customary choice when the pinnacle of a celebration has arrived; when toasting the wedding couple, or when the clock strikes midnight on New Year's Eve, glasses of bubbly are poured and down the hatch it goes. Beer is customarily served beforehand, after, and in-between. Where and why we drink beer is an ever-changing sociocultural experience and typically associated with relaxation and celebration. Session beer consumption has a well-established role in our society and it is extremely refreshing to see the rise of session beers in the craft world.

Shifting cultural norms not only affect the "where" and "why" we drink beer, but they also play a significant role in how we drink beer. For centuries, beer has been associated with casualness, comfort, and relaxing in American culture. How we relax is indicative of how breweries respond in terms of packaging. When it's time to pack the cooler for weekend getaways to the lake or river, cans of session beer fill ice chests. Bottles are heavy, break easily, and are more expensive to transport, making the beer can a perfect fit for summer festivities. Krueger Brewing Company sold the first beer in cans on January 24th, 1935 in Richmond, Virginia. Pre-Prohibition breweries were regional, selling most of their beer close to home. By the late 1930s, three-quarters of American breweries were selling and transporting at least some of their beer to other states (Ogle 2006, 215). Summer is hot, and many of the activities that go along with it require multiple, refreshing, lower-alcohol beers. From yard work to river trips, activities often associated with the weekend, refreshment is a constant necessity. The craft brewing industry has recognized the cultural shift of its consumers, who long for a more convenient package for their favorite craft brew.

Formerly, when American craft brewers were diligently focused on separating themselves from macro lager beer, using cans was not even considered. Glass had always symbolized a higher-quality product and did not carry the same stigma that canned beer did. Canned beer implied an inferior product associated with drinkers from a lower socioeconomic class. At college parties, the bottles always disappeared before the cans were touched, even if both contained the same brand of beer. Today, the stigma of canned beer is lifting and this is largely due to the introduction of canning beer in the craft brewing world. When consumers are choosing what beer to buy they may not consider how the package affects the beer. That is the brewery's responsibility. I am happy to see so many craft beers now offered in a can, because the advantages to both the beer and the brewery are massive. Kunze lists just some of the advantages of cans as follows: cans are unbreakable, lighter, easily stacked, cool rapidly, and able to be opened without a tool; a can also protects the beer from light and oxygen egress once sealed, and is easily recycled (Kunze 2004, 642). The advantages of cans are clear, and craft brewers' fear of being aligned with the macro breweries has vanished. For the craft brewing industry, cans have arrived and are here to stay. You will find canned craft beer at bars, package stores, restaurants, backpacking trips, and tailgating parties.

Many events and celebrations are conducive to lower-ABV beer offerings. According to my son Dylan Knab, a 10-year-old expert on all things sports, the average football, baseball, or basketball game lasts about two-and-a-half to three hours. For Americans, it is almost a rite of passage to tailgate before one of these events. In 2016, the kids and I strapped hot dogs under the hood and drove to the East Bay area to watch sadly while the Pirates beat the A's in Oakland. When we arrived the "engine dogs" were perfect and we were ready to relax with all the other fans and celebrate in the parking lot before the game, kids with their soda and parents with their session beer.

Fans who are not tailgating often choose a sports bar near the stadium or ballpark from where they can cheer on their favorite team. Once in the stadium, beer lines at every station are a mile long, no matter what the brewery is charging. The point is, national sporting events have been associated with drinking beer for decades. Company sponsorship and branding has always been a fundamental part of the macro brewing industry and its big money is evident throughout numerous sports. An example of a well-established relationship is the announcement that Dos Equis struck a multimillion dollar deal to become the official beer sponsor of the college football playoffs, the second most watched sport in America according to an ESPN poll.[2] Dos Equis' very popular ad campaign encourages fans to "Stay Thirsty" and is perfectly aligned with the amount of time most fans stay drinking before, during, and after watching college football. Session beer is an obvious beer to choose when long hours are to be spent drinking and enjoying a favorite team and time with friends. Craft brewing companies are starting to make a strong showing at stadiums and ballparks across America. In 2016, there was a nice selection of craft beer available at California's Oakland Coliseum and many of the beers offered were session beers.

When I think of session beer I think of a best friend. A best friend is one you can rely on to be there for you in any given situation. No matter what is happening in your life, you can count on a best friend; they are the very definition of dependable. Consistently, you return to a best friend and are greeted by comfort and security. However, beyond dependability, comfort, and safety, what draws you to a best friend is the history you share with

[2] "Dos Equis Becomes the Official Beer Sponsor of the College Football Playoff on ESPN," *PR Newswire*, December 7, 2015, http://www.prnewswire.com/news-releases/dos-equis-becomes-the-official-beer-sponsor-of-the-college-football-playoff-on-espn-300188649.html.

> *them. History is not created overnight and carries a weight incomparable to new relationships, which can often be fleeting. History cannot be replaced and must be built over a lifetime. Quality session beer is like that best friend, dependable, consistent, and comforting, time and time again.*

Creating a Culture of Responsible Drinking

Being part of a society requires a collective commitment and adherence by its members to a chosen set of rules. One fundamental part of the reasoning behind having societal rules is that they keep members of society safe and out of harm's way. In 2014 the Center for Disease Control (CDC) stated that approximately 10,000 people die each year due to accidents caused by drunk driving and over one million Americans are charged with driving while under the influence (DUI). The highest rate of both drunk driving-related fatalities and DUI charges are the 21–34 age group—the largest segment of craft beer consumers. Within this age group, men are three times more likely than women to drive while drunk; these men make up 85% of craft beer consumers. Since the mid-1980s state DUI laws have meted out progressively more severe punishment. The National Transportation Safety Board (NTSB) reports that, in 1980, there were 20,000 fatalities due to drunk driving when the limit for blood alcohol concentration (BAC) in many states was 0.15%. Mothers Against Drunk Driving (MADD) was established in September of 1980 and, along with other safety organizations around the nation, aggressively lobbied to reduce state BAC limit laws to 0.08%. In 2004, Delaware became the final US state to adopt a 0.08% BAC limit for DUI conviction. MADD is one of the strongest and most well-funded non-profits in the US, and it has had a major effect on state drinking and driving legislation. The Center for Disease Control (CDC) reported 9,967 fatalities relating to DUI charges for 2014, a 50% reduction on the same statistic from 1980.

As of 2017, there is a movement by the NTSB and the Association for the Advancement of Automotive Medicine (AAAM) to reduce the BAC from 0.08% to 0.05%. Utah is the first state to have voted in the BAC reduction and it is possible that other states may follow. The NTSB and the AAAM cite lower rates of drunk driving fatalities in other countries that have adopted a 0.05% BAC. Australia, Austria, Belgium, Bulgaria, Croatia, Denmark, Finland, France, Germany, Greece, Israel, Italy, the Netherlands, Portugal, South Africa, Spain, and Turkey have all adopted a BAC limit of 0.05%. Japan and Poland recently adopted a 0.03% BAC standard. Norway, Russia, and Sweden have essentially a zero-tolerance limit of 0.02% BAC. Limiting the BAC for drunk driving is just one way to try and control crashes and fatalities related to driving under the influence. Other control measures include installation of a breath-test device connected to the vehicle's ignition (alcohol ignition interlock device), severe financial penalties, driver-education classes, and revocation or suspension of driving privileges.

> *To say drinking and driving penalties have drastically changed since the 1980s is an understatement. I remember my father, who made his career as a popular sports writer during the 1970s in the Chicago area, had some very interesting interactions with the city police after leaving his favorite umpire's bar. He usually just had to tell the police officers who he was and how the Cubs were hitting, sign some autographs, and, after a pat on the back and a coffee in hand, was sent driving home.*

In California, the minimum penalties for a first time DUI offender involve a 30-day license suspension followed by a five-month license restriction, approximately $2,400 in court fines, three months of DUI education classes totaling about $550, the likelihood of an interlock device being installed in their vehicle, two days in jail (or the equivalent in a work release program), and a roughly 100% increase in monthly car insurance rates for the following three years. If a lawyer is retained to help ensure only the above minimum penalties are faced, then add a minimum of $2,000 in attorney fees. All in all, it costs approximately $10,000, not forgetting the jail time, for a first-time, minimum-conviction DUI in California.

So what does all this mean for the brewer and brewery owner? Since the demographic at the highest risk for driving drunk is the exact same population that fills the barstools at multi-tap establishments and brewpubs, as an industry, we should absolutely be promoting responsible drinking. The best way to encourage safe drinking behavior is through education and beer selection. Promoting access to and encouraging the use of safe transportation, such as the bus system, light rail, local taxis, and ride-share apps is a good option. Providing a tasty selection of low-alcohol session beer choices for conscientious drivers is also an excellent way to help control over-consumption. The average male of 160 lb. (73 kg), as described by the CDC, will reach the illegal driving limit of 0.08% BAC after consuming three 16 oz. pints of 5% ABV beer in one hour. The same 160 lb. man only has to consume two 16 oz. pints of 7% ABV beer in one hour to reach 0.08% BAC. Ensuring your staff are well trained is essential. They should be aware of all the beers' ABV content, along with the state's rules and penalties surrounding over-serving patrons. Creating a culture of responsible drinking will foster a safer environment for your staff, your community, and ensure that your patrons return.

Figure 4.1. Enjoying food with beer can help you enjoy a longer session. Photo © Getty Images/Rawpixel.

Food with Drinking Sessions

Serving food or having access to food near the brewery is another positive option to help maintain a legal BAC for driving. Promoting eating while drinking can help reduce the amount of alcohol that is released into the blood system. Up to 80% of alcohol is absorbed into the bloodstream through the small intestine, so slowing the rate that alcohol enters the small intestine helps slow the rate at which it is absorbed. During eating, partially digested food is churned in the stomach and then ejected through the pyloric valve, in small quantities at a time, into the duodenum of the small intestine. It doesn't take a lot of food to enter the duodenum before it quickly sends a signal back to the stomach that causes the pyloric valve to close until the duodenum is ready to accept more. This slows the rate at which the contents of the stomach empty into the small intestine. This is mainly why ingesting food along with drink slows the rate at which alcohol passes into the small intestine and is absorbed into the bloodstream.

If food is offered at your brewery, listing beer-pairing suggestions next to highlighted menu items is a great educational tool to help the customer have a wonderful culinary experience while they enjoy a tasty craft brew. *The Brewmaster's Table* by Garret Oliver is a fabulous book focused on beer and food pairing, and I reference it often when educating customers about how best to pair beer with food. Offering suggestions for a helles and salad pairing or, as Oliver suggests, helles with sandwiches, panini, or falafel, works great (Oliver 2003, 248). Oliver articulately and movingly describes one of the greatest session beer styles ever brewed, the German Pilsener, as follows: "Pilsner is a study in purity, simplicity, and cleanliness of flavor. With food, its lack of fruity, spicy, roasty, or caramelized flavors turns out to be no hindrance; sometimes characterful simplicity can be just what you want" (p.242). Beautiful simplicity that highlights high-quality malts and properly balanced, fresh hops can artfully compliment many creative, tantalizing food dishes and entice customers. The opportunities for pairing session beer with food are endless and way too large of a subject for this book. However, I think reviewing some of the basic principles could give some insight into just how versatile session beer and food pairing can be.

CAN A SESSION BEER BE INTENSE?

Intensity is the key when matching food with beer. Session beers can have high or low intensity. Just because the ABV is lower does not mean that the intensity of session beer must be lower as well. A domestic industrial lager lacks intensity in all forms. The malt flavor is negligible and the hops do not express themselves, leaving only some residual esters behind to provide any noticeable characteristic. On the opposite end of the spectrum would be, say, a craft-brewed Irish red ale aged in a whiskey barrel. The complex caramel malts should interweave with one another, dancing on the palate to create a beautiful malt sweetness. There is an interplay between the malts and the soft notes of vanilla, whiskey, and wood that tells the story of the barrel. Hops stand up like a beam, holding the structure together, but hidden under a drywall of malt complexity and barrel notes.

Could an Irish red ale aged in a whiskey barrel be a session beer? Absolutely. But only if the brewer had the proper skill set to constrain the ABV, understanding that more alcohol would be gained during the barrel-aging period. I would also suggest using a whiskey barrel that had aged other strong beer at least two turns prior to pull out most of the whiskey from the wood. I once began an imperial stout in a whiskey barrel, then a 6% ABV brown ale, and on the third turn laid down a 4% ABV amber ale, and it worked perfectly for all three beers.

Oliver states that balance is the most important component when matching beer with food. It should be a harmonic duet between the two, not a fierce battle. Impact is described by Oliver as the "weight" and "intensity of the food on the palate" (Oliver 2003, 49). We find intensity in many dynamic forms in both the food we eat and the beer we consume.

Session beer can have both high and low intensity. Just because the ABV is lower does not mean that the intensity of the session beer is lower too (see sidebar). Take, for example, a 4.5% ABV Irish red ale aged in a whiskey barrel. Not your typical session beer, but artfully created and produced with drinkability in mind. When paired with food, a grilled burger layered with sweet, caramelized onions and covered in melted, lightly smoked, young Gouda cheese would stand up to, but not destroy, the caramel malt flavors of the Irish red. The light Gouda holds itself up and compliments the low levels of smokiness expressed from the oak whiskey barrel and together make a delightful pairing.

The opposite of a barrel-aged Irish red ale might be a Belgian witbier. Bright, effervescent, and singing with carbonation, the intensity of this beer is much lower than the barrel-aged red and offers multiple opportunities for food pairings with lighter-weight foods. Oliver suggests beginning the day off right by forgoing the orange juice and having a witbier instead. Since witbier is produced with orange peel it works perfectly with many brunch items, as well as something simple like a perfectly grilled ham and cheese sandwich (Oliver 2003, 95). The important component to keep in mind, as Oliver stresses throughout his book, is balancing the food with the beer by pairing "light-bodied, lightly hopped, bright-tasting beers with delicately flavored foods" (p.50).

Since session beers have low alcohol, the body of the beer is light to medium. Therefore, food intensity must be carefully considered when creating the perfect pairing for your guests. Notice earlier I mentioned a lightly smoked and young Gouda cheese for the barrel-aged Irish red ale and loaded burger pairing. A heavily smoked and well-aged Gouda would destroy the delicately bold flavors of the beer. Delicately bold means flavor without huge body and can be done with detailed attention to the brewing process and proper ingredient manipulation.

Another great session beer for matching with food is German Pilsener. This is an incredibly versatile session beer that simply loves to be married to a multitude of menu items, from ham dishes and shellfish to Mexican food. Session beer pairing opportunities are endless and should not be forgotten when it is time to design the new menu or advertise the next brewmaster's dinner.

Session Beers for Every Season

How, why, when, where, and what people decide to drink depends on a lot of different factors. Weather plays a huge role in what we grab from the refrigerator. The fact that Brock Wagner from Saint Arnold Brewing Company named his delightful Kölsch Fancy Lawnmower Beer was no mistake. When the weather is hot and the grass is high, what better beer to quench one's thirst with than a light session Kölsch? Once the leaves start changing and people gravitate toward more indoor activities, their beer choices often change. Session beer can still be the highlight of a beer menu no matter what season it is.

In colder weather, a dry Irish stout by the fire can warm the bones while refreshing the palate all evening long. As the snow melts or the rains begin to clear and the days get longer, change is in the air once again. Change is a dependable and constant force in life. As we witness the seasons predictably rolling through each year, with traditional holidays in tow, beer menus follow suit to help keep the customers coming back for an old friend or one of your newest creations. Accompanying weather changes and holidays with roll outs of seasonal beers has been part of craft brewing culture since the beginning. Because session beer encompasses such a wide spectrum of beer styles, it is simple enough to always have two or three session beers on tap that highlight the time of year and excite your regulars. Saisons are great for springing out of winter as new flowers push up through the ground. When the heat of summer lies heavy over the land, Pilsners and wheat beers are vital for keeping refreshed. From Gose and Berliner weisse to Bavarian wheat beers and hoppy German Pilseners, the choice is endless for what to brew during the hot summer months. As leaves begin to change and school buses reappear on the streets, caramel malt starts arriving at the brewery and wort color changes once again. Vienna lagers and amber and brown ales help usher in the fall and fill the glasses of holiday tables. Session beers are truly beers for all seasons and can round out a beer menu, always providing a great lower-alcohol beer choice for those who want to quaff a few or just simply get home safely.

Education Is Key

The world is full of stress and anxiety. In fact, anxiety is America's number one mental health disorder, affecting an estimated 43 million adult Americans—that's 18% of the adult population.[3] By the time work is over and it's finally time

---

[3] "Any Mental Illness (AMI) Among U.S. Adults," National Institutes of Mental Health, accessed April 22, 2017, http://www.nimh.nih.gov/health/statistics/prevalence/any-mental-illness-ami-among-us-adults.shtml.

to enjoy a beer, stress is something folks are looking to relieve, not increase. It is becoming extremely common in the modern craft beer bars to see large LED screens listing 20-plus beers. As you read through the board, crazy names appear with little description as to what exactly the six-to-nine-dollar pint tastes like. It can be downright intimidating. Even if you're lucky enough to get a server or bartender to help you, they may race through a list of the beers on draught, or hand out a bottle list a mile long written in super-small font—this too can be a nerve-wracking experience. When did ordering a beer become so complicated?

I have noticed that many beer bars list, or at least the staff know, each beer's ABV, and customers sometimes make their decision based on ABV alone. If you happen to be the designated driver for the night and are planning on having something other than soda or water, a beer with lower alcohol is usually a good choice. Or maybe you plan on spending two to three hours having beers with friends, so choosing a lower-alcohol beer can be a good way to go. While there are numerous factors influencing a beer drinker's selection, alcohol content remains one of the most important.

Properly training your staff about the beer produced or sold at your establishment is a fundamental part of growing the craft beer market and keeping customers happy. Intimidation evokes stress in people. The last thing anyone wants to experience is stress when they go to relax and enjoy the new taproom or brewpub in their town. Customers that walk in the door will differ in their beer knowledge, from the novice, first-time craft beer drinker, to the well-educated beer aficionado. A properly trained staff member who can quickly evaluate the level of knowledge each customer brings when ordering goes a long way to providing a fun, inviting experience. An educated server can competently introduce the new craft beer drinker to their first craft beer, as well as explain the combination of dry hops used to infuse the grapefruit character when questioned by a craft beer buff. When introducing a new session beer to your staff, it is important to highlight all the wonderful characteristics that make up the beer's flavor profile. Focusing on high ABV as a selling point when there are other offerings can create a culture of prejudice toward beers under 5% ABV. I suggest embracing all beer styles and celebrating each one for its unique nuances and features expressed. There is a time and place for all beers, and knowing how to sell many differing beer styles only helps increase total sales. Attitude and culture are created everyday within the craft beer world. Staying positive with language regarding session beers, as well as the stronger beers, presents an open-minded environment that's welcoming to customers, no matter what their preference or mood is.

One way to demonstrate a non-biased attitude toward lower-alcohol beers is by keeping the price the same as other craft beer on tap. There is a trend among craft beer establishments to price beer according to ABV. Typically, higher priced beers contain more alcohol and are therefore also served in smaller-sized glassware. This pricing technique can be a positive educational opportunity or a slippery slope. If the beer created by the hard-working brewer takes longer to produce, such as a barrel-aged beer, then by all means a higher price may very well be warranted. Similarly, a higher price might be necessary for certain beers that cost a lot more to produce, such as a triple IPA that required a pallet of hops just for the first dry hop alone.

The message of how the new, special beer was artfully created and honed, and perhaps the history behind the unique style that inspired the brewers to try brewing it, can be passionately delivered by your servers to the customers, helping them to understand more about the world of craft beer. Pricing such beers higher than your regular tap lineup can be appropriate and it does provide the opportunity to talk about beer at the table. However, simply reducing the price of a beer based solely on a lower alcohol content gives the message of subpar quality and can establish a culture that session beer is of lesser quality then higher-alcohol beers. I hope to encourage and inspire a positive pricing scale that supports all craft styles, no matter what the ABV. For additional reading regarding educating your staff, I suggest picking up or downloading a copy of the *Beer Server Training for Brewpubs* manual written by the Brewers Association brewpub subcommittee.[4]

---

[4]   Further details about the *Beer Server Training for Brewpubs* manual can be found on the Brewers Association website, http://www.brewersassociation.org/educational-publications /beer-server-training-for-brewpubs/.

5

The Cost of
Doing Business

One thing that it is impossible to do is to tell a craft brewer to invent a different style of beer for the sole purpose of saving money. The foundation of the entire craft brewing industry is built on freedom of expression. Having such prolific liberty has delivered peanut butter oatmeal cookie stout, white porter, key lime Gose, and raspberry Belgian IPA into our reality. Exploring endless flavor combinations is what sustains the vitality of craft brewing and excites conversation at pubs and multi-tap houses everywhere. Amid daily life, which can often be mundane and repetitive, discussing (and trying!) the newest creations the local brewers have tapped can bring a refreshing break to the monotony of our world. Many new recipes are artfully executed at the lower end of the alcohol spectrum, while others smash you over the tongue and dare you to be able to drink the entire pint. The weekly production schedule for a craft brewery can change radically from day to day. Monday could be a double IPA brew, Tuesday a dry Irish stout, Wednesday a German Pilsener, and Thursday a Belgian-style dubbel. All great beer styles, but with radically differing expenditures. Calculating the cost of production is a challenging task for any brewery owner.

Fiscal and Community Responsibility

During my twenty-year tenure at Salt Lake Brewing Company, Jeff Polychronis and Peter Cole promoted and encouraged a company-wide, triple bottom line philosophy, otherwise known as the "three Ps": people, planet, and profit. First coined in 1994 by John Elkington, a British business consultant, the basic tenet is that companies should prepare three bottom line reports, the first being a traditional account of profit and loss, a second that measures impact of business practices in regard to social responsibility to their employees and community, and a third that exhibits the effect of doing business on the environment.[1] Making a healthy profit gives a company the ability to better take care of its people and planet. If a company is not profitable, nothing works and the company will die.

For Squatters, session beer production was first perceived as a restriction, a 4% ABV muzzle that was strapped on us by a religiously governed state. However, under this ABV cap, something beautiful was born. As creative craft brewers, we flourished, producing as many wonderful session beer creations as we could. The cost saving was a hidden benefit that helped the company grow strong. Offering many types of diverse, high-quality beers will always be the flagship of the modern craft brewery. Placing session beers on the tap lineup is common sense because it makes good business sense—it gives your customers the opportunity to socialize with friends longer.

Cost of Ingredients

Craft beer in America has built a strong reputation for quality, diversity, and flavor. Craft beer provides an alternative to standard light lager beers that have dominated marketplace shelves for decades. Quality has to be first and foremost, but quality often comes at a premium. Sourcing the finest malted barley and freshest hops rapidly inflates the cost of making craft beer. A typical beer, whether considered craft or not, includes four basic ingredients:

---

[1]   "Triple bottom line," Online Extra, *Economist*, November 17, 2009, http://www.economist.com/node/14301663.

malted barley and/or cereal grain, hops, water, and yeast. According to the United States Department of Agriculture (USDA) National Agricultural Statistics Service, historical data reveal the average price the farmer received for malting barley increased from $2.21 per bushel in the 1982–86 period to $6.03 per bushel in 2011–15. Although there are market fluctuations caused by supply and demand, weather, inflation, and other economic impacts, the real price brewers pay for malted barley has risen over the three decades.

Hop pricing also has increased over the last three decades. A variety of market impacts, such as production costs and the development of new hop varieties, have drastically raised the price of specific hops over others. According to Ann George, executive director at the Hop Growers of America, a large increase in the demand for aroma varieties over the last five years has driven many American growers to expand the necessary infrastructure that helps guarantee high-quality aroma hops. Sudden hop fame combined with limited availability also greatly distresses the volatile hop market, particularly in recent years; all the while, prices for other traditional hop varieties steadily increase per pound, slowly and consistently, year after year. Hopping rates per barrel have also grown exponentially since 2007. In a presentation at the 61st Annual American Hop Convention, Brewers Association (BA) supply chain specialist, Chris Swersey, reported a 42% increase in hop usage per barrel from 2007 to 2016. One thing brewers can always depend on is the rising cost of doing business when it comes to their ingredients, especially if high-quality ingredients are being sourced.

Water is a crucial ingredient in making beer and must be considered when calculating the cost of production. The amount of water used to produce a barrel of beer varies depending on total volume of beer produced by a given brewery. For a large-scale brewery, target water usage goal is around 3.5 bbl. water per barrel of beer produced. However, for a brewery that produces under 10,000 barrels annually, the scale of operation makes such a target more difficult and water usage rises, typically to 4.5 or 5.0 bbl. water per barrel of beer produced (Palmer and Kaminski 2013, 205). No matter how much capacity a brewery has, water should be viewed as a precious resource and monitored in all departments. Water usage remains constant in many areas of the brewery for all beer brands, no matter what the ABV is. For instance, all vessels, such as bright tanks and fermentors, need to be cleaned in the same manner under the brewery's standard operating procedures, regardless of alcohol content. The cellar and brewhouse floors need to be sprayed down in a similar fashion, and water requirements for filtration and packaging remain equal across the board. When different beer styles are produced in the same brewhouse is where water usage can vary greatly.

The volume of water used for mashing and sparging depends on the grain volume needed to reach the desired original gravity. The average liquor-to-grist ratio producing a 20% (i.e., 20°P) first wort is roughly 300 L of water to every 100 kg of malt, that is to say, a liquor-to-grist ratio of 3 to 1 (Kunze 2004, 235). Therefore, the more malt used to achieve higher original gravities for higher ABV in the final beer, the more water needed in mashing. There are numerous techniques used to extract fermentable sugars from a mash, such as multi-step decoction mashes or using a mash filter. Vessel design and dimensions, and the mashing system employed all greatly influence time needed and concentration of wort extracted.

For our purpose, the common single step infusion mash will be used to demonstrate water requirements for creating wort at varying original gravities. After the mash rest and *vorlauf* is complete, with conversion and proper clarification achieved, the first wort is run to the kettle. After the first wort is successfully lautered, a considerable amount of extract still resides in the grains and must be sparged to extract the remaining sugar. Sparge water usage increases as the strength of the first wort rises. For instance, if the percent concentration of first wort is 16%, the sparge water ratio to first wort will be 1.2, whereas for a first wort concentration of 20% the sparge water to first wort ratio increases to 1.5 (Kunze 2004, 256). Therefore, extraction of a higher-gravity wort requires increased volumes of sparge water.

Calculation Explanations

As a practicing craft brewer, I have come to the realization that there are many ways to skin a cat. Meaning, it is not always a straight line when it comes to scaling and recipe design. Subjectivity, brewing experience, cost, and access to ingredients all play a critical role when deciding how to create a new beer or invigorate an old one. The following discussion is an exercise on cost, not on recipe development. For the sole purpose of demonstrating the cost savings for beer brewed at different strengths of alcohol, the recipe employed will be kept as simple as possible. By no means am I suggesting this is how you should brew this particular style of beer. For great examples to help with recipe development, please refer to the recipes found in chapters 6, 7, and 8. A mock IPA recipe will be used for the example recipe below, due to this style's immense popularity throughout America among craft beer consumers and brewers alike.

For the examples below, we'll be making the following assumptions. The cost demonstrations that follow will be for IPAs of varying ABV. They use 100% two-row American barley for the grist. Bittering hops are Chinook pellets with an alpha acid percentage (% AA) contribution of 13%; IBUs derived from the early boil addition will be 50% of total IBUs. The aroma hops for this exercise are 13% AA Simcoe pellets, which make up the rest of the IBU percentage. Kettle utilization will be held at 30% for the boiling hops and 10% for the end-of-boil Simcoe addition, and total boil time will be 90 minutes. The alcohol and IBU targets will be at mid-range and are based on the BA's 2015 beer style guidelines for the GABF. Bitterness units will be calculated using a standard IBU formula developed and taught by the faculty at the American Brewers Guild:

$$\text{hop addition in grams} = \frac{\text{IBU desired for addition} \times \text{liters of wort} \times 0.001}{\text{\% hop utilization rate} \times \text{\% alpha acid of hop}}$$

Lastly, the liquor-to-grist ratio used in all calculations is 3 to 1, based on common brewing practice, with the understanding that this ratio is not always achievable or desired given diverse mashing systems and grist charges.

To successfully achieve the desired specific original gravity in the brewhouse, the rate of evaporation must be determined. Wort boiling accomplishes many goals, including concentration of wort, color formation, removal of unwanted aroma substance, sterilization, and hop alpha acid isomerization. It was once thought a high evaporation rate exceeding 10% was indicative of good kettle performance (Kunze 2004, 284). However, boiling for longer consumes more energy and energy usage must be considered when trying to maximize cost savings. Common brewing practice for achieving the basic goals of the boil is to boil between one and two hours, depending on brewing system and beer style being produced. If boil goals are met within 60 minutes and the target original gravity is achieved, boiling longer only costs the brewery more money for no practical gain. The heat source used in the brewhouse greatly affects kettle performance and subsequently the rate of evaporation. Evaporation rates can vary from 4% to 10% depending on heat source and kettle design. For the purpose of this discussion, an evaporation rate of 6% will be used in the following calculations.

Efficiency in the brewhouse is a key component for maximizing profit and reducing waste. Brewhouse efficiency, as defined by John Mallett in his book, *Malt*, is the ability to recover potential extract from the grain (Mallett 2014, 12–13). Mash tun dimensions and design, and liquor-to-grist ratios play a critical role in determining the efficiency of a brewhouse. Mallett also states that, as wort strength increases, efficiency will inevitably decline (Mallett 2014, 13). The grain bill must increase to achieve higher original gravities due to the mash's ability to hold back potential extract.

Kunze states that brewhouse efficiency "indicates what percentage of the grist charge is available as extract content in the cast wort" (Kunze 2004, 323). Factors affecting brewhouse efficiency are raw materials, brewhouse equipment, mash process, and lautering operations. Brewhouse efficiency varies greatly depending on these factors, and usually falls somewhere between 75%–94% of the maximum efficiency.

The definition of brewhouse efficiency can be expanded in scope to include how much actual wort is finally delivered to the fermentor. From my personal experience working on various brewing systems producing countless styles of beer, I have witnessed declining efficiency volumes in the fermentor in direct correlation to the amount of hops used in the kettle and/or whirlpool vessel. Once again, absorption is the culprit.

In the following cost calculations, the brewhouse efficiency percentage will be manipulated up or down depending on starting original gravity and quantity of hops used. The efficiency calculation utilizes the hot water extraction (HWE) measurement indicated by the maltster on a typical malt analysis sheet as percent extract coarse grind, as-is (CGAI). Since only American two-row will be used in the grist charge to simplify the example, CGAI will remain constant at 78%.

Pricing Explanations

There has certainly been a large shift from how craft brewers in America once bought ingredients in the early 1990s versus how they are bought today. Back in 1993, all one had to do was pick up the phone and order 44 pounds of Centennial and poof!—magically a delivery person would show up two days later with your box of fresh hops at a fair price. Nowadays, hop contracts plague the mind of the brewmaster, and forecasting capacity and brand growth must be calculated in order to secure the correct amount of fresh ingredients necessary to keep the ship afloat. Malt contracts are also heavily encouraged and bulk malt supply is in high demand. Economies of scale and buying power play a massive role in whether a brewery receives better prices for ingredients. When a brewery grows to a regional level, its buying power greatly increases and its costs inevitably decline. However, since the bulk of American craft breweries are under the 15,000 bbl./year mark, and for the purpose of demonstrating rising expenses with rising alcohol, the following pricing will be used in the calculation of ingredient cost: bulk two-row barley will be priced at $0.35/lb., Chinook hops at $8/lb., and Simcoe hops at $12.62/lb. These are generally representative of 2016 prices and may, of course, change over the years.

Any increase in water usage will be noted, but not factored into the final cost differences due to the wide range of water and sewer prices around the United States. However, when reviewing the charts that follow, you should take into account any increase in your water needs. According to Palmer and Kaminski, typical water usage is "5–8 volumes of water per volume of beer produced and about 3 pounds of saturated spent grain per gallon of beer" (2013, 218).

Brewpub Numbers

In 2015, the BA reported 1,650 brewpubs were operating in the United States. The BA's definition for a brewpub is as follows:

> A restaurant-brewery that sells 25 percent or more of its beer on site. The beer is brewed primarily for sale in the restaurant and bar. The beer is often dispensed directly from the brewery's storage tanks. Where allowed by law, brewpubs often sell beer "to go" and/or distribute to off-site accounts. Note: BA re-categorizes a company as a microbrewery if its off-site (distributed) beer sales exceed 75 percent. ("Craft Beer Industry Market Segments," Brewers Association, accessed April 23, 2017, http://www.brewersassociation.org /statistics/market-segments/)

The following calculations are based on a brewpub producing 1,000 bbl./year, with their flagship IPA accounting for 40% of total sales.

BREWPUB COST COMPARISON

	Flagship Session IPA	Flagship IPA	Flagship Double IPA
Batch size	10 bbl. KO	10 bbl. KO	10 bbl. KO
Original gravity	11.2°P	16.5°P	21.0°P
Final gravity	2.8°P	3.0°P	3.5°P
ABV	4.4%	7%	9%
IBU	48	60	85
Brewhouse efficiency	85%	80%	75%
Evaporation	6%	6%	6%
Liquor-to-grist ratio	3:1	3:1	3:1
Mash water required	164 gal.	262 gal.	362 gal.
Two-row malt required	456 lb.	730 lb.	1007 lb.
Total malt price	$160	$256	$352
Bittering hop required	Chinook 1.6 lb.	Chinook 2.0 lb.	Chinook 2.7 lb.
Aroma hop required	Simcoe 4.7 lb.	Simcoe 5.9 lb.	Simcoe 8.2 lb.
Dry hop required	Simcoe 2 lb./bbl. = 20 lb.	Simcoe 3 lb./bbl. = 30 lb.	Simcoe 3.5 lb./bbl. = 35 lb.
Total hop price	$323	$469	$567
Total cost of 10 bbl. batch	$483	$725	$919
Total annual cost of 400 bbl.	$19,320	$29,000	$36,760

Note all prices in US dollars and representative of 2016 prices.
bbl., US beer barrel (31 US gal.); gal., US gallon; KO, knockout; lb., US pound; °P, degrees Plato.

Microbrewery Numbers

In 2015, the BA reported 2,397 microbreweries were operating in the United States. The BA's definition of a microbrewery is as follows:

A brewery that produces less than 15,000 barrels (17,600 hectoliters) of beer per year with 75 percent or more of its beer sold off-site. (Ibid.)

The calculations below are based on a microbrewery producing 10,000 barrels per year, with their flagship IPA accounting for 40% of total sales.

MICROBREWERY COST COMPARISON

	Flagship Session IPA	Flagship IPA	Flagship Double IPA
Batch size	30 bbl. KO	30 bbl. KO	30 bbl. KO
Original gravity	11.2°P	16.5°P	21.0°P
Final gravity	2.8°P	3.0°P	3.5°P
ABV	4.4%	7%	9%
IBU	48	60	85
Brewhouse efficiency	90%	85%	80%
Evaporation	6%	6%	6%
Liquor-to-grist ratio	3:1	3:1	3:1
Mash water required	465 gal.	741 gal.	1018 gal.
Two-row malt required	1294 lb.	2061 lb.	2832 lb.
Total malt price	$453	$721	$991
Bittering hop required	Chinook 4.69 lb.	Chinook 5.92 lb.	Chinook 8.39 lb.
Aroma hop required	Simcoe 14.07 lb.	Simcoe 17.77 lb.	Simcoe 25.17 lb.
Dry-hop required	Simcoe 2 lb./bbl. = 60 lb.	Simcoe 3 lb./bbl. = 90 lb.	Simcoe 3.5 lb./bbl. = 105 lb.
Total hop price	$978	$1,407	$1,710
Total cost of 30 bbl. batch	$1,431	$2,128	$2,701
Total annual cost (4,000 bbl.)	$190,795	$283,733	$360,132

Note all prices in US dollars and representative of 2016 pricing.
bbl., US beer barrel (31 US gal.); gal., US gallon; KO, knockout; lb., US pound; °P, degrees Plato.

Brewhouse Efficiency and Small-Scale Systems

Four major factors that affect brewhouse efficiency are mash parameters, mill settings, lautering techniques, and mash pH. My experience in several small brewhouses and several large brewhouses has taught me many lessons on why larger breweries tend to be more efficient. Small breweries often run with limited brewing staff and usually, after some success, grow their brewery by installing a larger, more efficient brewhouse. New brewing companies typically start off small, learning valuable lessons along the way while cutting their teeth on smaller batches of craft beer and honing their skill set. When production increases, which requires more employees and a greater focus on cost reduction, brewhouse efficiency is often a hot topic. Mill settings are dialed in, lautering techniques improve with experience and advancement in equipment design, and stricter pH and other mash parameters are met to help increase efficiency. I am by no means saying that a small brewing system can't be extremely efficient, especially given the plethora of brewhouse manufacturers, but this is not typically the case. Therefore, brewhouse efficiency has been increased by 5% for the microbrewery numbers.

Final Financial Contemplations

The above cost exercise is to provide readers a quick glimpse into the significant financial impact creating bigger beers can have. The cost exercise specifies the use of water in volume, but not in cost. Water, in terms of sewer prices and regulations, can vary immensely depending on location and size of brewery. Although cost was not calculated due to this variability, it is important to factor in how water is paid for at your brewery and, more importantly, how your brewery handles wastewater. A severe wastewater surcharge is often levied on breweries discharging effluent that is high in biological oxygen demand (BOD), chemical oxygen demand (COD), and total suspended solids (TSS). When big beers are being produced, the last worts are stopped high in gravity at the end of runoff so as not to dilute the strength of the kettle original gravity, thus sending a higher-strength BOD to the drain and incurring additional costs for total brewery operations. Larger craft breweries have sophisticated wastewater systems in place to manage all effluent discharged from the brewery. Many smaller microbreweries and brewpubs, however, are ill-equipped to neutralize wastewater pH, reduce BOD load, and properly control other load factors that impact wastewater costs.

Operating an environmentally friendly brewery is a key ingredient in a recipe for long lasting success. Knowing your brewery's water and wastewater demands and associated costs is crucial for making key expenditure decisions when it comes to calculating the bottom line. Other considerations need to be factored in when calculating the cost of producing big beers versus session beers. For example, high-gravity beers require a huge amount of yeast, and dry hops can often present problems for both wastewater systems and loss of beer yield.

An additional consideration when deciding one's brand line-up is how many turns are anticipated in the brewhouse each day. Creating higher-gravity beers can slow down brewhouse throughput significantly. By no means should cost alone dictate a brewer's every move when it comes to building their dream brewery, but it is clear that blindly choosing beer styles to create, market, and sell without contemplating the related costs is imprudent.

The tall price of producing high-gravity beer is both quantitative and qualitative. What is difficult to measure, but clearly has significant financial impact on a brewery, is how the customer enjoys beer. It is fair to say the lower the amount of alcohol a beer has, the more one can drink. When blood alcohol remains low for a longer duration it enables the customer to stay in better control and stay in the bar. Therefore, it is my belief that session beers promote increased consumption, generating higher sales and profitability for the brewery. Many craft beer enthusiasts hold craft session beers in the same regard as other craft beers, regardless of alcohol content. Bellying up to a multi-tap house LED screen or chalkboard to navigate the sea of choices is what customers are used to. They expect to pay high prices for special barrel-aged project beers, limited releases, and beers over 9% ABV. When it comes to craft beer selections drifting between 3.5% ABV to 8.5% ABV, the price point is usually very similar. If a long night of drinking is in store, certain consumers will sometimes select lower ABV beers first and have several, before ordering a higher-alcohol style. Alternatively, customers will have a couple of high-alcohol beers before settling into an evening filled with session beer rounds. Regardless of fluctuating drinking patterns, quality session beer has a noteworthy place on any tap list. There is certainly a time and place for all different beer styles, and having several session beer choices for customers to choose from is always a good decision for both them and the brewery.

SECTION II

Session Beer Recipes

The next three chapters contain a collection of great modern-day session beers currently produced at craft breweries around the United States. There will be an introduction to the brewery and sometimes to the people behind these great beers. Let's admit it, without the brewers there would be no beer. We could say the same thing about the yeast, but that's another book.

Recipe Specifications and Assumptions

The Recipes

The beer style is indicated when there is one and the basic specifications of the beer are listed. Recipes are first outlined using grain bill percentages and hop alpha-acid percentages that commercial breweries use, and the yeast strain.

Underneath this are notes on brewing that include information on mashing, fermentation, maturation, and carbonation; additional information, such as water treatment, may be given if such details are known or extra advice is warranted.

The first recipe outline is then followed by the same recipe, this time adjusted for a five-gallon batch size. The homebrewing software program, BeerSmith™ (http://beersmith.com), was used to convert the recipes from percentages to quantities appropriate for five-gallon batch size, and some of the amounts have been slightly manipulated for rounding purposes. I have done my best to uphold the recipe's integrity and true flavor profile. The five-gallon batch recipe is then accompanied by the same notes on brewing as before, so it stands as a complete recipe on its own.

Specifications and Units

- Original gravity and final gravity (terminal gravity) are given as specific gravity followed by degrees Plato (°P) in parentheses.
- Bitterness units are calculated and listed as international bitterness units (IBU).
- Alcohol content is given as percent alcohol by volume (ABV).
- Temperatures are given in degrees Fahrenheit (°F) followed by degrees Celsius (°C) in parentheses.
- Weights and volumes given in pounds (lb.), ounces (oz.), gallons (gal.), and beer barrels (bbl.) are US units of measure. (Note: one US beer barrel equals 31 gal.)
- Other measures use metric units, such as liter (L), milliliter (mL), kilograms (kg), and grams (g).
- Concentrations are given in parts per million (ppm), parts per billion (ppb), or, in the case of carbonation, grams per liter (g/L) or volumes CO_2.

Hops and Bitterness Units

- Hops are calculated and listed as "Type 90" (T90) pellets, unless otherwise indicated by the brewer.
- If the information was made available, the recipe indicates how many bitterness units (by percentage of total IBU) come from each hop addition.
- Addition times (e.g., @ 60) have taken into consideration typical utilization rates and may need to be adjusted for your specific equipment design and function.

- The BeerSmith program was used to assign an industry appropriate alpha acid percentage (% AA) to each varietal listed in their database.

Yeast

- If indicated by the brewer, the specific yeast strain is listed; if a specific yeast strain was not provided, then a generic yeast is suggested.
- Pitch rates should assume 1 million cells per milliliter of wort per degree Plato (million cells/mL/°P) and pitched as a reclaimed yeast slurry, unless otherwise stated.

Brewing Notes

- Mashing techniques are outlined if provided; if not, then assume a single-step, infusion mash.
- Conversion and lautering assumptions are a 20-minute rest, 15-minute vorlauf, or as needed to achieve clarity and run off to kettle.
- Wort pH to the kettle should not rise above 5.75 to reduce the level of astringent malt polyphenol extraction.
- If water treatment is provided by the brewer, it will be indicated; if not, then the necessary calcium or other minerals per specific style recommendations should be added. (Since styles of session beers range broadly, further research may be needed by the brewer to replicate the exact beer style's water treatment.)

Enjoy your session beer journey!

6

North American
Session Beer Recipes

What a great time to be a craft beer drinker in America. With over 5,000 craft breweries nationwide, it's hard to throw a rock these days and not hit a fermentor. So much beer, so little time is what I always say, and with all this competition, everyone is sprinting for the next hot, new trend that makes the front page. Some trends come and go, whereas some arrive and never leave. I am certain that craft session beer is here to stay. I will admit, for a short time, it was difficult to find a craft beer under 6% ABV on tap, but thankfully those days are over. It did not take long for most craft breweries to realize it takes a lot of craft session beer to keep our industry strong and people on their bar stool. Americans have always encouraged and applauded hard work, and what better way to celebrate the end of a tough work day than with a cold session beer. The wonderful thing is, session beers in America now come in many different flavors and styles. From artfully crafted cream ales to a tart Berliner weisse, or even a dry-roasted Irish stout, there is a craft session beer on tap for everyone.

Sun King Brewing Company

Sun King Brewing Company began, like most great breweries do, over numerous conversations and numerous beers. Dave Colt and Clay Robinson worked together at The Ram brewery in downtown Indianapolis. After enjoying many after-work beers and conversations together, they decided that they formed a great partnership and started developing the concept behind Sun King. Initially, they explored opening a brewpub, but they then realized that Indianapolis did not have a production brewery to call its own. That was what Colt and Robinson really wanted to do, make great beer for their great city. Both had roughly a decade of professional brewing experience and realized that running a brewery was their life's passion. This culture of part production brewery and part brewpub was a large part of the Sun King dialogue from the beginning. It just happened to work out that when their start-up funds diminished and a final wall could not be built between the brewery's production area and the taproom it would end up being a blessing in disguise. Having the production area visible to the taproom brought the customers closer to the process and created a great synergistic energy for Sun King.

Sun King opened in downtown Indianapolis in the summer of 2009 with a 12-tap tasting room and a 15-barrel brewhouse. With growth in mind, they continued to add warehouse square footage in the surrounding buildings to keep up with high demand for their delicious beers. In 2015 a second location was opened north of Indianapolis in Fisher, Indiana, not more than a 30-minute drive from their downtown brewhouse. The 6,000-square foot Fisher location currently is home to a second taproom and a three-barrel pilot system. Robinson and Colt make a dynamic and successful partnership; Robinson runs the sales and marketing side of Sun King while Colt manages and oversees production and taproom operations. Their focus on culture, quality beer, and support for their local community is steadfast and true.

Sun King continues to be recognized for their astute business practices and award-winning beers. Colt and Robinson are truly living their dream, creating both new and creative craft beers alongside traditional favorites, while at the same time partnering with community and environmental support groups. Sunlight Cream Ale, one of the year-round offerings and flagship beers at Sun King, exemplifies their celebration of traditional brewing heritage; winning a Silver in the Golden/Blonde Ale category at the WBC in 2010 and Gold in the same category at GABF in 2015. Sunlight Cream Ale brings harmonious balance to the pallet with light, malt complexity artfully intermingled with a delicate hop backbone.

Sun King Sunlight Cream Ale (Commercial)

Cream Ale

Original gravity: 1.044 (11°P)
Final gravity: 1.006–1.007 (1.5–1.8°P)
Bitterness: 18 IBU
ABV: 5%–5.2%
Attenuation: 85%
Boil (min): 70

MALTS
90% two-row pale malt
4% flaked oats
6% white wheat

HOPS
Warrior (15% AA) @ 70
U.S. Liberty (4.3% AA) @ 20

YEAST
California/American ale yeast (Wyeast 1056)

BREWING NOTES
Mashing: Single step infusion rest at 152°F (67°C).
Primary Fermentation: 68°F (20°C).
Fermentation/Maturation: Ferment until you pass diacetyl rest then crash to 32°F (0°C).
Finishing: Bright with no haze. Sun King uses a centrifuge to achieve this desired clarity.
Carbonation: 2.50–2.70 volumes CO_2.

Sun King Sunlight Cream Ale (Five-Gallon Batch)

Cream Ale

Original gravity: 1.044 (11°P)
Final gravity: 1.006–1.007 (1.5–1.8°P)
Bitterness: 18 IBU
ABV: 5%–5.2%
Attenuation: 85%
Boil (min): 70

MALTS
7 lb. 12 oz. (3.5 kg) two-row pale malt
6 oz. (170 g) flaked oats
0.5 lb. (230 g) white wheat

HOPS
0.25 oz. (7 g) Warrior (15% AA) @ 70
0.25 oz. (7 g) Liberty (4.3% AA) @ 20

YEAST
California/American ale yeast (Wyeast 1056)

BREWING NOTES
Mashing: Single step infusion rest at 152°F (67°C).
Primary Fermentation: 68°F (20°C).
Fermentation/Maturation: Ferment until you pass diacetyl rest then crash to 32°F (0°C).
Finishing: Bright with no haze. Sun King uses a centrifuge to achieve this desired clarity.
Carbonation: 2.50–2.70 volumes CO_2.

Auburn Alehouse

Auburn Alehouse is located in the historic old town section of Auburn, California, just off Interstate 80 about 33 miles north of Sacramento. Brian and Lisa Ford opened the doors to their brewpub on July 24th, 2007. The Fords are not afraid of hard work and are the definition of hands-on owners. While Lisa manages the restaurant side, running food to her bustling brewpub, Brian is behind the scenes keeping things running on the production side, all the while coming up with new ideas for the brewery. It's not hard to find either Ford, or both of them, somewhere in the building on a daily basis.

For the last nine years, Auburn Alehouse has been serving American-brewpub cuisine and great craft beers to locals and travelers, who are usually on their way to Tahoe. Brian, a graduate of the American Brewers Guild, served his internship at Rubicon Brewing before beginning his professional brewing career. To say Brian loves to make things is an understatement. When he is not at the brewery laying out a new label design or developing the next seasonal rotation, Brian is pouring concrete somewhere. If not otherwise occupied, he can be found tearing up the race track on his Yamaha YZ250. Brian has a love for all things hoppy, but he has enjoyed crafting session beers since he opened the doors.

Auburn is situated along the Sierra Nevada foothills in Placer County, the heart of Gold Country. Many of the Auburn Alehouse beer names come from historical references to the gold mining history of the area. Pre-Prohibition lager has been flowing throughout California's Gold Country since the mid-nineteenth century. After James Marshall discovered the first gold in 1848 in Coloma, California, thousands of miners from all over the world flooded into the area to find their riches. Mining is hard work and requires long hours in the hot sun. As soon as any new town was erected to support the influx of gold seekers and immigrants, building a local brewery was the first order of business so as to quench the thirst of local miners.

Brian thought it fitting to continue the long history of brewing pre-Prohibition lager in Gold Country and really enjoys the unique flavor profile this beer style brings. Gold Country Pilsner is a beautiful medium-bodied, straw-colored Pilsner with an elegant hop bitterness and lingering aroma. A touch of maize lends a subtle sweetness and light body.

Auburn Alehouse Gold Country Pilsner (Commercial)

Pre-Prohibition Lager

Original gravity: 1.048 (12°P)
Final gravity: 1.010 (2.6°P)
Bitterness: 42 IBU
ABV: 4.9%
Attenuation: 80%
Boil (min): 90

MALTS

71% two-row pale malt
19% flaked maize
10% wheat

HOPS

German Magnum (14% AA) @ 90
German Magnum (14% AA) @ 30
Mt. Hood (6% AA) @ 5
Czech Saaz (3.75% AA) @ 5
Czech Saaz (3.75% AA) @ 0

YEAST

Lager yeast

BREWING NOTES

Mashing: Single step infusion rest at 154°F (68°C).
Primary Fermentation: The optimum primary fermentation temperature will depend on the house lager yeast that is selected. Please refer to the recommendations from your yeast supplier.
Fermentation/Maturation: Once fermentation is complete, carry out a 24-hour diacetyl rest before cooling. Cool beer to 33°F (0.5°C). Beer is aged for nine days before filtration. Remove yeast often to avoid autolysis.
Finishing: Beer is filtered bright.
Carbonation: 2.52 volumes CO_2.

Auburn Alehouse Gold Country Pilsner (Five-Gallon Batch)

Pre-Prohibition Lager

Original gravity: 1.048 (12°P)
Final gravity: 1.010 (2.6°P)
Bitterness: 42 IBU
ABV: 4.9%
Attenuation: 80%
Boil (min): 90

MALTS
6 lb. 11 oz. (3 kg) two-row pale malt
1 lb. 12 oz. (800 g) flaked maize
15 oz. (425 g) white wheat

HOPS
0.3 oz. (8.5 g) German Magnum (14% AA) @ 90
0.2 oz. (6 g) German Magnum (14% AA) @ 30
3 oz. (85 g) Mt. Hood (6% AA) @ 5
2 oz. (57 g) Czech Saaz (3.75% AA) @ 5
1 oz. (28 g) Czech Saaz (3.75% AA) @ whirlpool

YEAST
Lager yeast

BREWING NOTES
Mashing: Single step infusion rest at 154°F (68°C).
Primary Fermentation: The optimum primary fermentation temperature will depend on the house lager yeast that is selected. Please refer to the recommendations from your yeast supplier.
Fermentation/Maturation: Once fermentation is complete, rack to secondary for a 24-hour diacetyl rest before cooling. Cool beer to 33°F (0.5°C) and age for nine days before serving.
Carbonation: 2.52 volumes CO_2.

New Glarus Brewing Company

Dan Carey, a Diploma Master Brewer, is by far one of the finest craft brewers in the world. He is brewmaster for the employee-owned New Glarus Brewing Company in New Glarus, Wisconsin. Dan has honed his brewing skills and education in the brewing industry over the last two decades and his successful brewing company is direct evidence of that. He earned a bachelor's degree in Food Science with an Emphasis in Malting and Brewing Science from the University of California, Davis (UC Davis) in 1983, before serving his apprenticeship at a small brewery near Munich, Germany. When attending the Siebel Institute Course in Brewing Technology in 1987, Dan was awarded valedictorian of his class. Dan's hunger for brewing knowledge did not stop there—in 1990 he passed the Institute of Brewing and Distilling Diploma Examination, followed by the Master Brewer Examination in 1992. Dan is highly regarded by his peers and the beers he has created have earned many awards. He won the Association of Brewers Small Brewer of the Year award in 2003, and Mid-Size Brewer of the Year in 2005 and 2006. One of Dan's greatest recognitions came in 2006 when he was presented the Russell Schehrer Award for Innovation in Craft Brewing at the Brewers Association annual conference.

It was truly a perfect match when Deborah met her future partner in life, Dan Carey. Deborah Carey is founder and president of the New Glarus Brewing Company, becoming the first women to establish and operate a brewery in the United States. A native of Wisconsin, she attended Carroll College in Helena, Montana, majoring in marketing and graphics. Deborah's marketing genius is unprecedented and quite evident in the evolution and continued success of the New Glarus beer brands. Deborah is the true definition of entrepreneur. She started and built the business side of New Glarus Brewing Company in tandem with her husband's fantastic beer. Together, the Careys led their Midwestern brewery to becoming one of the best breweries in the world. New Glarus Brewing Company's second location on the outskirts of New Glarus, Hilltop Brewery, pays tribute to the local farming community of the surrounding area in a modest European-style setting. Once inside, visitors can gaze in awe at the beautiful copper-clad brewhouse, slate flooring, and spiral staircase. The brewery is a state-of-the-art design and the Careys left no detail unturned. Hilltop Brewery has a 300,000-barrel capacity with room for expansion, and it produces excellent craft beers. Wisconsin residents are extremely lucky to have such an amazing brewery in their state.

Totally Naked lager is a pure, crisp beer with nothing to hide. Wisconsin two-row barley malt ensures a mellow and smooth body. New Glarus imports noble hop varieties from Germany and the Czech Republic to ensure a fine mature aroma with no coarse bitterness. Expect this beer to pour a delicate golden hue. Kick back, relax, and enjoy the simple unadorned flavor. This is beer at its most basic and refreshing.

New Glarus Totally Naked Lager (Commercial)

North American Lager

Original gravity: 1.040 (10.1°P)
Final gravity: 1.008 (2.0°P)
Bitterness: 11 IBU
ABV: 4.3%
Attenuation: 80%
Boil (min): 70

MALTS
100% American two-row malt
Malt Specifications
Total protein: ≤11%
Soluble protein: ≤5%
Color: 2 (±0.2) SRM

HOPS
27% IBUs Celeia (4.5%) @ 60
37% IBUs Czech Saaz (3.75% AA) @ 60
18% IBUs Czech Saaz (3.75% AA) @ 10
18% IBUs Hallertau Mittelfrüh (4% AA) @ 10

YEAST
Lager yeast (Fermentis SafLager™ W34/70)

BREWING NOTES
Water Treatment: alkalinity ≤35 ppm, calcium hardness 60 ppm, magnesium
    hardness 24 ppm.
Liquor-to-Grist Ratio: 3.5 to 1
Kettle Boil: 70 min. with 6% evaporation
Fermentation/Maturation:
    48–58°F (9–11°C) approximately 100 hours
    Hold at 58°F (14°C)
    Close tank at 3.2°P and 0.9 bar
    Draw off yeast often and as needed
    At 2.5°P, cool 58–41°F (14–15°C)
    Hold until VDK ≤0.10 ppm (circa 1 week)
    Crash cool to 32°F (0°C)
    Hold ≥1 week
Finishing: Filter to clarify.
Carbonation: Natural to 2.7 (±0.1) volumes CO_2

New Glarus Totally Naked Lager (Five-Gallon Batch)

North American Lager

Original gravity: 1.040 (10.1°P)
Final gravity: 1.008 (2.0°P)
Bitterness: 11 IBU
ABV: 4.3%
Attenuation: 80%
Boil (min): 70

MALTS
8 lb. 2 oz. (3.7 kg) American two-row malt

HOPS
0.25 oz. (7 g) Celeia (4.5%) @ 60
0.25 oz. (7 g) Czech Saaz (3.75% AA) @ 60
0.25 oz. (7 g) Czech Saaz (3.75% AA) @ 10
0.25 oz. (7 g) Hallertau Mittelfrüh (4% AA) @ 10

YEAST
Lager yeast (Fermentis SafLager W34/70)

BREWING NOTES
Water Treatment: Alkalinity ≤ 35 ppm, calcium hardness 60 ppm,
   magnesium hardness 24 ppm.
Liquor-to-Grist Ratio: 3.5 to 1
Fermentation/Maturation:
   48–58°F (9–11°C) approximately 100 hours
   Hold at 58°F (14°C)
   Draw off yeast often and as needed
   At 1.010 specific gravity (2.5°P), cool 58–41°F (14–15°C)
   Hold circa 1 week for diacetyl rest
   Crash cool to 32°F (0°C)
   Hold ≥1 week
Carbonation: Natural to 2.7 (±0.1) volumes CO_2 (up to 5.3 g/L CO_2)

Russian River Brewing Company

Surprisingly, one of the most popular craft breweries in America was started
by a winery on vineyard grounds in Guerneville, Sonoma County, California.
Korbel Champagne Cellars, original owners of Russian River Brewing
Company, eventually decided to exit the beer business and offered their brewmaster, Vinnie Cilurzo and his wife, Natalie, the opportunity to purchase the
brewing company in 2003. In April 2004, the Cilurzos first opened the doors
to their new brewpub located in downtown Santa Rosa. Since opening day,
the Russian River Brewing Company brewpub has become a landmark for
beer lovers from all over the nation and has established itself as one of the top
brewpubs in the United States in both sales and awards.

Cilurzo was raised in the wine business, working on his family's winery in
Temecula, California as a young man. Cilurzo taught himself homebrewing at
the age of 18, and by 1994 he had started his first brewery, Blind Pig Brewing
Company, with a business partner.

After relocating to Sonoma County in 1997 and brewing for Korbel,
Cilurzo began experimenting with wine barrels in the brewing process.
Cilurzo has always had a passion for brewing unique, funky sour beers as well
as amazing hop forward IPAs. While working for Korbel, Cilurzo developed

Russian River's flagship beer, Pliny the Elder, which is noted for being the first double IPA. Pliny the Elder is still an extremely sought after beer across the US, although it is only made in small production batches and sold in select markets. In 2008 Cilurzo opened a production brewery just a mile from the brewpub, allowing him to triple production and begin distributing. Cilurzo's main focus has always been on quality and innovation; growth comes second to happiness. It was not until 2016 that Russian River announced plans to build a new production brewery in the neighboring town of Windsor to allow for increased production and continued improvement on quality and experimentation. Russian River broke ground on this new production facility in May 2017.

Cilurzo's desire and passion for brewing amazingly delicious beers is unprecedented. His hunger for understanding and replicating some of the greatest Belgian beers, but applying his own twist and knowledge from the wine world, is awe-inspiring. It is this strong passion for beer that continues to drive Cilurzo to consistently produce some of the best beers I have ever had. His love for the craft is so strong and ingrained, it must be expressed. Cilurzo shares his knowledge freely with those around him, hoping to help and guide others to follow their own dreams in the beer world. His openness, along with his refined brewing skillset, was recognized during the 2008 Craft Brewers Conference when Cilurzo was awarded the Russell Schehrer Award for Innovation in Craft Brewing.

Although Russian River Brewing Company is best known for producing barrel-aged sour beers and strong IPAs, their beer board always offers a wide selection of diverse craft beer. The Aud Blonde has occupied a space on the Russian River tap list for over a decade and is one of the lightest beers offered at the brewpub. It is a beautifully refreshing blonde ale with a medium bitterness, and has a delicate fruit forward finish developed through the artful blend of hop varieties both old and new. Aud Blonde is consistently flavorful and it is easy to spend an entire night sipping a few pints. A favorite for many locals and staff, Aud Blonde is a testament to the philosophy that some of the greatest things in life are simple, pure, and beautiful.

Russian River Aud Blonde (Commercial)

Golden/Blonde Ale

Original gravity: 1.044 (11°P)
Final gravity: 1.010–1.011 (2.5–2.6°P)
Bitterness: 35–40 IBU
ABV: 4.5%
Attenuation: 78%
Boil (min): 90

MALTS

65% two-row malt
24% Pilsner malt
11% white wheat

HOPS

Crystal (3.5% AA) @ 90
Northern Brewer (8.5% AA) @ 30
Equinox (15% AA) @ whirlpool
Crystal (3.5% AA) @ whirlpool

YEAST

California ale yeast

BREWING NOTES

Mashing: Standard infusion mash, rest at 154–155°F (67–68°C).
Primary Fermentation: 68°F (154°C).
Finishing: Hold beer at 32°F (0°C) for 2 weeks then clarify with gelatin.
Carbonation: 2.52 volumes CO_2.

Russian River Aud Blonde (Five-Gallon Batch)

Golden/Blonde Ale

Original gravity: 1.044 (11°P)
Final gravity: 1.010–1.011 (2.5–2.6°P)
Bitterness: 35–40 IBU
ABV: 4.5%
Attenuation: 78%
Boil (min): 90

MALTS
5.5 lb. (2.5 kg) two-row malt
2 lb. (910 g) Pilsner malt
1 lb. (450 g) white wheat

HOPS
0.75 oz. (21 g) Crystal (3.5% AA) @ 90
0.5 oz. (14 g) Northern Brewer (8.5% AA) @ 30
0.5 oz. (14 g) Equinox (15% AA) @ whirlpool
0.25 oz. (7 g) Crystal (3.5% AA) @ whirlpool

YEAST
California ale yeast

BREWING NOTES
Mashing: Standard infusion mash, rest at 154–155°F (67–68°C).
Primary Fermentation: 68°F (154°C).
Finishing: Hold beer at 32°F (0°C) for 2 weeks then clarify with gelatin.
Carbonation: 2.5 volumes CO_2.

Firestone Walker Brewing Company

When you think of Firestone Walker Brewing Company two things usually come to mind, great beer and Matt Brynildson, their brewmaster. Brynildson has a passion and thirst for brewing knowledge, innovation, and producing awesome beer. His drive is unparalleled in the craft brewing industry and he has helped advance the world of brewing significantly since his entrance in the early 1990s. Brynildson graduated with a degree in chemistry from Kalamazoo College in 1993 and went to work for Kalamzoo Spice Extraction Company (KALSEC) as a hop chemist. Prior to joining Firestone Walker, Brynildson cut his teeth in the brewhouse and cellars at Goose Island Brewing in Chicago for four years, before moving to California to work for SLO Brewing in San Luis Obispo. After winning SLO the Best Small Brewpub award at the 2001 GABF, Brynildson went back to Chicago to open Piece Brewing with Bill Jacobs, hiring Jonathan Cutler to run the brewery. Cutler is still turning out fantastic beer at Piece Brewing, and Brynildson has retained his silent partnership. Not long after Piece Brewing opened, Brynildson came to work for Firestone Walker Brewing Company, situated in the Central Coast region of California.

David Walker co-founded Firestone Walker with his brother-in-law, Adam Firestone in 1996. Walker's native country was England, where he developed a love and appreciation for English ales. Firestone's roots grew out of the wine business and the first Firestone Walker brewery launched on vineyard grounds. Since the company's brewing roots were heavily influenced by English pale ales and the wine business, it seemed natural that oak barrels would be used in making great beer for the Central Coast. When Firestone Walker outgrew their first brewery and needed to expand, they purchased SLO Brewing's equipment and hired Brynildson to run the brewery, in a way making Brynildson's journey come full circle. Firestone Walker's flagship beer, DBA (Double Barrel Ale), is partially fermented in their version of the Burton Union system, presenting Brynildson with a challenging operation to manage and grow when he came on board.

Over the last fifteen years with Firestone Walker, Brynildson has won many awards. His greatest contribution to the craft brewing industry, however, is not his amazing beer, but his infectious love for brewing and his willingness to share it. When I needed barrels for a sour beer project, Brynildson was there to help out, sending me four used DBA barrels that are still producing Fifth Element today at Squatters Pub Brewery. When Brynildson talks about beer he smiles ear to ear and you can't help but get thirsty. He truly wants the brewers around him to make the best beer possible and is known for having both a wealth of knowledge and a willingness to bestow it upon others. In that spirit, Brynildson has shared with me, and so with you, the recipes for two of his favorite beers.

Extra Pale Ale has bold spicy and floral hops that dominate the nose, but the bitterness is balanced and not overdone. The light malt body supports the restrained bitterness and highlights the beautiful hop flavor and aroma. On the other hand, Easy Jack IPA exhibits a unique combination of German flavor hops and North American hops. No specific weights were provided for hopping either recipe, so many amounts that are provided are merely a suggestion from the author. They are combined in the boil, finish, and dry hopping to provide a full array of hoppy goodness. The medium bitterness, approachable body, and malt complexity makes for an enjoyable session.

Firestone Walker Extra Pale Ale (Commercial)

American Pale Ale

Original gravity: 1.040 (10°P)
Final gravity: 1.008 (2.0°P)
Bitterness: 38–40 IBU
ABV: 4.5%
Attenuation: 81%
Boil (min.): 60

MALTS
80% two-row pale malt
14% Munich malt 10°L
6% Carapils® (dextrin malt)

HOPS
American Fuggle (4.75% AA) @ 60
Chinook (13% AA) @ 10
Centennial (10% AA) @ whirlpool
Cascade (5.5% AA) @ whirlpool
Centennial (10% AA) (dry hop)

YEAST
English/London ale yeast

BREWING NOTES
Water Treatment: Reverse osmosis water treated and adjusted with calcium sulfate, calcium chloride, and phosphoric acid.

Mashing: Mash in at 145°F (63°C) and rest for 15 min. Ramp to 154°F (68°C) and rest for 20 min. or until conversion. Ramp to 169°F (76°C) prior to transferring to the lauter tun.

Fermentation: Cool in at 62.5°F (17°C) and ferment at 66°F (19°C).

Fermentation/Maturation: Yeast is harvested from non-hoppy beer and pitched at the peak of viability. Pitching rate is about 0.5 million cells/mL/°P, less in larger tanks that take longer to fill (or more turns of the brewhouse).

Dry Hop: Add dry hops to the top of the tank. Firestone Walker currently uses a hop cannon, but prior to that the hops were simply added through a port in the top of the tank. Hops are typically added on day 3 of the fermentation or just at the end of fermentation (0.2–0.3°P prior to final gravity). The heavy yeast at the bottom of the tank is removed prior to the addition of hops. The hops are left in the tank for three days then dumped along with any residual yeast at the bottom of the fermentor.

Finishing: Once the beer passes VDK (GC analysis*), typically day 6 or 7, the beer is crash-cooled to 30°F (−1°C) and filtered through diatomaceous earth. The beer can be served unfiltered, if clarity is not a priority.

Carbonation: 2.5 volumes CO_2, or 5 g/L CO_2.

---

* GC analysis: Gas chromatography (GC) analysis is a common type of chromatography used in analytical chemistry for separating and analyzing compounds that can be vaporized without decomposition. The threshold for VDK can vary depending on the brewery and the beer. In this case, VDK levels by GC analysis of <50 ppb at cooling and 30 ppb at packaging is probably an acceptable range, based on information supplied for Firestone's Easy Jack IPA recipe (*see* below).

Firestone Walker Extra Pale Ale (Five-Gallon Batch)

American Pale Ale

Original gravity: 1.040 (10°P)
Final gravity: 1.008 (2.0°P)
Bitterness: 38–40 IBU
ABV: 4.5%
Attenuation: 81%
Boil (min.): 60

MALTS
8.5 lb. (3.9 kg) two-row pale malt
1 lb. (450 g) Munich malt 10°L
0.5 lb. (225 g) Carapils (dextrin malt)

HOPS
0.75 oz. (21 g) American Fuggle (4.75% AA) @ 60
0.75 oz. (21 g) Chinook (13% AA) @ 10
0.75 oz. (21 g) Centennial (10% AA) @ whirlpool
0.75 oz. (21 g) Cascade (5.5% AA) @ whirlpool
2.0 oz. (57 g) Centennial (10% AA) (dry hop)

YEAST
English/London ale yeast

BREWING NOTES
Water Treatment: Reverse osmosis water, treated and adjusted with calcium sulfate, calcium chloride, and phosphoric acid.

Mashing: Mash in @ 145°F (63°C) and rest for 15 min. Ramp to 154°F (68°C) and rest for 20 min. or until conversion. Ramp to 169°F (76°C) prior to transferring to the lauter tun.

Fermentation: Cool in at 62.5°F (17°C) and ferment at 66°F (19°C).

Fermentation/Maturation: Yeast is harvested from non-hoppy beer and pitched at the peak of viability. Pitching rate is about 0.5 million cells/mL/°P.

Dry Hop: Add dry hops to the top of the tank. Firestone Walker currently uses a hop cannon, but prior to that the hops were simply added through a port in the top of the tank. Hops are typically added on day 3 of the fermentation or just at the end of fermentation (0.2–0.3°P prior to final gravity). The heavy yeast at the bottom of the tank is removed prior to the addition of hops. The hops are left in the tank for three days then dumped along with any residual yeast at the bottom of the fermentor.

Finishing: Crash cool day 6 or 7 to 30°F.

Carbonation: 2.5 volumes CO_2, or 5 g/L CO_2.

Firestone Walker Easy Jack IPA (Commercial)

Session India Pale Ale

Original gravity: 1.042 (10.5–11°P)
Final gravity: 1.007–1.008 (1.8–2.0°P)
Bitterness: 45 IBU
ABV: 4.5%
Attenuation: 82%
Boil (min.): 75

MALTS
74% two-row pale malt
7% Munich malt 10°L
7% wheat malt
6% light crystal
6% oats

HOPS
German Magnum (14% AA) @ 60
Amarillo (9.2% AA) @ 10
Amarillo (9.2% AA) @ whirlpool
Simcoe (13% AA) @ whirlpool
Mandarina Bavaria (8.5% AA) (dry hop)
Huell Melon (7.2% AA) (dry hop)
Mosaic (12.25% AA) (dry hop at end of fermentation)

YEAST
English/London ale yeast

BREWING NOTES
Water Treatment: Reverse osmosis water, treated and adjusted with calcium sulfate, calcium chloride, and phosphoric acid. Mash pH goal is 5.4 and knockout goal is 5.2.

Mashing: Mash in at 145°F (63°C) and rest for 30 min. Ramp to 154°F (68°C) and rest for 15 min. or until conversion. Ramp to 169°F (76°C) prior to transferring to the lauter tun.

Fermentation: Cool in at 62.5°F (17°C) and ferment at 66°F (19°C).

Fermentation/Maturation: Yeast is harvested from non-hoppy (<30 IBU) beer and pitched at the peak of viability. Pitching rate is about 0.5 million cells/mL/°P, less in larger tanks that take longer to fill (or more turns of the brewhouse).

Dry Hop: Add dry hops to the top of the tank. Firestone Walker currently uses a hop cannon, but prior to that the hops were simply added through a port in the top of the tank. Hops are typically added on day 3 of the fermentation or just at the end of fermentation (0.2–0.3°P prior to final gravity). The heavy yeast at the bottom of the tank is removed prior to the addition of hops. The hops are left in the tank for three days then dumped along with any residual yeast at the bottom of the fermentor.

Finishing: Once the beer passes VDK (GC analysis less than 50 ppb at cooling and 30 ppb at package), typically day 6 or 7, the beer is crash-cooled to 30°F (−1°C) and filtered through diatomaceous earth. The beer can be served unfiltered, if clarity is not a priority.

Carbonation: 2.5 volumes CO_2, or 5 g/L CO_2.

Firestone Walker Easy Jack IPA (Five-Gallon Batch)

Session India Pale Ale

Original gravity: 1.042 (10.5–11°P)
Final gravity: 1.007–1.008 (1.8–2.0°P)
Bitterness: 45 IBU
ABV: 4.5%
Attenuation: 82%
Boil (min.): 75

MALTS

6.5 lb. (2.95 kg) two-row pale malt
0.5 lb. (225 g) Munich malt 10°L
0.5 lb. (225 g) wheat malt
0.5 lb. (225 g) light crystal
0.5 lb. (225 g) oats

HOPS

0.5 oz. (14 g) German Magnum (14% AA) @ 60
0.5 oz. (14 g) Amarillo (9.2% AA) @ 10
0.5 oz. (14 g) Amarillo (9.2% AA) @ whirlpool
0.5 oz. (14 g) Simcoe (13% AA) @ whirlpool
1.5 oz. (43 g) Mandarina Bavaria (8.5% AA) (dry hop)
1.0 oz. (28 g) Huell Melon (7.2% AA) (dry hop)
0.5 oz. (14 g) Mosaic (12.25% AA) (dry hop at end of fermentation)

YEAST

English/London ale yeast

BREWING NOTES

Water Treatment: Reverse osmosis water, treated and adjusted with calcium sulfate, calcium chloride, and phosphoric acid. Mash pH goal is 5.4 and knockout goal is 5.2.

Mashing: Mash in @ 145°F (63°C) and rest for 30 min. Ramp to 154°F (68°C) and rest for 15 min. or until conversion. Ramp to 169°F (76°C) prior to transferring to the lauter tun.

Fermentation: Cool in at 62.5°F (17°C) and ferment at 66°F (19°C).

Fermentation/Maturation: Yeast is harvested from non-hoppy (<30 IBU) beer and pitched at the peak of viability. Pitching rate is about 0.5 million cells/mL/°P.

Dry Hop: Add dry hops to the top of the tank. Firestone Walker currently uses a hop cannon, but prior to that the hops were simply added through a port in the top of the tank. Hops are typically added on day 3 of the fermentation or just at the end of fermentation (0.2–0.3°P prior to final gravity). The heavy yeast at the bottom of the tank is removed prior to the addition of hops. The hops are left in the tank for three days then dumped along with any residual yeast at the bottom of the fermentor.

Finishing: Crash-cool to 30°F (−1°C).

Carbonation: 2.5 volumes CO_2, or 5 g/L CO_2.

Stone Brewing Company

Stone Brewing was founded by Steve Wagner and Greg Koch in 1996 in San Marcos, California. Since then, Wagner and Koch have helped build a craft beer empire that now has retail locations across southern California and employs over 1,100 people. As of 2017, Stone Brewing are the 10th largest craft brewery in the United States.

Stone Brewing paved the way in the extreme beer craze with beers from their Vertical Epic series and with Ruination, their double IPA. At an MBAA conference presentation on extreme beers in 2012, it was stated that 85% of Stone Brewing's production is over 16°P original gravity and 10% is over 20°P. What most craft beer aficionados don't know is that Stone Brewing has also been making session beers like Heat Seeking Wheat, Stone Session Ale, Lee's Mild, and Levitation since 1997.

Former brewmaster, Mitch Steele, joined Stone Brewing in 2006, commissioning the World Bistro & Gardens. He managed and grew Stone's brewing and packaging team to the powerhouse that it is today, overseeing a growth in production from 48,000 barrels to over 325,000 barrels. Steele earned his degree in fermentation science at UC Davis and is the 2014 recipient of the Russell Schehrer award for Innovation in Craft Brewing. He is also the author of *IPA: Brewing Techniques, Recipes and the Evolution of India Pale Ale* (Steele 2012).

Steele notes that Stone Brewing's Go To IPA is light golden in color and pours with a white frothy head. Hops are the key ingredient and are heavily used at end of boil, whirlpool, and dry hop to impart intense hop flavor and aromatics. While peach and melon flavors dominate the flavor and aroma of this beer, bitterness is medium to high. Go To IPA certainly bursts with fruity hoppiness, allowing for only a small amount of malt character to display itself and ending with a slightly dry finish. This was Stone Brewing's first attempt at hop bursting, a technique in which all or most of the bitterness comes from late addition hops. Stone Brewing had to go back and add some Magnum early to hit the IBU target and keep kettle foaming down.

On the other hand, Stone Levitation Ale pours a dark amber with a creamy off-white foam. A small amount of hop aroma presents itself, but your palate is soon overtaken by rich caramel and toast malt character. Although the alcohol is restrained, the body is bold. A small amount of citrus, pine, and earthy hop flavor mingles with malt complexity. Levitation has been retired by Stone Brewing, but now you can brew your own.

Stone Go To IPA (Commercial)

Session India Pale Ale

Original gravity: 1.044 (11.1°P)
Final gravity: 1.010 (2.5°P)
Bitterness: 65 IBU
ABV: 4.5%
Attenuation: 77.3%
Boil (min.): 90

MALTS
87% two-row pale malt
2.9% crystal 15°L
2.9% Victory malt
7.2% Carapils

HOPS
0.15 lb./bbl. German Magnum (14% AA) @ 1st wort
0.17 lb./bbl. Ahtanum (6% AA) @ 10
0.33 lb./bbl. Chinook (13% AA) @ 10
0.17 lb./bbl. Steiner #06300 or #06297 @ 10
0.14 lb./bbl. Cascade (5.5% AA) @ 10
0.10 lb./bbl. Magnum (14% AA) @ 10
0.17 lb./bb. Sterling (7.5% AA) @ whirlpool
0.17 lb./bbl. Crystal (3.5% AA) @ whirlpool
0.56 lb./bbl. Mosaic (12.25% AA) @whirlpool
0.34 lb./bbl. Amarillo (9.2% AA) @ whirlpool
0.34 lb./bbl. Ahtanum (6% AA) @ whirlpool
1.0 lb./bbl. Mosaic (12.25% AA) (dry hop)
0.6 lb./bbl. Citra (12% AA) (dry hop)
0.3 lb./bbl. Cascade (5.5% AA) (dry hop)

YEAST
White Labs WLP007 dry English ale yeast, or WLP002 English ale yeast

BREWING NOTES

Water Treatment: Carbon filter, target total hardness 120 ppm. Calcium 70–80 ppm.

Mashing: 154°F (68°C) for 45 minutes. Raise to 165°F (74°C) prior to lautering.

Fermentation: 72°F (22°C).

Fermentation/Maturation: Aerate wort to 10–12 ppm dissolved oxygen. Target 12–16 million cells/mL yeast pitch rate.

Dry-hop: Chill beer from 72°F (22°C) to 62°F (17°C). Dump as much yeast as possible. Dry hop and circulate three times (30–45 minutes) over 36 hours, then chill beer to 32°F (0°C).

Finishing: Hold at 32°F (0°C) for 3–7 days and dump yeast/hops that settle in the cone every other day.

Filtration/Clarification: Perlite filtration, no fining agents.

Carbonation: 2.5–2.65 volumes CO_2.

Stone Go To IPA (Five-Gallon Batch)

Session India Pale Ale

Original gravity: 1.044 (11.1°P)
Final gravity: 1.010 (2.5°P)
Bitterness: 65 IBU
ABV: 4.8%
Attenuation: 77.3%
Boil (min.): 90

MALTS

7 lb. 9 oz. (3.43 kg) two-row pale malt
4 oz. (115 g) crystal 15°L
4 oz. (115 g) Victory malt
10 oz. (280 g) Carapils

HOPS*

0.25 oz. (7 g) German Magnum (14% AA) @ 60

0.25 oz. (7 g) Ahtanum (6% AA) @ 10

0.5 oz. (14 g) Chinook (13% AA) @ 10

0.25 oz. (7 g) Steiner #06300 @ 10

0.25 oz. (7 g) Cascade (5.5% AA) @ 10

0.25 oz. (7 g) Magnum (14% AA) @ 10

0.25 oz. (7 g) Sterling (7.5% AA) @ whirlpool

0.25 oz. (7 g) Crystal (3.5% AA) @ whirlpool

1.0 oz. (28 g) Mosaic (12.25% AA) @whirlpool

0.88 oz. (25 g) Amarillo (9.2% AA) @ whirlpool

0.88 oz. (25 g) Ahtanum (6% AA) @ whirlpool

2.5 oz. (71 g) Mosaic (12.25% AA) (dry hop)

1.5 oz. (43 g) Citra (12% AA) (dry hop)

0.75 oz. (21 g) Cascade (5.5% AA) (dry hop)

YEAST

White Labs WLP007 dry English ale yeast, or WLP002 English ale yeast

BREWING NOTES

Water Treatment: Carbon filter, target total hardness 120 ppm. Calcium 70–80 ppm.

Mashing: 154°F (68°C) for 45 minutes. Raise to 165°F (74°C) prior to lautering.

Fermentation: 72°F (22°C).

Fermentation/Maturation: Aerate wort to 10–12 ppm dissolved oxygen. Target 12–16 million cells/mL yeast pitch rate.

Dry-hop: Chill beer from 72°F (22°C) to 62°F (17°C). Rack beer off yeast, then dry hop, circulating three times (30–45 minutes) over 36 hours, then chill beer to 32°F (0°C).

Finishing: Hold at 32°F (0°C) 3–7 days, and dump yeast/hops that settle in the cone every other day.

Carbonation: 2.5–2.65 volumes CO_2.

* **Hopping notes:** Stone Brewing provided the exact amount of hops as pound per barrel (lb./bbl.), as seen in the commercial recipe above. After feeding these amounts for each individual hop addition and the target IBU into the BeerSmith program, adjustments were made accordingly.

Stone Levitation Ale (Commercial)

Amber Ale

Original gravity: 1.046 (11.5°P)
Final gravity: 1.013 (3.2°P)
Bitterness: 45 IBU
ABV: 4.4%
Attenuation: 72.2%
Boil (min.): 90

MALTS

85% two-row pale malt
9% crystal 75°L
7.6% Briess C-120°L (or, if you can source crystal 150°L, use 5.2%)
0.8% black malt

HOPS

0.07 lb./bbl. Columbus or Warrior (14%–15% AA) @ 90
0.35 lb./bbl. Amarillo (9.2% AA) @ 10
0.35 lb./bbl. Crystal (3.5% AA) @ whirlpool
0.1 lb./bbl. Simcoe (13% AA) @ whirlpool
0.3 lb./bbl. Amarillo (9.2% AA) (dry hop)

YEAST

White Labs WLP007 dry English ale yeast, or WLP002 English ale yeast

BREWING NOTES

Water Treatment: Carbon filter, target total hardness 120 ppm. Calcium 70–80 ppm.
Mashing: 154°F (68°C) for 30 minutes. Raise to 165°F (74°C) prior to lautering.
Fermentation: 72°F (22°C).
Fermentation/Maturation: Aerate wort to 10–12 ppm dissolved oxygen. Target 12–16 million cells/mL yeast pitch rate.
Dry hop: Chill beer from 72°F (22°C) to 62°F (17°C). Dump as much yeast as possible. Add dry hops and circulate three times (30–45 minutes) over 36 hours, then chill beer to 32°F (0°C).

Finishing: Hold at 32°F (0°C) 3–7 days and dump yeast/hops that settle in the cone every other day.

Filtration/Clarification: Perlite filtration and no fining agents.

Carbonation: 2.5–2.65 volumes CO_2.

Stone Levitation Ale (Five-Gallon Batch)

Amber Ale

Original gravity: 1.046 (12°P)
Final gravity: 1.013 (3.2°P)
Bitterness: 45 IBU
ABV: 4.4%
Attenuation: 72.2%
Boil (min.): 90

MALTS
8 lb. (3.63 kg) two-row pale malt
13 oz. (370 g) crystal 75°L
12 oz. (340 g) Briess C-120°L (or, if you can source crystal 150°L, use 9 oz.)
1.25 oz. (35 g) black

HOPS
1.75 oz. (50 g) Columbus or Warrior (14%–15% AA) @ 90
0.75 oz. (21 g) Amarillo (9.2% AA) @ 10
0.75 oz. (21 g) Crystal (3.5% AA) @ whirlpool
0.25 oz. (7 g) Simcoe (13% AA) @ whirlpool
0.75 oz. (21 g) Amarillo (9.2% AA) (dry hop)

YEAST
White Labs WLP007 dry English ale yeast, or WLP002 English ale yeast

BREWING NOTES
Water Treatment: Carbon filter. Target total hardness 120 ppm. Calcium 70–80 ppm.
Mashing: 154°F (68°C) for 30 minutes. Raise to 165°F (74°C) prior to lautering.

Fermentation: 72°F (22°C).

Fermentation/Maturation: Aerate wort to 10–12 ppm dissolved oxygen. Target 12–16 million cells/mL yeast pitch rate.

Dry hop: Chill beer from 72°F (22°C) to 62°F (17°C). Rack off yeast. Add dry hops and circulate three times (30–45 minutes) over 36 hours, then chill beer to 32°F (0°C).

Finishing: Rack to secondary after fermentation is complete. Hold at 32°F (0°C) 3–7 days.

Carbonation: 2.5–2.65 volumes CO_2.

Squatters Craft Beers

Founded by Peter Cole and Jeff Polychronis, Squatters Pub Brewery has been a landmark in Salt Lake City since 1989. One night in Portland while throwing darts, eating pizza, and drinking IPA at Bridgeport Brewing, Cole and Polychronis had an awakening. Uninspired by their successful real estate business, they asked, "Why can't we open a great brewpub in Salt Lake City?" So that's just what they did. In a historic building in downtown Salt Lake City, just blocks from the Mormon temple, they began with four small fermentors and a seven-barrel brewhouse. With help from brewery consultant Peter Burrell and brewmaster Dan Burick, the first brewpub in Salt Lake City was opened. I joined Burick in 1991, and over the next twenty years I was fortunate to be part of the brewing team that brought the diversity of craft beer to the Utah community.

Although there is a 4% ABV cap on the amount of alcohol allowed in draught beer in Utah, it did not stop us from creating style after style; we simply committed to learning how to brew great session beer. Since craft beer was new to Salt Lake City, we placed a heavy emphasis on staff education, discussing the brewing process, historical styles, and innovative techniques any chance we got. The brewery was always open to tours and we visited many tables to introduce our newest creation or explain the dry-hop procedure recently implemented. Cole and Polychronis knew business and they knew it well. They had unbelievable trust in their team and gave us incredible leeway in the brewery. When it came to quality, there was no question: if it made the beer better, then we did it. This is not to say we were frivolous in our spending. There was a companywide philosophy that the customer came first and our goal was to provide the highest quality experience in every department. That meant buying malt, hops, and equipment we felt would further improve our beer.

One of the greatest lessons I learned while honing my brewing skills at Squatters is that the brewery is no place for big egos. Ego does not make better beer or a better company. Honesty, hard work, and perseverance do. And that's just what Cole and Polychronis did, they rolled up their sleeves and kept growing their successful brewing company. A draught only production brewery was quickly built in 1994 to supply the entire state with beer. The second Squatters retail location opened at the Salt Lake City International Airport in February 2000, followed by the opening of Squatters Roadhouse Grill in Park City six years later. With the reputation of Squatters beer on the rise and the need for a larger production brewery, Cole and Polychronis formed an alliance with Greg Schirf, owner of Wasatch Brewing, establishing the Utah Brewers Cooperative (UBC) and moved to a larger location in Salt Lake City in 2000.

With Burick at the helm, the production numbers kept increasing, quality was better than ever, and a great brewing team continued to excel. Although the founding members are gone, the brand they built, along with Burick's team, is still going strong and now enjoys nationwide distribution. Current UBC brewmaster Jon Lee joined the team as a keg washer in 1997, working in almost every brewery job over the years until taking the reins in 2000. Lee has witnessed immense changes during his time at Squatters, and by 2016 was managing production of over 60,000 barrels a year. His commitment to brewing both fabulous session beers and stronger offerings is undying.

In a fun tip of the hat to the challenging 4% ABV level, enjoy this rich, Northwest-style pale ale. Note that no hopping rates were provided for the boil, so those quantities are author suggestions. Squatters Full Suspension Pale Ale is a rare feat of balance. Unfiltered, dry-hopped, and 40 IBUs, it is a deliciously seasonable and sessionable beer. Full Suspension pours a hazy, light copper and presents a bouquet of floral Columbus hops. The bitterness is perfectly poised alongside the malt backbone, creating a beer full of harmonious flavor that leaves the heaviness behind.

Squatters Full Suspension Pale Ale (Commercial)

Pale Ale

Original gravity: 1.042 (10.5°P)
Final gravity: 1.011 (2.8°P)
Bitterness: 38–42 IBU
ABV: 4%
Attenuation: 73.3%
Boil (min.): 80

MALTS

66% two-row pale malt
10% Munich 10°L
11% dextrin-type malt
8% caramel 40°L
5% caramel 80°L

HOPS

Columbus (14% AA) @ 70
Columbus (14% AA) @ 45
Columbus (14% AA) @ 2
Columbus (14% AA) (dry hop)

YEAST

Fermenting with Wyeast 1318 London Ale III™ will create a dry finish. This beer was initially fermented with Wyeast 1187 Ringwood Ale™ yeast, which provided a bit more mouthfeel, but diacetyl management was difficult.

BREWING NOTES

Water Treatment: Calcium chloride to mash for increased calcium. Target all water to an alkalinity of 80–100 ppm.

Mashing: Mash in and hold at 155°F (68°C) for 30 min. If possible, mash off to 168°F (76°C) to aid in runoff and increase brewhouse yield. Liquor-to-grist ratio of 3 to 1.

Fermentation: 67–69°F (19–21°C).

Dry hop: All Columbus. Once fermentation is complete, reduce temp to 58°F (14°C) and remove as much yeast as possible prior to dry hopping. Dry hop at 50–60°F (10–16°C), 0.4–0.45 lb./bbl. If possible, recirculate hops in fermentor.

Finishing: This beer is unfiltered, but make sure it's not too yeasty before you serve it. Ready to serve 14–18 days from original brew date.

Carbonation: 2.6–2.7 volumes CO_2, or 5.13–5.33 g/L CO_2.

Squatters Full Suspension Pale Ale (Five-Gallon Batch)

Pale Ale

Original gravity: 1.042 (10.5°P)
Final gravity: 1.011 (2.8°P)
Bitterness: 38–42 IBU
ABV: 4%
Attenuation: 73.3%
Boil (min.): 80

MALTS

5 lb. 9 oz. (2.5 kg) two-row pale malt
13.5 oz. (380 g) Munich 10°L
1 lb. (450 g) dextrin-type malt
11 oz. (310 g) caramel 40°L
7 oz. (200 g) caramel 80°L

HOPS

0.5 oz. (14 g) Columbus (14% AA) @ 70
0.25 oz. (7 g) Columbus (14% AA) @ 45
0.25 oz. (7 g) Columbus (14% AA) @ 2
1 oz. (28 g) Columbus (14% AA) (dry hop)

YEAST

Fermenting with Wyeast 1318 London Ale III™ will create a dry finish. This beer was initially fermented with Wyeast 1187 Ringwood Ale™ yeast, which provided a bit more mouthfeel, but diacetyl management was difficult.

BREWING NOTES

Water Treatment: Calcium chloride to mash for increased calcium. Target all water to an alkalinity of 80–100 ppm.

Mashing: Mash in and hold at 155°F (68°C) for 30 min. If possible, mash off to 168°F (76°C) to aid in runoff and increase brewhouse yield. Liquor-to-grist ratio of 3 to 1.

Fermentation: 67–69°F (19–21°C).

Dry hop: Once fermentation is complete, reduce temp to 58°F (14°C) and remove as much yeast as possible prior to dry hopping. Dry hop at 50–60°F (10–16°C). If possible, recirculate hops in fermentor.

Finishing: This beer is unfiltered, but make sure it's not too yeasty before you serve it. Ready to serve 14–18 days from original brew date.

Carbonation: 2.6–2.7 volumes CO_2, or 5.13–5.33 g/L CO_2.

Wasatch Brewing Company

Greg Schirf was undoubtedly a visionary in 1986 when he opened the first brewery in Utah since General Brewing Company closed in 1967 (Vance 2006, 163). Schirf, a native of Milwaukee, had a love of beer from a young age, homebrewing during the seventies and visiting Munich to attend Oktoberfest in 1971. During a trip to Washington state while visiting Hart Brewing (now Pyramid Breweries, Inc.) in 1985, Schirf decided to open a brewery in Park City, Utah where his brother Skip lived. It had been fifty years since anyone tried to open a brewery in Utah, and to say Schirf was up against some godly obstacles would be an understatement. Schirf was steadfast in his conviction and employed Melanie Pullman as his brewmaster. Pullman studied brewing at UC Davis and completed an internship at Pyramid in Seattle. Just two years after Schirf opened his production brewery with Pullman in Park City, he went back to Capitol Hill in Salt Lake City and lobbied for legalizing brewpubs in Utah. After much debate and anguish, the bill was passed and the first brewpub in Utah was opened at the top of Main Street, Park City in 1988.

I have extremely warm feelings for Schirf Brewing Company because it was the very first brewery I ever set foot in. I was working at a call center for a non-profit human and environmental rights organization, spending my days and evenings behind a desk answering the phone. During my breaks, I walked across the parking lot on Iron Horse Drive and visited the Schirf Brewing tap room. The first brewer I ever met was Pullman and she was definitely an inspirational force in my brewing career. I sat in there on many an evening after my work was over, sipping Wasatch Gold or Premium Ale with Schirf's brewers, talking beer. After partnering with Cole and Polychronis to form the Utah Brewers Cooperative in 2000, Schirf's beer became an even stronger force in the Utah beer scene. Many new brands have since been formulated and sales distribution now covers 15 states in the US.

Enjoy a solid session in the form of Wasatch Premium ale. It's a clear, amber-brown Northwest ale, with both hop aroma and flavor of citrus, floral, and pine. This medium-bodied ale has a bready, caramel-malt backbone and finishes with a clean, firm bitterness.

Wasatch Premium Ale (Commercial)

American Brown Ale

Original gravity: 1.043–1.044 (10.7–11°P)
Final gravity: 1.012–1.014 (3.1–3.5°P)
Bitterness: 32–35 IBU
ABV: 4%
Attenuation: 70%
Boil (min.): 80

MALTS
67% two-row pale malt
21% Munich 10°L
11% caramel 80°L
1% dehusked roast barley

HOPS
Cascade (5.5% AA) @ 75
Cascade (5.5% AA) @ 45
Chinook (13% AA) @ 10
0.33–0.44 lb./bbl. 20% Chinooks and 80% Cascades (dry hop)

YEAST
Wyeast 1318 London Ale III

BREWING NOTES

Water Treatment: Calcium chloride to mash for increased calcium and the elevated chloride will enhance the malt. Target water alkalinity of 100–120 ppm.

Mashing: Mash in and hold at 155°F (68°C) for 30 min.

Fermentation: 67–69°F (19–21°C).

Fermentation/Maturation: Make sure tank is well vented and do not bung kegs too early.

Dry hop: Once fermentation is complete, reduce temperature between 58°F (13°C) and remove as much yeast as possible prior to dry hopping. Dry hop at 50–60°F (10–16°C) and, if possible, recirculate hops in fermentor.

Finishing: Cool to 32–34°F (0–1°C) when dry hop is complete or 2 days after hops are added. Once yeast has settled well, filter beer.

Carbonation: 2.6–2.7 volumes CO_2, or 5.13–5.33 g/L CO_2.

Wasatch Premium Ale (Five-Gallon Batch)

American Brown Ale

Original gravity: 1.043–1.044 (10.7–11°P)
Final gravity: 1.012–1.014 (3.1–3.5°P)
Bitterness: 32–35 IBU
ABV: 4%
Attenuation: 70%
Boil (min.): 80

MALTS

5 lb. 12 oz. (2.6 kg) two-row pale malt
2 lb. (910 g) Munich 10°L
1 lb. (450 g) caramel 80°L
1.5 oz. (40 g) dehusked roast barley

HOPS

0.5 oz. (14 g) Cascade (5.5% AA) @ 75
0.5 oz. (14 g) Cascade (5.5% AA) @ 45
0.5 oz. (14 g) Chinook (13% AA) @ 10
0.25 oz. (7 g) Chinook and 0.75 oz. (21 g) Cascades (dry hop)

YEAST
Wyeast 1318 London Ale III

BREWING NOTES
Water Treatment: Calcium chloride to mash for increased calcium and the elevated chloride will enhance the malt. Target water alkalinity of 100–120 ppm.
Mashing: Mash in and hold at 155°F (68°C) for 30 min.
Fermentation: 67–69°F (19–21°C).
Fermentation/Maturation: Make sure fermentor is well vented and do not package too early.
Dry hop: Once fermentation is complete, reduce temperature between 58°F (13°C) and remove as much yeast as possible prior to dry hopping. Dry hop at 50–60°F (10–16°C) and, if possible, recirculate hops in fermentor.
Finishing: Cool to 32–34°F (0–1°C) when dry hop is complete or 2 days after hops are added. Package after yeast has dropped out.
Carbonation: 2.6–2.7 volumes CO_2, or 5.13–5.33 g/L CO_2.

Bell's Brewery, Inc.

Larry Bell is a dynamic personality and passionate about his beer, his company, and his family. His resilient principles have paved the way for one of the most successful brewing companies in America and helped shape the success of the craft brewing industry. As a student at Kalamazoo College, Larry Bell developed an interest and passion for fermentation while working at Sarkozy Bakery in Kalamazoo, Michigan. He began expanding his knowledge base in fermentation through homebrewing, and opened a homebrew supply store under the name Kalamazoo Brewing Company in 1983. By 1985, Bell had a 15-gallon pot and a strong dream of selling beer.

Bell sold his first commercial keg of beer in September of 1985, establishing Kalamazoo Brewing Company as the first microbrewery in the Midwest. Larry Bell is unquestionably a man of his own conviction. Simply put, Bell makes beer he wants to drink and always speaks from the heart. Bell's creations soon took on a cult status within the homebrewing community that continues to this day. The Eccentric Café opened in 1993 onsite at the small brewery's downtown location, making it the first brewpub in Michigan. By 2001, high production entailing a seven-day weekly brew schedule demanded a larger brewery be built. Plans began for the Comstock

Brewery and a pivotal member of the Bell's Brewery team, John Mallett, was brought onboard.

As Director of Operations, Mallett is responsible for logistics, brewing, packaging, and brewery capital projects. Mallett, Russell Schehrer award recipient in 2002, is one of the most prominent members of the craft brewing community. His commitment and dedication to the growth of the craft brewing industry, and to technological innovation in brewing as a whole, is unparalleled. Mallett serves on numerous technical committees and boards, including the Master Brewers Association of the Americas, the Brewers Association, American Malting Barley Association, and the Hop Quality Group. This active role in the craft industry is just one of the ways Mallett demonstrates his fortitude to continually better the art and science of brewing and provide high-quality beer for everyone. The Bell's Brewery team Mallett has created is a direct reflection of his passion, proficiency, and unrelenting pursuit of great beer. He is a true leader, not just for the Bell's team, but for craft brewing as a whole.

Within the last decade, Larry Bell has brought his daughter, Laura, on board. Laura hit the ground running and excelled at learning her father's business. She now serves as CEO and co-owner of Bell's Brewery, and is extremely pivotal in day-to-day decision making regarding her vision for the brewery. She is an absolutely delightful person to know and will certainly continue to help lead Bell's Brewery to new heights. With Mallett at the helm, Laura steering the business, and Larry's strong beliefs firmly planted, the Bell's crew has charted a course of accelerated growth and unstoppable success.

Despite accelerated growth, Bell's has not lost its attention to detail regarding the varieties of beer they produce, and that extends to their session beers. Bell's Oarsman Ale is a slightly tart wheat ale. Extremely refreshing, the sourness is subdued, letting the citrus and lemon note of the cascade hops lightly express themselves. Oarsman Ale is made with finesse and care and makes for a great session beer experience for any occasion; it also pairs wonderfully with a variety of culinary dishes.

It's important to note that this beer receives its signature, tart, acidic, character from a hot side (brewhouse) addition of sour wort. This sour wort is produced in a *Lactobacillus* bio-reactor located in the Bell's brewhouse. The titratable acidity and pH of the reactor dictate the volume of the sour wort addition in the brew kettle. The apparent extract of the sour wort must be considered when formulating malt quantity totals to achieve the target original extract of $10.2°P$.

Bell's Oarsman Ale (Commercial)

Sour Wheat Ale

Original gravity: 1.040–1.041 (10°P–10.42°P)
Final gravity: 1.010 (2.6°P)
Bitterness: 10 IBU
ABV: 4%
Attenuation: 74%
Boil (min.): 64

MALTS
42.5% two-row pale malt
42.5% wheat
9% pale malt
6% Carapils (dextrine malt)

HOPS
60% of IBUs Cascade (5.5% AA) @ 42
40% of IBUs Cascade (5.5% AA) @ 27

YEAST
Bell's house ale yeast and either sour wort or *Lactobacillus* must be used in the production of a mock Oarsman recipe in order to impart the tart, light sour flavor that defines this beer. See also discussion above on p.166.

BREWING NOTES
Water Treatment: Municipal water with calcium chloride added to mash vessel for increased calcium.

Mashing: Mash in very thin at a liquor-to-grist ratio of 4.1 to 1. Mash in at 144°F (62°C). Ramp to 149°F (65°C) and hold for conversion rest. Ramp to mash off at 172°F (78°C).

Fermentation: 71.6°F (22°C). The quantity of malt in the recipe, and the target original gravity, needs to be calculated while taking into consideration the apparent extract and volume of sour wort that will be added.

Fermentation/Maturation: Crash to 34.7°F (1.5°C) once diacetyl rest is complete and final gravity is reached (generally 6 or 7 days).

Carbonation: 2.6–2.7 volumes CO_2, or 5.13–5.33 g/L CO_2.

Bell's Oarsman Ale (Five-Gallon Batch)

Sour Wheat Ale

Original gravity: 1.040–1.041 (10°P–10.42°P)
Final gravity: 1.010 (2.6°P)
Bitterness: 10 IBU
ABV: 4%
Attenuation: 74%
Boil (min.): 64

MALTS

3 lb. 5 oz. (1.5 kg) two-row pale malt
3 lb. 5 oz. (1.5 kg) wheat
11 oz. (310 g) pale malt
7.5 oz. (215 g) Carapils (dextrine malt)

* Boil 22 minutes before first hop addition. Be careful of boil over during this time due to no hops.

HOPS

0.25 oz. (7 g) Cascade (5.5% AA) @ 42
0.25 oz. (7 g) Cascade (5.5% AA) @ 27

YEAST

Bell's house ale yeast and either sour wort or *Lactobacillus* must be used in the production of a mock Oarsman recipe in order to impart the tart, light sour flavor that defines this beer. See also discussion above on p.166.

BREWING NOTES

Water Treatment: Municipal water with calcium chloride added to mash vessel for increased calcium.

Mashing: Mash in very thin at a liquor-to-grist ratio of 4.1 to 1. Mash in at 144°F (62°C). Ramp to 149°F (65°C) and hold for conversion rest. Ramp to mash off at 172°F (78°C).

Fermentation: 71.6°F (22°C). The quantity of malt in the recipe, and the target original gravity, needs to be calculated while taking into consideration the apparent extract and volume of sour wort that will be added.

Fermentation/Maturation: Crash to 34.7°F (1.5°C) once diacetyl rest is complete and final gravity is reached (generally 6 or 7 days).

Carbonation: 2.6–2.7 volumes CO_2, or 5.13–5.33 g/L CO_2.

7

German-Inspired Session Recipes

Some of the most beautiful session beers in the world are brewed in Germany. Beer has been, and will always be, an integral part of German culture and is woven into the fabric of German society. It is not uncommon to see men and women standing at a beer kiosk, enjoying a refreshing weissbier while waiting for the train to work on a Monday morning. Germans celebrate life often, hoisting liters of Pilsener, helles, or weissbier throughout the thousands of beer gardens covering the countryside. Beer drinking in Germany is a time to be shared with friends, family, and community over long hours, requiring a low to moderate alcohol level to help the day often stretch into night. One of my personal favorite German traditions is where local patrons are guaranteed a seat at a special, communal large table, the *Stammtisch*, at their favorite beer hall. Session beer is what Germans love and German brewmasters have truly mastered the art of producing them.

Urban Chestnut Brewing Company

Behind every great brewing company you are sure to find an amazing brew-master. Florian Kuplent is just that. Kuplent, born and raised in Bavaria, developed a passion for beer and took his first brewing job as an apprentice brewer at Brauerei Erharting in Bavaria. While there, Kuplent gained a deep love and appreciation for artisan-based brewing, going on to earn his master's degree in Malting and Brewing from the Technical University of Munich, Weihenstephan. He learned the academic essentials of brewing science and sharpened his practical knowledge by working in many prestigious breweries throughout London, Germany, and Belgium. He highlights one of his greatest small brewing lessons as helping build, launch, and operate Meantime Brewing Company's first brewery in Greenwich, London. Kuplent later took on the challenge of working for one of the world's largest brewing companies, Anheuser-Busch. During his tenure there, Kuplent refined his skills in yeast propagation, quality control, and batch consistency. In addition, he was granted enormous creative freedom, enabling him to develop many award-winning recipes under the Michelob brand.

Although Kuplent's tenure at Anheuser-Busch taught him many valuable skills, his heart was drawn back to local, handcrafted beer. Utilizing his wide range of brewery experiences and education, Kuplent built and opened Urban Chestnut Brewing Company's (UCBC) first location in St. Louis, Missouri, in January 2011. One of its primary philosophies established early on by UCBC is their mission of "beer divergency." The beer divergency approach, defined by UCBC, is a New World meets Old World brewing ideal. They developed two primary series of beers under the beer divergency vision: the Revolution Series, representing the modern craft beer movement, and the Reverence Series, paying tribute to classic European brewing. Their first location, Midtown Brewery and Biergarten, honors the Reverence Series by brewing traditional European styles. Urban Chestnut's instant success led them to open their second location, Grove Brewery and Bierhall, in February, 2014. The Grove Brewery, representing the Revolution Series, tackles the bulk of UCBC's production and packaging. In 2015, UCBC opened their third location in Kuplent's Bavarian hometown of Wolnzach, Germany, situated in the world's largest hop-growing region, the Hallertau. Urban Chestnut's Hallertauer Brauerei added an additional element to their beer divergent philosophy, producing small batches of traditional Bavarian beer.

Chestnut trees have been used for centuries in Germany to protect *bier-gartens* (beer gardens) and *bierkellers* (beer cellars) from the sun. Kuplent honors the heritage and tradition of the chestnut tree by incorporating it in his company's name. As Kuplent witnessed the explosive growth of modern craft beer in cities around the United States, it seemed only natural to fuse Old World brewing tradition with the new modern craft movement to create high-quality craft beers for his local community. One of the most impressive company values that UCBC embraces is their commitment to their local community and environment, what they call "Urban Efforts." Urban Chestnut's sustainability methods include water conservation techniques, recycling, composting, and solar power. The Grove Brewery was the first LEED-certified brewery in St. Louis.[1] In addition, UCBC is actively engaged with a plethora of not-for-profit organizations in and around the St. Louis area.

Kellerbier and *Zwickelbier* are unfiltered versions of their lager counterpart. Typically, a Kellerbier is usually a traditional German helles served unfiltered; however, brewers also produce Kellerbiers from unfiltered dunkels, Dortmunders, and other German styles. Although the Kellerbier style remains, for the most part, unknown in North America, it is one of the most consumed styles of beer throughout the beer gardens of Bavaria, especially the unfiltered Pilsener version. Slightly cloudy from the remaining yeast in suspension, Kellerbier brings all the fantastic flavors of a filtered German Pilsener with a little added body, and sometimes a light sulfur character derived from the remaining yeast. Urban Chestnut's Zwickel beer, a helles style, is their flagship beer and is an excellent example of the traditional Kellerbier served throughout Bavaria.

---

[1] Leadership in Energy and Environmental Design.

Urban Chestnut Zwickel (Commercial)

Bavarian-Style Lager

Original gravity: 1.048 (12° P)
Final gravity: 1.010–1.012 (2.5–3°P)
Bitterness: 19 IBU
ABV: 5.2%
Attenuation: 75–80%
Boil (min.): 90

MALTS

98% German Pilsener malt
1% light caramel (2–3°L)
1% pale caramel (8–12°L)

HOPS

30% of IBU Hallertau Perle (8.25% AA) @ 90
50% of IBU Hallertau Mittelfrüh (4% AA) @ 30
20% of IBU Hallertau Mittelfrüh (4% AA) @ 0

YEAST

German lager yeast

BREWING NOTES

Water Treatment: Sparge at 176°F (80°C). Add calcium chloride to target about 75 ppm of dissolved calcium in the water.

Mashing: Mash in at 122°F (50°C) and heat up to 144°F (62°C). After 15 min at 144°F (62°C), pull decoction mash. Heat the decoction mash to 162°F (72°C) and rest for 15 min., then heat the decoction mash to a boil, boiling for 10 min. Combine mashes—target temperature is 162°F (72°C). Hold at 162°F (72°C) for 30 min., then heat up to 172°F (78°C) and mash off.

Fermentation: Pitch healthy yeast at 12 million cells per mL. Wort temperature at pitch should be 46°F (8°C); the temperature should be allowed to rise to 50°F (10°C) during fermentation.

Finishing/Maturation: At 0.5–1°P before hitting attenuation, slowly cool to 41°F (5°C) and transfer for maturation (make sure diacetyl has been sufficiently reduced). Hold at 41°F (5°C) for 24 hours, then cool to 32°F (0°C) or colder. Mature for at least 3 weeks.

Filtration/Clarification: None.

Carbonation: Carbonate naturally to 2.5 volumes CO_2.

Urban Chestnut Zwickel (Five-Gallon Batch)

Bavarian-Style Lager

Original gravity: 1.048 (12° P)
Final gravity: 1.010 (2.5–3°P)
Bitterness: 19 IBU
ABV: 5.2%
Attenuation: 75–80%
Boil (min.): 90

MALTS
7.25 lb. (3.3 kg) German Pilsener malt
1oz. (28 g) light caramel 2–3°L
1oz. (28 g) pale caramel 8–12°L

HOPS
0.15 oz. (4 g) Perle (8.25% AA) @ 90
1.75 oz. (50 g) Hallertau Mittelfrüh (4% AA) @ 30
1.25 oz. (35 g) Hallertau Mittelfrüh (4% AA) @ 0

YEAST
German lager yeast

BREWING NOTES
Water Treatment: Add calcium chloride to target about 75 ppm of dissolved calcium in the water.

Mashing: Mash in at 122°F (50°C) and heat up to 144°F (62°C). After 15 min at 144°F (62°C), pull decoction mash. Heat the decoction mash to 162°F (72°C) and rest for 15 min., then heat the decoction mash to a boil, boiling for 10 min. Combine mashes—target temperature is 162°F (72°C). Hold at 162°F (72°C) for 30 min., then heat up to 172°F (78°C) and mash off.
Fermentation: Ferment cold starting at 46°F (8°C) and let rise to 50°F (10°C).
Finishing/Maturation: Mature at 30–32°F (−1–0°C) for 3–4 weeks.
Filtration/Clarification: None.
Carbonation: Carbonate naturally to 2.5 volumes of CO_2.

5 Rabbit Cervecería

5 Rabbit Cervecería is the first Latin-inspired brewery concept in the United States. Andrés Araya was working as a business consultant for various beverage companies when he had an epiphany one night while tasting beers with clients. He was puzzled as to why Latin-American food was so full of flavor, diversity, and liveliness yet beers from the region lacked the same vitality. The idea gestated with Araya, finally leading him, his wife, and other partners to turn his Latin-inspired brewery concept into reality. The team opened in Chicago due to its large Latin population, vibrant food scene, and enthusiasm for craft beer. In 2010, they brought renowned beer author, educator, and Chicago resident Randy Mosher on board. With these forces together, the Latin-inspired craft brewery concept was destined for success.

> *I was first introduced to 5 Rabbit's beer while visiting Chicago on a business trip for the Cicerone Program. I walked over to a downtown taproom and ordered one of my favorite styles of beers, a Vienna lager. I was impressed with the quality, flavor, and story behind 5 Rabbit and their beers.*

The 5 Rabbit name comes from Aztec mythology. The Aztec legend tells of 400 rabbits born to Mayahuel, goddess of the maguey plant and fertility, and Pantecatl, god of fermentation. Maguey is a sacred plant from the agave plant family that has deep roots in Latin-American culture and cuisine. 5 Rabbit was one of the leaders of the 400 rabbits and symbolized excess and indulgence.

Some might find it incredibly odd that a Latin-inspired craft brewery produces a phenomenal classic German Vienna lager, but if you look into the history of Viennese lager, it actually makes a lot of sense. In the mid-nineteenth century and early twentieth century there was a large influx of German immigrants to the American Southwest, particularly the Texas–Mexico border area (Fix and Fix 1991, 14). One of the most influential brewers of the time for this region was a Mexican citizen, Santiago Graf, who was well aware of the brewing advances made by Anton Dreher and Gabriel Sedlmayr. Graf began producing great German-inspired beers, such as Vienna lager, throughout the region of Mexico using imported, high-quality ingredients (Fix and Fix 1991, 20). Therefore, a Latin-inspired brewery producing a high-quality Vienna lager actually makes perfect sense when reviewing the fascinating world history of brewing.

La Bici by 5 Rabbit is a toast to classic Viennese-style lager, with a deep, red color and complex malt flavor, hopped just enough to support the caramel and toasted malt notes. La Bici is perfectly balanced, finishing with a delicate malt sweetness, leaving your empty glass yearning for another pour.

5 Rabbit La Bici (Commercial)

Vienna Lager

Original gravity: 1.054 (13.5°P)
Final gravity: 1.014 (3.5°P)
Bitterness: 25 IBU
ABV: 5.2%
Attenuation: 74%
SRM: 12
Boil (min.): 75

MALTS
54% Pilsner malt
28% two-row pale malt
16% Bonlander® Munich malt
0.8% caramel 40°L
1.2% Briess Midnight wheat

HOPS

17% of IBU Tettnang (4.5% AA) @ 75
34% of IBU Celeia (4.5% AA) @ 15
42% of IBU Tettnang (4.5% AA) @ 0
7% of IBU Celeia (4.5% AA) @ 0

YEAST

Omega Yeast Labs' Bayern Lager 114. Low sulfur and low diacetyl producing yeast.

BREWING NOTES

Water Treatment: Calcium chloride to mash for increased calcium. Target all
water to an alkalinity of 80–100 ppm.

Mashing:

Step 1: Mash-in to achieve a 140°F (60°C) rest for 1 minute.

Step 2: Ramp to 152°F (67°C) and rest for 60 minutes.

Step 3: Ramp to 165°F (74°C) and rest for 10 minutes, then transfer to lauter tun.

Fermentation: 65–67°F (18–19°C).

Finishing: Cool aging maturation and filter for clarity.

Carbonation: Carbonate to 2.5 volumes CO_2.

5 Rabbit La Bici (Five-Gallon Batch)

Vienna Lager

Original gravity: 1.054 (13.5°P)
Final gravity: 1.014 (3.5°P)
Bitterness: 25 IBU
ABV: 5.2%
Attenuation: 74%
SRM: 12
Boil (min.): 75

MALTS

6 lb. (2.7 kg) Pilsner malt
3 lb. (1.36 kg) two-row pale malt
1 lb. 11 oz. (0.77 kg) Bonlander Munich malt
1.5 oz. (42 g) caramel 40°L
2.5 oz. (71 g) Midnight wheat (Make sure your black malt addition comes dehusked.)

HOPS

0.25 oz. (7 g) Tettnang (4.5% AA) @ 75
1.25 oz. (35 g) Celeia (4.5% AA) @ 15
2 oz. (57 g) Tettnang (4.5% AA) @ 0
0.5 oz. (14 g) Celeia (4.5% AA) @ 0

YEAST

Omega Yeast Labs' Bayern Lager 114. Low sulfur and low diacetyl producing yeast.

BREWING NOTES

Water Treatment: (Mash/Sparge) Calcium chloride to mash for increased calcium. Target all water to an alkalinity of 80–100 ppm.

Mashing:
Step 1: Mash-in to achieve a 140°F (60°C) rest for 1 minute.
Step 2: Ramp to 152°F (67°C) and rest for 60 minutes.
Step 3: Ramp to 165°F (74°C) and rest for 10 minutes then transfer to lauter tun.

Fermentation: 65F–67°F (18-19°C).

Finishing: Cool aging maturation and filter for clarity.

Carbonation: Carbonate to 2.5 volumes CO_2.

Red Rock Brewing Company

Six years after Utah granted the legal right to operate brewpubs, Red Rock Brewing Company opened its doors. Initially, a total of eleven partners started Red Rock Brewing Company in March of 1994 in an old dairy warehouse of downtown Salt Lake City. The brewing company has under gone many owner-ship and management changes throughout the last two decades and currently just two people now retain ownership of the brewpub side of the company. One of the original owners, Eric Dunlap, a pivotal member of the group, managed day-to-day brewing activity and designed the first recipes. Red Rock has received many accolades over the last twenty years for both its session beers and beers made at higher strength, most notably winning Large Brewpub of the Year at the 2007 GABF. Behind the outstanding beers at Red Rock is a great brewing team that actively participates in both the Utah and national craft beer scene.

Standing behind this successful brewing team is brewmaster Kevin Templin. Hired by Dunlap in 2000, Templin has developed dozens of great session beers, as well as beautiful barrel-aged sours and higher strength offerings. He never dances around how he feels about a beer and provides real feedback to help brewers figure out how to make the beer better. Templin's leadership and creativity in the brewhouse has paved the way for Red Rock's healthy sales and continued growth. Since opening its first brewpub in 1994, Red Rock has built two additional retail locations and a production brewery. It has established itself firmly in the Utah beer scene and produces some of the best session beers in the country.

> I had the distinct pleasure of brewing just two blocks away from Red Rock, allowing Templin and me to share stories, knowledge, and many beers with each other over the years. He embodies the spirit of craft brewing in every sense. He is a selfless brewer and truly devotes himself to making the highest quality craft beer he can at every turn.

Red Rock's Black Bier is a German-style dark lager that is very easy drinking, with medium body and low bitterness. A variety of high-quality German malts and thirty-five days of lagering give this award winning schwarzbier its dark color and extremely smooth flavor. A fantastic black session lager for any time of day or for any season.

Red Rock Black Bier (Commercial)

Schwarzbier

Original gravity: 1.040 (10°P)
Final gravity: 1.009 (2.3°P)
Bitterness: 28 IBU
ABV: 4%
Attenuation: 77%
Boil (min.): 90

MALTS

85% Pilsner malt
9.5% Munich malt
3.5% dehusked black malt
1.5% Special "B"
1% roast malt

HOPS

Tettnang (4% AA) @ 60
Tettnang (4% AA) @ 30
Hallertauer Mittelfrüh (4% AA) @ whirlpool

YEAST

Lager yeast (2124 Wyeast)

BREWING NOTES

Water Treatment: Adjust reverse osmosis water pH with lactic acid. No
   calcium is added.
Mashing: Rest at 148–149°F (64.4–65°C), thin mash.
Fermentation: 48–49°F (8.9–9.4°C).
Finishing/Maturation: Cool aging for 28 days at 36°F (2°C). Diatomaceous
   earth filter for clarity.
Carbonation: Carbonate to 2.5 volumes CO_2.

Red Rock Black Bier (Five-Gallon Batch)

Schwarzbier

Original gravity: 1.040 (10° P)
Final gravity: 1.009 (2.3°P)
Bitterness: 28 IBU
ABV: 4%
Attenuation: 77%
Boil (min.): 90

MALTS
7 lb. (3.18 kg) Pilsner malt
12 oz. (340 g) Munich malt 10°L
5 oz. (140 g) dehusked black malt
1.5 oz. (43 g) roast malt

HOPS
0.75 oz. (21 g) Tettnang (4% AA) @ 60
0.75 oz. (21 g) Tettnang (4% AA) @ 30
1.5 oz. (43 g) Hallertauer Mittelfrüh (4% AA) @ whirlpool

YEAST
Lager yeast (2124 Wyeast)

BREWING NOTES
Water Treatment: Adjust reverse osmosis water pH with lactic acid. No
   calcium is added.
Mashing: Rest at 148–149°F (64.4–65°C), thin mash.
Fermentation: 48–49°F (8.9–9.4°C).
Finishing/Maturation: Once primary fermentation is complete, rack the
   beer off the yeast and age in the coldest place you have, 33–36°F (0.5–2°C)
   is optimal. Since it is only 4% ABV do not cool below 33°F (0.5°C). Rack
   again into a Cornelius keg or bottle.
Carbonation: Carbonate to 2.5 volumes of CO_2.

Saint Arnold Brewing Company

Saint Arnold Brewing Company is the oldest craft brewery in Texas. Brock Wagner and Kevin Bartol decided Houston, then the largest city in the country without a brewery, needed a craft brewery, and since they lived there, it was a perfect fit. The first keg of Saint Arnold beer was shipped June 9th, 1994 and since then a fantastic brewing company has emerged that epitomizes the craft spirit. Bartol has moved on, but Wagner is still leading the team. Wagner was surrounded by great beer his whole life, growing up in two very beer-focused cities, Cincinnati, Ohio and Brussels, Belgium. His great, great, great grandfather from Alsace arrived in America in the mid-nineteenth century and opened up Wagner's Beer Hall (now called The Saloon) in San Francisco. Wagner began homebrewing while attending Rice University, and after graduating with a degree in economics he joined the ranks of investment banking. Despite his career success, Wagner's true calling was steeped in brewing, leading him to build the Saint Arnold Brewing Company and live his dream.

Wagner notes that Saint Arnold's philosophy is rooted in brewing balanced beers. There can be a strong emphasis on a component or flavor, but at the end of the day there should be balance. "But," says Wagner, "within the balance, there should always be complexity as well. We are Texas' oldest craft brewery, a title we earned by outlasting the other early breweries here" (Wagner, pers. comm.).

Saint Arnold takes climate into consideration when designing beers. Fancy Lawnmower Beer is produced year-round and has garnered four awards at the GABF to date: a bronze medal in 2000 and 2006, and a gold in 2007 and 2010 in the German-style Kölsch category. A testament to the German Kölsch style, which originated in Cologne, Fancy Lawnmower Beer is crisp and refreshing, yet has a delicate malt body with a slight sweetness. Well balanced by a complex, citrus hop character, Saint Arnold uses a special Kölsch yeast (an ale yeast that ferments at lager temperatures) to provide a slightly fruity flavor and clean finish. Truly refreshing and thirst quenching after some strenuous activity, such as mowing your lawn in Texas on a hot day!

Saint Arnold Fancy Lawnmower Beer (Commercial)

Kölsch-Style Beer

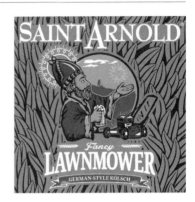

Original gravity: 1.045 (11.25°P)
Final gravity: 1.008 (2°P)
Bitterness: 17–19 IBU
ABV: 4.9%
Attenuation: 83%
Boil (min.): 75

MALTS
91% two-row pale malt
9% wheat malt

HOPS
Hallertauer Hersbrucker (4% AA) @ 60
Hallertauer Hersbrucker (4% AA) @ 30
Hallertauer Hersbrucker (4% AA) @ 0
Hallertauer Hersbrucker (4% AA) @ whirlpool

YEAST
Kölsch yeast

BREWING NOTES
Water Treatment: Siebel salts* and calcium chloride.
Mashing: Rest at 151°F (66°C).
Fermentation: 60°F (16°C).
Finishing/Maturation: Crash beer to 31°F (−0.5°C) once diacetyl levels have been cleared by sensory or VDK analysis. Clarified bright through centrifuge and diatomaceous earth filter.
Carbonation: Carbonate to 2.7–2.8 volumes CO_2.

* **Siebel salts:** Although the exact ratios are not known to the author, Siebel salts is a mixture of calcium sulfate, magnesium sulfate, magnesium carbonate, and ammonium carbonate (a.k.a. bakers salt). Siebel salts are not commonly used, but Brock Wagner does use them to make Saint Arnold's Kölsch.

Saint Arnold Fancy Lawnmower Beer (Five-Gallon Batch)

Kölsch-Style Beer

Original gravity: 1.045 (11.25°P)
Final gravity: 1.008 (2°P)
Bitterness: 17–19 IBU
ABV: 4.9%
Attenuation: 83%
Boil (min.): 75

MALTS
8 lb. (3.6 kg) two-row pale malt
1 lb. (450 g) wheat malt

HOPS
1 oz. (28 g) Hallertauer Hersbrucker (4% AA) @ 60
0.25 oz. (7 g) Hallertauer Hersbrucker (4% AA) @ 30
0.25 oz. (7 g) Hallertauer Hersbrucker (4% AA) @ 0
0.25 oz. (7 g) Hallertauer Hersbrucker (4% AA) @ whirlpool

YEAST
Kölsch yeast

BREWING NOTES
Water Treatment: (Mash/Sparge) Siebel salts* and calcium chloride.
Mashing: Rest at 151°F (66°C).
Fermentation: 60°F (16°C).
Finishing/Maturation: Crash beer to 31°F (−0.5°C) once both fermentation and diacetyl rests are complete.
Carbonation: Carbonate to 2.7–2.8 volumes of CO_2.

---

* Siebel salts: Although the exact ratios are not known to the author, Siebel salts is a mixture of calcium sulfate, magnesium sulfate, magnesium carbonate, and ammonium carbonate (a.k.a. bakers salt). Siebel salts are not commonly used, but Brock Wagner does use them to make Saint Arnold's Kölsch.

Hollister Brewing Company

Eric Rose, co-owner and brewmaster of Hollister Brewing Company, began homebrewing while attending University of California, Santa Barbara. After receiving a bachelor of arts degree in history, Eric's heart was still drawn to brewing and he accepted an assistant brewer position at the Santa Barbara Brewing Company. Eric's talent and motivation to make great beer quickly propelled him into the lead brewer position within his first year. During the six years he spent at Santa Barbara Brewing, Eric honed his brewing skills, allowing him to garner many GABF awards and brewing accolades. It didn't take him long to realize that brewing was his true calling.

Eric's father, Marshall Rose, has always been an active member in the Santa Barbara community where he was born and raised. After graduating UC Berkley in Business Administration, Marshall joined his father, Lou Rose, in running the family-owned retail apparel business. The Lou Rose stores were sold in the early 1990s, and Marshall decided to accept the position of executive director at the Santa Barbara Downtown Organization, where he worked for a decade. With Marshall's savvy business skills and Eric's brewing expertise, it was a perfect match for success.

Eric and Marshall Rose decided to build Hollister Brewing Company in the town of Goleta, adjacent to UC Santa Barbara. Besides attracting the large student population from the university to their awesome craft beer and delicious food, Hollister is also located in the center of the technology district of Santa Barbara County. Hollister is devoted to quality, craft, and community. The brewpub provides a diverse and delicious menu to pair beautifully with its 15 rotating tap lineup. Their mission is simple and noble. Hollister celebrates and honors both the artisan and the environment by sourcing local, high-quality ingredients and reducing its environmental impact downstream whenever possible. Eric, although extremely humble in character, has a very strong belief system rooted in traditional brewing. His deep conviction for brewing high-quality traditional and creative beers has led Hollister Brewing Company to becoming a hugely successful mainstay of the Santa Barbra County community.

Tiny Bubbles is one of Eric's finest examples of his undying commitment to brewing tasty, traditionally inspired beers, winning silver in German-Style Sour Ale at the 2010 GABF. This is a nice, tart, German wheat beer, brewed in the traditional fashion. A small amount of coriander and French sea salt gently flavor this refreshing Gose. Very few hops are used in the brewing process, allowing the delicate wheat and Pilsner malts to complement the slightly sour, citrus, and dry finish.

Hollister Tiny Bubbles (Commercial)

Traditional Gose

Original gravity: 1.042–1.044 (10.5–11°P)
Final gravity: 1.008–1.010 (2–2.5°P)
Bitterness: Extremely low, possibly 2–3 IBU
ABV: 4%–4.5%
Attenuation: 81%
Boil (min.): 45

MALTS

53% pale wheat malt
26% Pilsner malt
9% Munich (light)
9% acidulated malt
3% rice hulls

HOPS

0.25 lb./bbl. or 4 oz./bbl. aged whole leaf Saaz (3.75% AA) added to the mash (no hops in the boil)
3 handfuls Indian coriander (super oily) @ 40
14 oz. of French sea salt @ 40

BACTERIA AND YEAST

Lactobacillus delbrueckii
Bavarian hefeweizen yeast

BREWING NOTES

Boil Time: 45 minutes
Mashing: Rice hulls added to mash. Single step mash, 149–150°F (65–66°C).
Fermentation Temperature: *Lactobacillus* fermentation temperature is 95°F (35°C). Drop temperature to 78°F (25.5°C) for the hefeweizen yeast pitch.

Fermentation: Grow 1 L starter of *Lactobacillus delbrueckii* for approximately 1 week prior to brew day (amount is sized for a 10 bbl. batch brew). Pitch the *L. delbrueckii* at 95°F (35°C) on brew day and let flavors develop for 3–4 days or until desired tartness or pH is achieved. No oxygen added at any point! Drop temperature to 78°F (25.5°C) and pitch standard quantity (1 Cambro bucket) of second-generation Bavarian hefeweizen yeast through top of tank and allow beer to ferment approximately 8–10 days until all fermentation activity has ceased.

Finishing/Maturation: Rest 2–3 days warm before doing a four-stage drop to 34°F (1°C). Cold condition beer for 5–7 days and transfer to serving vessel. Do not add any fining or clarifying agents. Should be ready to drink within three weeks of brew day if all goes well. Beer can be served the day following transfer, but continues to clear up for 3–4 weeks, at which point it is usually crystal clear. Pours with a thick head that quickly dissipates, so get it to the customer fast. Big lemon notes develop around the third week. Enjoy!

Carbonation: Carbonate to highest possible level (≥ 3 volumes CO_2).

Special Cleaning Instructions: The fermentor must be thoroughly cleaned and then heat-sterilized with 208°F (98°C) water. Any plastic gaskets must be removed and thrown away. Boil all removable metal fittings and door gasket. Always brew an extremely hoppy beer into the fermentor used to produce the Gose on next brew cycle, which takes advantage of the hops' antibacterial properties and helps prevent any further growth of lactobacilli. This intense cleaning and sterilizing regime is to prevent cross contamination of *L. delbrueckii* with any other clean beers in production or entering the fermentor next. I also suggest using dedicated hoses when working with any bacteria to avoid cross contamination.

Hollister Tiny Bubbles (Five-Gallon Batch)

Traditional Gose

Original gravity: 1.042–1.044 (10.5–11°P)
Final gravity: 1.008–1.010 (2–2.5°P)
Bitterness: Extremely low, possibly 2–3 IBU
ABV: 4%–4.5%
Attenuation: 81%
Boil (min.): 45

MALTS
4.5 lb. (2 kg) pale wheat malt
2.5 lb. (1.14 kg) Pilsner malt
1 lb. (450 g) Munich (light)
12 oz. (340 g) acidulated malt
4 oz. (115 g) rice hulls

HOPS
0.75 oz. (21 g) aged whole leaf Saaz (3.75% AA) added to the mash (no hops in the boil)
2 oz. (57 g) Indian coriander (super oily) @ 40
0.21 oz. (6 g) of French sea salt @ 40

BACTERIA AND YEAST
Lactobacillus delbrueckii
Bavarian hefeweizen yeast

BREWING NOTES
Mashing: Rice hulls added to mash. Single step mash, 149–150°F (65–66°C).

Fermentation Temperature: *Lactobacillus* fermentation temperature is 95°F (35°C). Drop temperature to 78°F (25.5°C) for the hefeweizen yeast pitch.

Fermentation: Grow *Lactobacillus delbrueckii* starter approximately 1 week prior to brew day. It will be necessary for you to find a very warm place in or around your home to ferment the wort with *L. delbrueckii.* Consider brewing this beer in the heat of summer and perhaps ferment the *L. delbrueckii* in the garage. Pitch the *Lactobacillus* starter at 95°F (35°C) on brew day and let flavors develop for 3–4 days or until desired tartness or pH is achieved. Don't allow oxygen exposure at any point! Before adding the Bavarian hefeweizen yeast on day 3 or 4, move fermentor to a slightly cooler location in your home, but still warm enough to support the warm hefeweizen fermentation. Stabilize temperature to 78°F (25.5°C) and pitch a standard quantity of second-generation Bavarian hefeweizen yeast into the fermentor and allow beer to ferment approximately 8–10 days until all fermentation activity has ceased.

Finishing/Maturation: Rest 2–3 days warm before doing a four-stage drop to 34°F (1°C). Cold condition beer for 5–7 days and transfer to serving vessel. Do not add any fining or clarifying agents. This beer should be ready to drink within three weeks of brew day if all goes well. Big lemon notes develop around the third week.

Carbonation: Since high carbonation is a major flavor component of the beer, do not bottle. It is very dangerous to try and force 3.2 volumes CO_2 into a regular beer bottle. If you are adamant about bottling the beer, then heavy glass bottles must be used, such as a champagne bottle, to protect you and others from explosion. The safer option would be to keg the beer in a Cornelius keg. To dispense the beer properly, higher amounts of CO_2 will be needed to draw beer out of the keg to limit excessive foaming.

Special Cleaning Instructions: Note the intense cleaning and sterilizing regime recommended for the commercial recipe (above). Brewing with bacterial strains like *L. delbruekii* puts your equipment at risk of cross contamination when you next come to brew a clean beer. Of course, space and financial constraints may apply to some homebrew set-ups, but I recommend a separate set of fittings, gaskets, and hoses for any beer you produce with lactobacilli. Always brew an extremely hoppy beer into the fermentor used to produce the Gose on next brew cycle, which takes advantage of the hops' antibacterial properties and helps prevent any further growth of lactobacilli.

Sierra Nevada Brewing Company

Ken Grossman, one of the founding fathers of the craft brewing movement in America, began as most brewers do, by homebrewing. In 1976, Ken opened The Homebrew Shop in downtown Chico, California. He and his friend Paul Camusi brewed at every opportunity, constantly trying to better their beer. Ken's home-brew was so popular he decided to piece together his first brewery. With used dairy equipment he sourced throughout northern California and Oregon, Ken started Sierra Nevada Brewing Company in 1979. Small-scale brewing was non-existent in the United States at the time. As a result, Ken had to teach himself many skills, such as refrigeration and welding, in order to build his first brewing system. By the fall of 1980, Ken was ready to brew his first batch for release: a stout. The current stout recipe is very close to the original recipe Ken wrote all those years ago, and remains part of the Sierra Nevada year-round lineup. The next beer style Ken brewed, and relentlessly refined to perfection, is his famous pale ale. Today, Sierra Nevada Pale Ale is one of the most popular and widely sold craft beers in America.

Ken Grossman's desire for using pure ingredients started early. His love for fresh, citrusy hops sent him on countless road trips to Washington's Yakima hop fields to select the finest whole-leaf Cascade hops, which continue to define the signature flavor at Sierra Nevada. Quality ingredients is just one of many core company values Ken instilled early on. Sierra Nevada demonstrates an unrelenting pledge to quality, innovation, invention, and commitment to the environment and community. Its beers are timeless and consistently wonderful to drink. Traditional brewing techniques, such as open fermentation and bottle conditioning, are still employed today, while Sierra Nevada continues to advance and innovate, providing new creative ways to bring fresh craft beer to the world.

High-quality, flavorful beers have been the hallmark of Sierra Nevada, leading the company to break ground in 1987 at its 20th Street brewery in Chico. Sierra Nevada has grown into the third-largest craft brewery and the seventh-largest brewery overall in the United States, according to the April 2016 Brewers Association annual listing of the Top 50 US Craft Breweries. Numerous expansions have transpired over the last several decades at the 20th Street brewery. Eventually, Sierra Nevada's desire to bring the freshest beer possible to the East Coast led it to build a brewery east of the Mississippi, in Mills River, North Carolina in 2015.

Ken Grossman's passion and promise for providing the highest quality craft beer, currently available in over 15 countries, has been passed down to his son Brian, who manages the Mills River brewery. Many of the new, up-and-coming brewers today opening craft breweries in their local communities grew up watching their parents drink Sierra Nevada Pale Ale. Grossman did not just build a successful brewing company, he changed how Americans think about beer. He taught us that beer is not just one thing, it is diverse, fresh and flavorful. There is no doubt that Sierra Nevada will continue to lead the craft brewing movement, inspiring us all to drink better beer.

Ken Grossman comments in *Modern Brewing Age* about his new beer release, Otra Vez:

> *The consumer palate is going away from kicking in your teeth, going towards something they can have a couple of. Otra Vez suits that. It has the citrus everyone is looking for, but also a lot of individual identity. It's the most complicated beer we have ever done. ("Sierra Nevada rolls out Otra Vez Gose nationwide,"* Modern Brewery Age, *January 18, 2016, 1.)*

In the same article, Brian Grossman adds that Otra Vez is a "very crushable beer." Otra Vez is a Gose-style ale, refreshingly dry, citrusy with tart notes and comes in at 4.5% ABV and just 5 IBU. A variation of the traditional Gose-style, incorporating grapefruit, cactus and coriander, Otra Vez is light bodied and extremely thirst quenching, making it a perfect session beer. The prickly pear cactus and grapefruit provide a unique tangy fruit experience, complementing the tart and refreshing nature of a traditional Gose. Prickly pear in many forms can be sourced on Amazon or your local culinary supply store. Otra Vez was recently released in Sierra Nevada's year-round lineup, and won gold in the Session Beer Category at the WBC in 2016. Try using light amounts of coriander, grapefruit, and prickly pear cactus at the end of boil for enhanced fruit flavor.

Sierra Nevada Otra Vez (Commercial)

Gose-Style Sour Ale

Original gravity: 1.040–1.044 (10–11°P)
Final gravity: 1.006–1.008 (1.5–2°P)
Bitterness: 5 IBU
ABV: 4.2%–4.8%
Attenuation: varies
Boil (min.): 60

MALTS
60% two-row pale malt
40% wheat malt

HOPS
80% of IBUs Cascade (5.5% AA) @ 60
20% of IBUs Hopsteiner experimental variety or other low-alpha hop
   (3–4 % AA) @ 60

BACTERIA AND YEAST
Lactobacillus strain
House ale yeast (White Labs 001 California Ale, or Wyeast 1056)

BREWING NOTES

Mashing: Single step infusion

Fermentation: Pitch the *Lactobacillus* starter into unhopped, unboiled wort at 100°F (38°C). Let the flavors develop for 3–4 days or until the sour wort reaches desired acidity. Don't allow oxygen exposure at any point! The sour wort is pitched into the kettle with the standard wort to make 25% of the total volume. Stabilize temperature to 72°F (22°C) and pitch a standard quantity of ale yeast into the fermentor and allow beer to ferment approximately 8–10 days until all fermentation activity has ceased.

Finishing/Maturation: Cool to cellar temperature of 40°F (4°C) before packaging. Do not chill proof.

Carbonation: Carbonate to >2.6 volumes CO_2.

Sierra Nevada Otra Vez (Five-Gallon Batch)

Gose-Style Sour Ale

Original gravity: 1.040–1.044 (10–11°P)
Final gravity: 1.006–1.008 (1.5–2°P)
Bitterness: 5 IBU
ABV: 4.2%–4.8%
Attenuation: varies
Boil (min.): 60

MALTS

5 lb. (2.27 kg) two-row pale malt
3 lb. (1.36 kg) wheat malt

HOPS

0.12 oz. (3 g) whole-flower Cascade (5.5% AA) @ 60
0.12 oz. (3 g) Hopsteiner experimental variety or other low-alpha hop (3–4 % AA) @ 60

BACTERIA AND YEAST

Lactobacillus strain
House ale yeast (White Labs 001 California Ale, or Wyeast 1056)

BREWING NOTES

Mashing: Single step infusion

Fermentation: Using an appropriate *Lactobacillus* strain of your choosing, grow a starter approximately 1 week prior to brew day. It will be necessary for you to find a very warm place in or around your home to ferment the wort with *Lactobacillus*. Consider brewing this beer in the heat of summer and perhaps ferment the lactobacilli in the garage. Pitch the *Lactobacillus* starter at 100°F (38°C) on brew day and let flavors develop for 3–4 days or until desired tartness or pH is achieved. Don't allow oxygen exposure at any point! Before adding the ale yeast on day 3 or 4, move fermentor to a slightly cooler location in your home that is suitable for the ale yeast fermentation. Stabilize temperature to 72°F (22°C) and pitch a standard quantity of ale yeast into the fermentor and allow beer to ferment approximately 8–10 days until all fermentation activity has ceased.

Finishing/Maturation: Cool to cellar temperature of 40°F (4°C) before packaging. Do not chill proof.

Carbonation: Carbonate to >2.6 volumes CO_2.

Special Cleaning Instructions: Brewing with bacterial strains like *Lactobacillus* puts your equipment at risk of cross contamination when you next come to brew a clean beer. Of course, space and financial constraints may apply to some homebrew set-ups, but I recommend a separate set of fittings, gaskets, and hoses for any beer you produce with lactobacilli. Always brew an extremely hoppy beer into the fermentor used to produce the Gose on next brew cycle, which takes advantage of the hops' antibacterial properties and helps prevent any further growth of lactobacilli.

8

Other International
Session Beers

The global brewing community is chock full of beer culture, flavor, and diversity. It is a bottomless mine brimming full of gold nuggets. Brewing inspiration can come from anywhere on the planet, at any time, and to say the world is your oyster (stout) is an understatement. Session beer has deep historical roots and spans every continent. When language becomes a barrier in communication, beer reaches across the divide. The commonality of beer culture is spoken in many different dialects, and displays countless faces. Certain brewing fundamentals persist steadfastly throughout most nations and tribes worldwide, and session beer is one of them.

Traveling abroad as a brewer was a life-changing event. It was inspiring to witness firsthand how family, brewing, and culture weave together to create community. As American craft brewers in the twenty-first century, we are humbled to have such amazing international brewing history and knowledge to draw upon and feed our own creative juices. However, no matter how off the rails brewers seem to drift in recipe formulation—whether out of boredom, unchartered territory, or just following a new trend—many American brewers find themselves returning to established and timeless traditional beer styles.

Allagash Brewing Company

One word best describes Rob Tod: visionary. He was truly ahead of his time when he began producing Belgian-inspired beers before most Americans had ever had a chance to experience them. Tod's passion for the art of brewing was not by way of homebrewing, but rather it was born out of discovering the craft brewing business first and craft beer second.[1] Tod graduated with a bachelor of science degree in geology and attended graduate school in Vermont. Prior to opening Allagash, he worked at Otter Creek Brewing in Middlebury, Vermont.

When Allagash Brewing Company was founded in 1995 in Portland, Maine, Tod was the only employee for quite some time. From managing the business and developing marketing, to performing all the brewing and cellaring duties, it was up to Tod to get it all done. One of the true pioneers of Belgian-style beer in America, Tod brought an entirely different element to the craft brewing industry. For one, he used a Belgian yeast. Most craft beers in the mid-1990s used generic ale and lager yeast, representing either English or German-influenced beers. However, Tod was drawn to beers with different flavors, such as Celis White, produced at the time by Pierre Celis out of Austin, Texas.

Tod began with a small 15-barrel system, selling his first batch the summer of 1995. Sales growth wasn't the number one focus for Allagash, rather the focus was always on quality and innovation. Over the first 10 years Allagash grew slowly to 3,000 barrels. Tod's vision for his company never wavered and as the craft world's eyes turned toward the wonderful flavors of Belgian-style beer, Allagash's numbers began to take off. By 2014, barrelage hit 70,000, which allowed Allagash to invest more in staff, community, and adherence to quality than ever before.[2]

One of the first employees Tod hired is the current brewmaster, Jason Perkins. Perkins was instantly drawn to the art and science of brewing when he started as a homebrewer. Starting in 1998, he has helped build the creative lineup of Allagash beers, and he is regarded as one of the industry's brightest stars. Perkins is motivated daily by his desire to produce the highest quality beer

[1]   "Interview with Rob Tod of Allagash," by Ashley Routson, *Drink With The Wench* (blog), April 30, 2010, http://drinkwiththewench.com/2010/04/interview-with-rob-tod-of-allagash/.

[2]   "Beer Town: Rob Tod Talks about Allagash Brewing," by Bob Townsend, *Atlanta Journal-Constitution*, November 5, 2014, http://atlantarestaurants.blog.ajc.com/2014/11/05/beer-town-rob-tod-talks-about-allagash-brewing/.

possible. Perkins not only dedicates his time to his brewery and his family, but to the craft industry as a whole. From his participation as a judge at the GABF and WBC, to speaking at both the BA and MBAA annual conferences, it came as no surprise when Perkins was recognized for his commitment to innovation in the craft brewing industry with the Russell Scherher Award at the 2016 Craft Brewers Conference in Philadelphia, Pennsylvania. With Tod and Perkins in charge, there is no doubt the Allagash team will continue to produce some of the world's finest Belgian-inspired beers that are brewed from the soul.

Allagash beers have collected many awards over the years, with the flagship beer alone, Allagash White, winning nine awards combined at the GABF and WBC. Refreshing and light, this Belgian-inspired witbier offers a slight fruitiness with hints of spice and citrus. Slightly cloudy in appearance and extremely delicious, Allagash White is one beer you can certainly drink all day long.

Allagash White (Commercial)

Belgian-Style Witbier

Original gravity: 1.048 (12°P)
Final gravity: 1.010 (2.5°P)
Bitterness: 21 IBU
ABV: 5.1%
Attenuation: 84%
Boil (min.): 75

MALTS
50% Pilsner malt
25% unmalted white wheat
19% malted red wheat
6% oats

HOPS
Hallertau Perle (8% AA) @ 75
Tettnang (4.5% AA) @ 30
Saaz (3.75% AA) @ 0

YEAST
Proprietary yeast strain—Allagash recommends using a commercially avail-able Belgian-style *wit* strain.

BREWING NOTES
Water Treatment: Adjust mash water to hit pH 5.3.
Mashing: Standard infusion mash, rest at 150°F (66°C).
Spices/Other: Coriander, Curaçao orange peel, house secret spice.
Fermentation: Dependent on strain, but Allagash recommends a rising
   fermentation temperature, for example, starting at 65°F (18°C) and rising
   to 72°F (22°C).
Finishing/Maturation: Diacetyl rest is recommended. Finished beer should be
   hazy. Haze can be controlled by waiting for yeast to settle, or by filtering a
   portion of the beer and transferring a portion to maintain a consistent haze.
Carbonation: 2.5 volumes CO_2 or higher.

Author's note on spice additions:
The variety of coriander and orange peel, how fine the grind, and when they
are added to the boil will all greatly affect the amount an individual brewery
uses. Therefore, a range of quantities is offered here as a starting point, which
will need to be adjusted by the brewer to meet their desired preference. For a
10 bbl. batch try 0.5–1.0 lb. Curaçao orange peel added at 10 minutes before
the end of boil and 1–2 lb. freshly ground coriander added 2 minutes before
the end of boil. Some classic witbiers also have grains of paradise added,
which imparts a hint of citrus and pepper to the beer. It is important to keep
a light hand with the grains of paradise—a suggested rate is 0.5–1.0 lb. freshly
ground grains of paradise at 2 minutes to end of boil. Any spices used can
also be added at whirlpool for a slightly lighter flavor.

Allagash White (Five-Gallon Batch)

Belgian-Style Witbier

Original gravity: 1.048 (12°P)
Final gravity: 1.010 (2.5°P)
Bitterness: 21 IBU

ABV: 5.1%
Attenuation: 84%
Boil (min.): 75

MALTS
4.75 lb. (2.15 kg) Pilsner malt
2.5 lb. (1.14 kg) torrified or unmalted white wheat
1.75 lb. (800 g) malted red wheat
9 oz. (260 g) flaked oats

HOPS
0.5 oz (14 g) Hallertau Perle (8% AA) @ 75
0.25 oz. (7 g) Tettnang (4.5% AA) @ 30
0.25 oz. (7 g) Saaz (3.75% AA) @ 0

YEAST
Proprietary yeast strain—Allagash recommends using a commercially available Belgian-style *wit* strain.

BREWING NOTES
Water Treatment: Adjust mash water to hit pH 5.3.
Mashing: Standard infusion mash, rest at 150°F (66°C).
Spices/Other: Coriander, Curaçao orange peel, house secret spice.
Fermentation: Dependent on strain, but Allagash recommends a rising fermentation temperature. Perhaps starting at 65°F (18°C) and rising to 72°F (22°C).
Finishing/Maturation: Diacetyl rest is recommended. Finished beer should be hazy. Haze can be controlled by waiting for yeast to settle and transferring a portion to maintain a consistent haze.
Carbonation: 2.5 volumes CO_2 or higher.

Author's note on spice additions: For a five-gallon batch size I suggest adding 0.5 oz. Curaçao orange peel 10 minutes before the end of boil and 0.5 oz. freshly ground coriander 2 minutes before the end of boil. If you decide to try your hand at adding grains of paradise, the suggested usage rate for this African pepper is 0.25 oz. freshly ground grains of paradise added 2 minutes before the end of boil. Spices added at whirlpool will give a slightly lighter flavor.

Jolly Pumpkin Artisan Ales

Some brewers concentrate heavily on the science of brewing, others chase trends and numbers. Ron Jeffries does neither. Jeffries is an artist and his brewery is his canvas, allowing him to express his creative spirit. His heart is warm and his mind open, just like his fermentors. Born and raised in Ann Arbor and a graduate of the University of Michigan, Jeffries had a life-long dream of opening a brewery long before he ever brewed his first batch of beer. Jeffries began his professional brewing career in 1995 and spent the next nine years working in many breweries, refining his skills and learning the fundamentals of brewing, all the while formulating his plan of one day creating his own line of beers. By 2003, Jeffries had officially formed his company. Seven months later, Jolly Pumpkin Artisan Ales began brewing in a warehouse space in Dexter, Michigan, located just outside Ann Arbor.

Jeffries always wanted to add a taproom to the brewery so that his customers could come and enjoy his newest creations or sample old favorites. However, every time Jolly Pumpkin would acquire an additional suite in the warehouse space, it would end up being used to house more barrels. Finally, in May of 2009, after forming a partnership with some good friends, Jolly Pumpkin opened their first restaurant and taproom located on Michigan's Old Mission Peninsula, just north of Traverse City. Six months later, Jolly Pumpkin's second restaurant-taproom location was opened in Ann Arbor; after that, the Jolly Pumpkin Detroit pizzeria and taproom opened in the spring of 2015.

Most brewers start out making classic ales and lagers, and only then spread their wings to take on more difficult tasks, like barrel aging. One thing is for sure, Jeffries is not like most brewers. Jolly Pumpkin was the first brewery in the United States producing 100% oak-aged beer. It was not until Jeffries himself thirsted for a fresh IPA at one of his pubs that he finally decided to produce a beer fermented and conditioned in an all-stainless steel vessel. Jeffries expresses his alter ego by producing these beers made in stainless steel vessels under different brand names, such as the North Peak and Grizzly Peak series.

Jeffries uses the age-old art of blending to make Jolly Pumpkin beers. He also relies on the naturally occurring flora of the town of Dexter to inspire secondary fermentations in barrels and foudres after primary fermentation has completed in one of his open fermentors. The artwork on the Jolly Pumpkin beer labels is representative of the art that goes into making the beer. The labels are some of the most beautiful and mystical ever produced, inviting the customer to explore the distinctive complexity of flavors that each beer exhibits.

Oddly enough, it was while the craft brewing industry was going through the extreme beer craze that Jeffries decided to do the polar opposite, producing a session beer. Bam Biére, a farmhouse ale, won a bronze medal in the Session Beer category at the 2009 GABF. Extremely refreshing with layers of flavor, Bam Biére epitomizes the fact that a beer does not have to be high in alcohol to display wonderful complexity. Simple yet complex, light yet full of flavor, golden and cloudy in presentation (no filtration or clarification aids), Bam Biére exhibits a slight fruitiness and complexity from the mixed fermentation, oak aging and bottle conditioning, and from the dry hop. A perfect beer to pair with flavorful cheeses.

Jolly Pumpkin Bam Biére (Commercial)

Farmhouse Ale

Original gravity: 1.037 (9.25°P)
Final gravity: 1.004–1.006 (1.0–1.5°P)
Bitterness: 24 IBU
ABV: 4.5%
Attenuation: 84%
Boil (min.): 75

MALTS
55% Pilsner malt
27% two-row pale malt
10.5% wheat malt
6.5% flaked barley
0.8% crystal 75°L
0.2% black malt

HOPS
Cascade (5.5% AA) @ 75
Crystal (3.5% AA) @ 30
Crystal (3.5% AA) @ 0
Crystal (3.5% AA) (dry hop)

YEAST
White Labs WLP 550, plus house wild cultures

BREWING NOTES
Water Treatment: (Mash/Sparge) Some calcium sulfate and calcium chloride, but "not much," says Jeffries.
Mashing: 147–149°F (64–65°C).
Fermentation: Free rise to 80°F (27°C) and above.
Fermentation Notes: Do not control temperature during fermentation.
Finishing/Maturation: Step down to 50–55°F (10–13°C). Age in oak for a minimum of one or two months.
Carbonation: Bottle condition to high carbonation levels, >2.65 volumes CO_2.

Jolly Pumpkin Bam Biére (Five-Gallon Batch)

Farmhouse Ale

Original gravity: 1.037 (9.25°P)
Final gravity: 1.004–1.006 (1.0–1.5°P)
Bitterness: 24 IBU
ABV: 4.5%
Attenuation: 84%
Boil (min.): 75

MALTS
4 lb. Pilsner malt
2 lb. two-row pale malt
0.75 lb. wheat malt
0.5 lb. flaked barley
1 oz. crystal 75°L
0.25 oz. black malt

HOPS
0.5 oz. Cascade (5.5% AA) @ 75
0.75 oz. Crystal (3.5% AA) @ 30
0.75 oz. Crystal (3.5% AA) @ 0
0.5 oz. Crystal (3.5% AA) added at ambient temperature (dry hop)

YEAST
White Labs WLP 550, plus house wild cultures

Author's Notes: Produced with a cultured abbey ale yeast, this beer also benefits from a mixed fermentation of a house wild culture, most likely including *Brettanomyces* and various *Lactobacillus* strains. Using the bottle dregs from a Bam Biére to inspire a secondary fermentation in a small oak barrel is probably the best way to try and recreate this beer at home. The other option is to purchase a mixed culture packet and some oak cubes or spirals from the local homebrew shop and add it to a secondary carboy after primary fermentation.

BREWING NOTES
Water Treatment: (Mash/Sparge) Some calcium sulfate and calcium chloride, but not much.
Mashing: 147–149°F (64–65°C).
Fermentation: Free rise to 80°F (27°C) and above.
Fermentation Notes: Do not control temperature during fermentation.
Finishing/Maturation: Step down to 50–55°F (10–13°C).
Carbonation: Bottle condition to high carbonation levels. Heavy glass bottles must be used, such as a champagne bottle, to protect you and others from explosion. The safer option would be to keg the beer in a Cornelius keg. To dispense the beer properly, higher amounts of CO_2 will be needed to draw beer out of the keg to limit excessive foaming.

Brooklyn Brewery

Steve Hindy, co-founder of Brooklyn Brewery, spent five and a half years as a foreign war correspondent in the Middle East working for the Associated Press. His hotel in Beirut was hit by mortars, and a piece of shrapnel that he picked up while it was still warm resides on his desk today as a reminder of his experience. While over in the Middle East, many of Hindy's diplomatic friends homebrewed, because of the limited availability and choice of beer in a region where, for reasons of religion, many choose not to drink alcohol. Upon returning to Brooklyn, Hindy began homebrewing himself and was so excited about creating great beer that he recruited his friend and neighbor, Tom Potter, a banker, to start a brewery with him. Potter and Hindy, eager to get their business off the ground, met with a renowned graphic designer, Milton Glaser. Glaser was impressed with their business ideas and enthusiasm and came on board. Yet another partnership and friendship was born, and Glaser continues to create all of Brooklyn Brewing's fabulous labels.

Once the Brooklyn Brewery logo was designed and the funds were raised, it was time to find a brewmaster to brew the beer. The team contracted the F.X. Matt Brewing Company out of Utica, New York to brew their first batches. It was William M. Moeller, a former head brewer at Philadelphia's Schmidt Brewery, who spent copious hours working on the Brooklyn Lager recipe; Potter and Hindy were able to deliver their first cases of this beer to Brooklyn locals in 1988. Over the next six years the Brooklyn brand grew to be very popular around local bars, theaters, and music venues and quickly developed a solid reputation for great beer.

Garrett Oliver, previously brewmaster at Manhattan Brewing Co., was brought onboard as brewmaster in 1994 to head up Brooklyn's brewing operations and build a new brewery in the Williamsburg neighborhood. In 1996, the New York City mayor, Rudy Giuliani, cut the ribbon at the new Williamsburg site, and in the tasting room Oliver's newly released Brooklyner Weisse was poured to celebrate the proud moment. Over the next two decades Oliver established himself as a leader in the craft brewing community. He is an international beer judge, speaker, author, and recipient of both the 2014 Russell Schehrer Award for Innovation in Craft Brewing and the prestigious James Beard Award for Outstanding Wine, Beer, or Spirits Professional. Oliver continues to lead the Brooklyn Brewery into new and exciting markets with his creative and amazingly delicious craft beer offerings and collaborations.

Brooklyn Brewery has focused on relationship building since its inception, supporting and collaborating with many artisans spanning the art, music, and food world. They were one of the first breweries in the world to pursue collaborations with other brewers. From the organic inception and humble roots of Hindy's dream came the dynamic, innovative, and internationally acclaimed Brooklyn Brewery of today. Selling beer in 30 countries makes foreign sales half of Brooklyn's current total volume. In 2014 it opened (with Carlsberg) Nya

Carnegiebryggeriet in Stockholm, and in August of 2016 it opened the newly renovated E.C. Dahls brewery in Trondheim, Norway. In addition, the barrel room at Brooklyn Brewery in Williamsburg has over 2,000 barrels full of beer, and the brewery continues to lead the way in bottle re-fermentation.

At 3.4% ABV, Brooklyn ½ Ale is a light "table saison" that harkens back to the days when saisons were light, refreshing beers meant for farm workers. Highly aromatic, it drinks much bigger than its actual weight. The trick to the flavor here is relatively high IBUs plus low finishing gravity, avoiding a thin-tasting beer because the aromatics are pronounced and pleasant. Lightly hazy and highly carbonated, this table saison drinks beautifully any time of day or night.

Brooklyn ½ Ale (Commercial)

Table Saison

Original gravity: 1.032 (8°P)
Final gravity: 1.008 (2°P)
Bitterness: 30 IBU
ABV: 3.4%
Attenuation: 75%
Boil (min.): 75

MALTS
98.5% German Pilsner malt
1.5% dark Munich malt (Weyermann® Munich Type 2)

HOPS
Sorachi Ace (13% AA) @ 75
Challenger (7.5% AA) @ 75
Sorachi Ace (13% AA) @ 30
Challenger (7.5% AA) @ 30
Sorachi Ace (13% AA) @ 0
Amarillo (9.2% AA) dry hop

YEAST
Belgian saison or other attenuative Belgian yeast at 4–5 million cells.

BREWING NOTES

Water Treatment: Depending on water type, an addition of calcium chloride can be considered to increase palate fullness.

Mashing: A 10 minute rest at 118°F (48°C) is followed by a rapid ramp-up to 158°F (70°C), and held for 40 minutes. This is then ramped up to 168°F (76°C) "mash off." Avoid over-sparging and high sparge water temperatures.

Hop Notes: The majority of the bitterness comes from the finishing hops. The hop charge is back loaded with the majority of Sorachi Ace hops in the whirlpool.

Dry-hop Information/Usage: Usage rate of 1.5lb./bbl. Dry hop at 60°F (15.5°C) for 3 days.

Fermentation: 70°F (21°C).

Finishing/ Maturation: Within 96 hours or when full attenuation is reached.

Filtration/Clarification: Allow the yeast to drop out naturally, no clarification procedure is necessary. If desired, centrifuge to 2.5–8 SRM. Light haze is desirable.

Carbonation: 2.7 volumes CO_2.

Brooklyn ½ Ale (Five-Gallon Batch)

Table Saison

5 lb. (2.27 kg) German Pilsner malt
1.25 lb. (570 g) Weyermann Munich Type 2

HOPS

0.1 oz. (3 g) Sorachi Ace (13% AA) @ 75
0.1 oz. (3 g) Challenger (7.5% AA) @ 30
0.1 oz. (3 g) Sorachi Ace (13% AA) @ 30
0.75 oz. (21 g) Sorachi Ace (13% AA) @ 3
0.75 oz. (21 g) Sorachi Ace (13% AA) @ 0
4 oz. (115 g) Amarillo (9.2% AA) dry hop

YEAST

Belgian saison or other attenuative Belgian yeast at 4–5 million cells/mL.

BREWING NOTES

Water Treatment: Depending on water type, an addition of calcium chloride can be considered to increase palate fullness.

Mashing: A 10 minute rest at 118°F (48°C) is followed by a rapid ramp-up to 158°F (70°C), and held for 40 minutes. This is then ramped up to 168°F (76°C) "mash off." Avoid over-sparging and high-sparge water temperatures.

Hop Notes: The majority of the bitterness comes from the finishing hops. The hop charge is back loaded with the majority of Sorachi Ace hops in the whirlpool.

Dry-hop Information/Usage: Use 4 oz. Amarillo (9.2% AA) at 60°F (15.5°C) for 3 days.

Fermentation: 70°F (21°C).

Finishing/ Maturation: Within 96 hours or when full attenuation is reached.

Filtration/Clarification: Allow to drop naturally, no clarification procedure is necessary. If desired, centrifuge to 2.5–8 SRM. Light haze is desirable.

Carbonation: 2.7 volumes CO_2.

Yards Brewing Company

Yards Brewing Company began like most great brewing companies do: two guys homebrewing in their dorm room at Western Maryland College and talking about beer. Having love for beer really is a simple thing, but starting and growing a successful brewing company is the difficult part. Tom Kehoe and Jon Bovit had a huge admiration and respect for classic English ales and gave their best at trying to replicate them through their homebrewing. Being proud young brewers wanting to share and talk about their new creations, they decided to sell some of their first batches on Shakedown Street at the Grateful Dead concert in Franklin D. Roosevelt Park in Philly, where it was well received. By October 1994, Yards Brewing Company became a reality and a 3.5-barrel system was installed in its first location in Manayunk, Pennsylvania. Some of the first releases are still in Yards' year-round lineup, such as the flagship Extra Special Ale, best enjoyed on a traditional cask hand pump. Other early releases included an imperial stout, barleywine, and an authentic entire porter. In 1997, Yards moved to the Roxborough region of Philadelphia, where they collaborated with Philadelphia's historic City Tavern and began re-creating original recipes brewed by the founding fathers, Thomas Jefferson and George Washington.

In 2002 demand for Yards beer was continuing to grow, so a new brewery with a 10,000-barrel capacity was built in the Kensington neighborhood, where it continued to flourish. At the new brewery, Philadelphia Pale Ale was born and quickly became a local favorite. The year 2008 proved to be a momentous year for Yards and their beloved city. The Phillies won the World Series and Kehoe moved the brewery to their current location in North Liberties in central Philadelphia.

Yards has always felt very connected to their community, and when the Phillies won the World Series, Yards was there, handing out Extra Special Ales at the parade to help the crowd celebrate. Yards' Brew Unto Others campaign was started in 2015, highlighting its commitment to hard work, having fun, and giving back to the community. Yards Brewing is a true American success story. From the early days of brewing at college, growing the company on a commitment to quality, community and family, it is no surprise that Yards has reached such great heights, producing over 41,500 barrels a year by 2015.

Kehoe's dedication and respect for traditional English ales is unwavering amidst an ever-changing and trendy craft brewing world. His classic ales are delicious and highly drinkable. Brawler mild, one of Yards' most popular brews, honors the very traditional session beer style of mild, winning a silver medal in the English-Style Mild Ale category at the 2013 GABF. The ruby-red colored Brawler is an extremely approachable English ale, with hops kept at bay enough to allow the toast and caramel malt flavors to shine through.

Yards Brawler (Commercial)

English Mild

Original gravity: 1.044 (11°P)
Final gravity: 1.012 (3°P)
Bitterness: 12 IBU
ABV: 4.2%
Attenuation: 73%
Boil (min.): 60

MALTS
79% two-row pale malt
10% Weyermann® Melanoidin malt
4% flaked oats
2% crystal 65°L
2% amber malt
2% Caravienne
1% roast barley

HOPS
50% of IBU Nugget (13% AA) @ 60
50% of IBU Nugget (13% AA) @ 30

YEAST
The real key to this beer is a poorly attenuating English ale yeast. And the difficulty in crafting this recipe was to make the beer malty without being sweet. This is a very uncharacteristically complicated recipe for Yards.

BREWING NOTES
Water Treatment: Depending on water type, an addition of calcium chloride can be considered to increase palate fullness.
Mashing: Depending on highly attenuating your yeast selection is, 154–156°F (68–69°C). It is very important to not attenuate the beer too dry.
Fermentation: 68°F (20°C).
Filtration/Clarification: This beer style can be filtered or fined, but should have little to no yeast haze.
Carbonation: Depends if beer is cask, on draught, or bottled. 2.0–2.5 volumes CO_2.

Yards Brawler (Five-Gallon Batch)

English Mild

Original gravity: 1.044 (11°P)
Final gravity: 1.012 (3°P)
Bitterness: 12 IBU
ABV: 4.2%

Attenuation: 73%
Boil (min.): 60

MALTS
7 lb. (3.2 kg) Maris Otter or two-row pale malt
1 lb. (450 g) Weyermann Melanoidin malt
0.25 lb. (115 g) flaked oats
0.25 lb. (115 g) crystal 65°L
0.25 lb. (115 g) amber malt
0.25 lb. (115 g) Caravienne
0.25 lb. (115 g) roast barley

HOPS
0.14 oz. (4 g) Nugget (13% AA) @ 60
0.14 oz. (4 g) Nugget (13% AA) @ 30

YEAST
The real key to this beer is a poorly attenuating English ale yeast. And the difficulty in crafting this recipe was to make the beer malty without being sweet. This is a very uncharacteristically complicated recipe for Yards.

BREWING NOTES
Water Treatment: Depending on water type, an addition of calcium chloride can be considered to increase palate fullness.
Mashing: Depending on how highly attenuating your yeast strain is, 154–156°F (68–69°C). It is very important to not attenuate the beer too dry.
Fermentation: 68°F (20°C).
Filtration/Clarification: This beer style can be filtered or fined, but should have little to no yeast haze.
Carbonation: Depends if beer is cask, on draught, or bottled. 2.0–2.5 volumes CO_2.

Stone Brewing Company
Please see chapter 6, "North American Session Beer Recipes," for more about the story of Stone Brewing Company. The former brewmaster at Stone Brewing, Mitch Steele, has kindly submitted another recipe, this time for an English

mild. There were only 300 cases of Stone Brewing's Lee's Mild ever released. Named after the head brewer at the time, Lee Chase, Lee's Mild garnered the Brewers' Choice award at the 1999 Real Ale Festival in Chicago.

Stone Lee's Mild Ale (Commercial)

English Mild

Original gravity: 1.040 (10°P)
Final gravity: 1.011 (2.9°P)
Bitterness: 25–30 IBU
ABV: 3.8%
Attenuation: 71%
Boil (min.): 90

MALTS
82.9% two-row pale malt
7.6% brown malt
7% crystal 150°L
2.5% pale chocolate

HOPS
0.29 lb./bbl. Northern Brewer (8.5% AA) @ 90

YEAST
White Labs WLP007 dry English ale yeast or WLP002 English ale yeast are closest to Stone Brewing's proprietary yeast

BREWING NOTES
Water Treatment: Carbon filter, target total hardness 120 ppm, calcium 70–80 ppm.
Mashing: 154°F (68°C) for 60 minutes. Raise to 165°F (76°C) prior to lautering.
Fermentation: 72°F (22°C).
Fermentation Notes: Aerate wort to 10–12 ppm dissolved oxygen. Target 12 million cells/mL yeast pitch rate.

Maturation/Cooling: Hold at 32°F (0°C), 3 days minimum, 7 days maximum, and dump yeast/hops that settle in the cone every other day.

Filtration/Clarification: Perlite filtration, no fining agents.

Carbonation: 2.5 volumes CO_2. The only Lee's Mild that was produced by Stone Brewing was bottle conditioned.

Stone Lee's Mild Ale (Five-Gallon Batch)

English Mild

Original gravity: 1.040 (10°P)
Final gravity: 1.011 (2.9°P)
Bitterness: 25–30 IBU
ABV: 3.8%
Attenuation: 71%
Boil (min.): 90

MALTS

6 lb. 10 oz. (3 kg) two-row pale malt
10 oz. (285 g) brown malt
9 oz. (255 g) crystal 150°L
3 oz. (85 g) pale chocolate

HOPS

0.75 oz. (21 g) Northern Brewer (8.5% AA) @ 90 minutes

YEAST

White Labs WLP007 dry English ale yeast or WLP002 English ale yeast are closest to Stone Brewing's proprietary yeast

BREWING NOTES

Water Treatment: Carbon filter, target total hardness 120 ppm, calcium 70–80 ppm.

Mashing: 154°F (68°C) for 60 minutes. Raise to 165°F (76°C) prior to lautering.

Boil time: 90 minutes

Fermentation: 72°F (22°C).

Fermentation Notes: Aerate wort to 10–12 ppm dissolved oxygen. Target 12 million cells/ml yeast pitch rate.

Maturation/Cooling: Hold at 32°F (0°C), 3 days minimum, 7 days maximum, and then rack to secondary.

Filtration/Clarification: No fining agents.

Carbonation: 2.5 volumes CO_2. The only Lee's Mild that was produced by Stone Brewing was bottle conditioned.

Carl Heron

It is unthinkable to pen a book about session beer without including an authentic English ale in the recipe section. Who better to donate a recipe then Carl Heron? Heron currently resides in Norfolk, England and is the craft sales manager for Northern England and Scotland at Crisp Malting Group.

Heron's career on the production side of beer has been long and varied. Heron's first position was laboratory technician at Webster's Brewery in Halifax, Yorkshire. Webster's, then part of Grand Metropolitan, was the first brewery outside of the United States to produce Budweiser, and Heron's role demanded strict focus on specifications and quality standards. After a short stint at another Yorkshire brewery, Tetley's, Heron returned to Webster's as a bottling line manager. Following successive takeovers, the Webster's Halifax site was closed, so Heron took his skillset to Scotland as a packaging manager for Belhaven, a small Scottish regional brewery, where Heron was soon promoted to process brewer, being responsible for everything from raw materials handling to bright beer. While honing his brewery management skills, he acquired his Master Brewer diploma from the Institute of Brewing and Distilling in 1999.

Heron had reached his promotional ceiling at Belhaven and decided to return to corporate brewing. Heron's career again witnessed several takeovers and mergers in the UK brewing industry. He initially moved to the Tennent's brewery in Glasgow, joining as part of Bass PLC. Heron was soon promoted to processing area manager at the Samlesbury Brewery near Preston, Lancashire in 2003, this time working for Interbrew (later to become InBev) after Bass PLC had divested its brewing business. After many successful projects under InBev ownership, Heron was promoted once again in 2008 to become product and process development specialist for InBev in Europe working out of Leuven.

By 2012, Heron had done about as much traveling as he cared to do and decided to get back to his roots in England. Wanting to get closer to the brewing process again, he took the head brewer position at Sharp's Brewery in Cornwall. For the best part of three years Heron enjoyed his days running Sharp's and brewing many fabulous craft beers, such as Doom Bar bitter, the top selling cask ale in the UK since 2013. Looking for a new challenge and wanting to increase his knowledge base about craft brewing, Heron took his current position with Crisp Malting Group in 2014.

Heron has designed and overseen production of many fabulous English ales during his illustrious career, and offers here a recipe that is very popular throughout all of England. This classic English amber ale recipe may taste familiar to those having traveled to England. Well-balanced and drinkable, this beer's delicate caramel malt flavors add nice malt sweetness and mesh artfully with subtle hop aroma.

Carl Heron's English Amber Ale (Commercial)

Classic Amber Ale

Original gravity: 1.040 (10°P)
Final gravity: 1.009 (2.25°P)
Bitterness: 20 IBU
ABV: 4%
Attenuation: 77.5%
Boil (min.): 90

MALTS
91% English pale malt
6% crystal 150°L
2.5% caramalt 15°L
0.5% roast barley

HOPS
5% of IBU Perle (8% AA) @ 90
5% of IBU Perle (8% AA) @ 20
30% of IBU Aurora (8.25% AA) @ 0
30% of IBU Perle (8% AA) @ 0
30% of IBU Northern Brewer (8.5% AA) @ 0

YEAST
Fermentis SafAle™ US-05 (dry yeast)

BREWING NOTES
Water Treatment: Burtonize your water with brewing salts.
Mashing: 154.5°F (68°C).
Fermentation: Send wort to fermentor at 64°F (18°C) and set temperature control to 70°F (21°C) to allow for optimum yeast growth.
Filtration/Clarification: The use of both auxiliary and isinglass finings is recommended at a rate to suit the brewery's equipment, if the beer is to be presented as a cask beer. Finings are not necessary for bottles and kegs.
Carbonation: 2.0–2.5 volumes CO_2, depending on whether beer is cask, on draught, or bottled.

Carl Heron's English Amber Ale (Five-Gallon Batch)

Classic Amber Ale

Original gravity: 1.040 (10°P)
Final gravity: 1.009 (2.25°P)
Bitterness: 20 IBU
ABV: 4%
Attenuation: 77.5%
Boil (min.): 90

MALTS
7.5 lb. (3.4 kg) Crisp pale ale malt
0.5 lb. (225 g) crystal 150°L
0.25 lb. (115 g) caramalt 15°L
1 oz. (28 g) roast barley

HOPS

0.07 oz. (2g) Perle (8% AA) @ 90
0.07 oz. (2g) Perle (8% AA) @ 20
0.5 oz. (14 g) Aurora (8.25% AA) @ 0
0.25 oz. (7 g) Perle (8% AA) @ 0
0.25 oz. (7 g) Northern Brewer (8.5% AA) @ 0

YEAST

Fermentis SafAle US-05 (dry yeast)

BREWING NOTES

Water Treatment: Burtonize your water with brewing salts.
Mashing: 154.5°F (68°C).
Fermentation: Send wort to fermentor at 64°F (18°C) and set temperature control to 70°F (21°C) to allow for optimum yeast growth.
Filtration/Clarification: For bottles and kegs, finings are not necessary.
Carbonation: 2.0–2.5 volumes CO_2, depending on whether beer is on draught or bottled.

Drop-In Brewing Company

Steve Parkes began his career in brewing in the United Kingdom. After graduating from the prestigious brewing and distilling school at Heriot-Watt University in Edinburgh, Scotland, Parkes honed his brewing skills in the UK over the next six years, winning many brewing accolades. In 1988, Parkes decided to take his career to the United States, opening the British Brewing Company in a suburb of Baltimore, Maryland. Although the beers Parkes created and brewed were fantastic, especially his popular Oxford Class Organic Amber Ale, he decided to sell the brewery in 1992. Parkes then joined Humboldt Brewing Company as brewmaster. Over the next five years Parkes expanded the brewery, taking Humboldt Brewing from a microbrewery to a regional brewery and producing the award-winning Red Nectar Amber Ale, still produced today by Firestone Walker.

Humboldt Brewery formed a working relationship with the American Brewers Guild (ABG) located in Davis, California. The brewery and brewing staff mentored students attending ABG who were preparing for a career in the craft brewing industry. In 1997, Parkes took a full-time faculty position with

ABG and immediately started designing course material and lectures, all geared toward helping students prepare for a successful craft brewing career. In 1998, Parkes developed what was then the only internet-based educational program available for craft brewers. One year later, the owners of ABG offered to sell the school to Parkes and he gladly accepted. During his early years of ownership and development of ABG, Parkes took a position as quality control manager at Wolaver's Certified Organic Ales, a national contract brewing company. Parkes audited, developed, and implemented quality control systems for breweries producing beer for Wolaver's. In 2003, Wolaver's purchased Otter Creek Brewery in Middlebury, Vermont and Parkes became the brewmaster, once again winning many awards at the GABF while increasing beer sales by 50%.

As ABG grew, so too did Parkes' desire to have a teaching brewery of his own, dedicated to educating and training the future brewers of America and to provide fresh, high-quality craft beers for the state of Vermont. With the support, assistance, and perseverance of his wife, Christine McKeever, Parkes' dream came true in 2012 with the creation of the Drop-In Brewing Company. The Drop-In brewery serves as a home to ABG, offering intensive brewing science and engineering courses for professional brewers; the brewery also produces fantastic beers. Parkes embodies the true spirit of craft beer in every way and in 2009—you may be noticing a trend by now—Parkes was awarded the Russell Scherer Award for Innovation in Craft Brewing.

When session beer is the topic of discussion, many traditional brewers adamantly state the original session beer is the ordinary bitter. The bitter style is a very elusive one and is discussed at greater length in chapter 1. Not many recipes for the classic bitter style are being brewed in the United States, therefore, I turned to my friend Steve Parkes to help present an authentic bitter recipe.

Drop-In Tisbury Local (Commercial)

English Bitter

Original gravity: 1.038 (9.5°P)
Final gravity: 1.006–1.008 (1.5–2°P)
Bitterness: 30 IBU
ABV: 4%
Attenuation: 81.5%
Boil (min.): 90

MALTS
95.3% Maris Otter
4.6% medium crystal
0.1% roast barley

HOPS
75% of IBU Fuggle (4.5% AA) @ 90
25% of IBU East Kent Goldings (5% AA) @ 5

YEAST
English ale yeast

BREWING NOTES
Water Treatment: Adjust water with gypsum to 100 ppm calcium.
Mashing: 149.5°F (65°C) with a 60-minute mash stand.
Fermentation: 68–72°F (20–22°C).
Carbonation: 2.0–2.5 volumes CO_2, depending on whether beer is cask, on draught, or bottled.

Drop-In Tisbury Local (Five-Gallon Batch)

English Bitter

Original gravity: 1.038 (9.5°P)
Final gravity: 1.006–1.008 (1.5–2°P)
Bitterness: 30 IBU
ABV: 4%
Attenuation: 81.5%
Boil (min.): 90

MALTS
6 lb. 14 oz. (3.12 kg) Maris Otter
5.0 oz. (140 g) crystal 60°L
0.1 oz. (3 g) roasted barley

HOPS
1.0 oz. (28 g) Fuggle (4.5% AA) @ 90
1.75 oz. (50 g) East Kent Goldings (5% AA) @ 5

YEAST
English ale yeast

BREWING NOTES
Water Treatment: Adjust water with gypsum to 100 ppm calcium.
Mashing: 149.5°F (65°C) with a 60-minute mash stand.
Fermentation: 68–72°F (20–22°C).
Carbonation: 2.0–2.5 volumes by CO_2. Depends whether beer is cask, on draught, or bottled.

Jennifer Talley

During my brewing career, I have had the distinct pleasure and freedom to create numerous session beers. One of the most popular rotating specials for many brewpubs across America is an interpretation of a traditional dry Irish stout. Although many brewers have their own twist and style when it comes to brewing an Irish stout, the basic parameters are simple and definitive.

Jennifer Talley's Dry Irish Stout (Commercial)

Dry Irish Stout

Original gravity: 1.038 (9.5°P)
Final gravity: 1.006–1.008 (1.5–2°P)
Bitterness: 29 IBU
ABV: 4%
Attenuation: 81.5%
Boil (min.): 110

MALTS
64% American two-row
12% flaked barley
7% roast barley
7% acidulated malt
5% rice hulls
3% dehusked black malt
2% chocolate malt

HOPS
50% of IBU German Magnum (14% AA) @ 110
50% of IBU German Magnum (14% AA) @ 55

YEAST
English ale yeast, or California ale yeast

BREWING NOTES
Water Treatment: Adjust water to 40 ppm calcium with gypsum in the kettle.
Mashing: 152°F (67°C).
Fermentation: 68–72°F (20–22°C).
Filtration/Clarification: Finings or filtration for clarification. The final beer should be free of yeast and haze.
Carbonation: 2.0–2.4 volumes CO_2. Depends whether beer is cask, draught, or bottled.

Jennifer Talley's Dry Irish Stout (Five-Gallon Batch)

Dry Irish Stout

Original gravity: 1.038 (9.5°P)
Final gravity: 1.006–1.008 (1.5–2°P)
Bitterness: 29 IBU
ABV: 4%
Attenuation: 81.5%
Boil (min.): 110

MALTS

5.5 lb. (2.5 kg) American two-row
1 lb. (450 g) flaked barley
0.75 lb. (340 g) roast barley
0.5 lb. (225 g) acidulated malt
0.5 lb. (225 g) rice hulls
0.25 lb. (115 g) dehusked black malt
0.25 lb. (115 g) chocolate malt

HOPS

0.25 oz. (7 g) German Magnum (14% AA) @ 110
0.25 oz. (7 g) German Magnum (14% AA) @ 55

YEAST

English ale yeast, or California ale yeast

BREWING NOTES

Water Treatment: Adjust water to 40 ppm calcium with gypsum in the kettle.
Mashing: 152°F (67°C).
Fermentation: 68–72°F (20–22°C).
Filtration/Clarification: Use finings for clarification. The final beer should be free of yeast and haze.
Carbonation: 2.0–2.4 volumes CO_2. Depends whether beer is on draught or bottled.

Afterword

Evacuation

One day at 2:47 p.m. the children and I arrived home after watching my son's football team, the U10 Jr. Miners, barely lose 15–18 to Pleasant Grove. I received a phone call I have never had before. The Nevada County sheriff's office was calling to inform our family that the Osborne Hill area was under a forced evacuation due to the wildfire burning at Empire Mine, one block from our home. Both my children decided to get what they needed if asked to evacuate. My son grabbed all his baseball gear and his 49ers hat, and my daughter grabbed her teddy bear, Mr. Softy Fuss Love. I went into each room to grab items that were important to us. From the family room I grabbed our photo albums, from the living room I took the computer, and from my bedroom my jewelry box and safe. After packing up the car, I still had not received the call that our street was evacuating, so I stood in all the rooms again and realized—it's just extra stuff. In fact, a lot of the stuff the kids argue over or that clutters-up the house gets in the way of our special family time. What is important to me are my children and my health. Once the kids were off to their friend's house, and the photo albums, baseball gear, and Mr. Softy were packed in the car, we were good.

Session beer is always on my mind, especially since I have been writing this book. I thought to myself, brewing a great session beer is much like preparing to evacuate. As a session beer brewer, ask yourself: What is important to this beer? It's about making sure things do not get in the way of enjoyment. The ingredients need to be fresh, yeast handling perfect, the fermentation healthy, temperatures accurate, dissolved oxygen managed, and balance obtained. A great session beer is not cluttered with too much bitterness, excessive sweetness, staling components, acetaldehyde, diacetyl, or other off flavors. It is simple, pure, and enjoyable. As pen hits paper to design your next session beer, ask yourself what matters to the beer. What do you really need and what just gets in the way? More is not better in the world of session beer. When all is said and done, focus on the essentials: quality and simplicity, flavor and balance. As we walk around the rooms of our life and look for what is important to us, we begin to strip away the layers of stuff we surround ourselves with. In the end, we find the simple, basic elements of life are what we hold dear, what brings us quality of life. Bring these elements to your beer.

Bibliography

Alworth, Jeff. 2016. "All Styles Evolve: The Guinness Example." *All About Beer* (online), August 16. http://allaboutbeer.com/styles-evolve-guinness-example/.

AHA (American Homebrewers Association). 2017. "Patersbier: The Lawnmower Beer of Trappist Monks." Boulder: AHA. Accessed April 7. http://www.homebrewersassociation.org/how-to-brew /patersbier-the-lawnmower-beer-of-trappist-monks/.

ASBC. 2017. "Methods of Analysis." American Society of Brewing Chemists. Accessed April 10. http://methods.asbcnet.org/.

Arnold, John Paul and Frank Penman. 1933. *History of the Brewing Industry and Brewing Science in America: Prepared as Part of a Memorial to the Pioneers of American Brewing Science, Dr. John E. Siebel and Anton Schwarz*. University of Michigan: G.L Peterson.

Biendl, Martin, Bernhard Engelhard, Adrian Forster, Andreas Gahr, Anton Lutz, Willi Mitter, Roland Schmidt, and Christina Schonberger. 2014. *Hops: Their Cultivation, Composition, and Usage.* Nuremburg: Fachverlag Hans Carl. 93–116.

Bradee, Lawrence, Will Duensing, Scott Halstad, Ray Klimovitz, and Andy Laidlaw. 1999. "Adjuncts." In *The Practical Brewer*, edited by John T. McCabe, 75–98. Wauwatosa, Wisconsin: Master Brewers Association of the Americas.

Briggs, D.E., J.S. Hough, R. Stevens, and T.W. Young. 1981. *Malt and Sweet Wort.* 2nd ed. Vol. 1 of *Malting and Brewing Science.* New York: Kluwer Academic / Plenum.

Bryson, Lew. 2017. *The Session Beer Project* (blog). Accessed April 11. http://sessionbeerproject.blogspot.com/

BYO (Brew Your Own). 2002. "Schwarzbier: Style Profile." *Brew Your Own,* November 2002. Accessed March 4, 2017. http://byo.com/hops/item/1351-schwarzbier-style-profile.

Burnsed, Justin. 2011. "Brew a Gose." *Brew Your Own.* May/June. http://byo.com/hops/item/2349-gose.

Cornell, Martyn. 2017. *Zythophile: Beer now and then* (blog). Accessed April 12. http://zythophile.co.uk/.

De Keukeleire, Denis. 2000. "Fundamentals of Beer and Hop Chemistry." *Quimica Nova* 23(1): 108–112.

Dornbusch, Horst. 1997. *Prost: The Story of German Beer.* Boulder: Brewers Association.

———. 2000. *Bavarian Helles.* Boulder: Brewers Publications.

Dr. Rainer Wild Foundation. 2008. *Geschmäcker sind verschieden: Wie sich Geschmackspräferenzen prägen und entwickeln.* Heidelberg: Dr. Rainer Wild-Stiftung (Dr. Rainer Wild Foundation). http://www.gesunde-ernaehrung.org/images/Dr_Rainer_Wild_Stiftung/07_Presse/Themenpapier/pdf/Geschmaecker_sind_verschieden.pdf.

Fahy, Ann, and Jim Spencer. 1999. "Wort Production." In *The Practical Brewer: A Manual for the Brewing Industry*. 3rd ed. Edited by John T. McCabe, 99–146. Wauwatosa, Wisconsin: Master Brewers Association of the Americas.

Fix, George J., and Laurie Fix. 1991. *Vienna, Märzen, Oktoberfest*. Boulder: Brewers Publications.

Foster, Terry. 1990. *Pale Ale*. Boulder: Brewers Publications.

———. 1992. *Porter*. Boulder: Brewers Publications.

Fowle, Zach. 2016. "The new IPA." *Draft*. July 18. http://draftmag.com /the-new-ipa-2/.

Gastl, M., S. Hanke, and W. Back. 2008. "'Drinkability'—Balance and Harmony of Components as Well as an Incentive for Continuing to Drink." *Brauwelt International* 26(3): 148–53.

Hanke, S., V. Ditz, M. Herrmann, W. Back, T. Becker, and M. Krottenthaler. 2010. "Influence of Ethyl Acetate, Isoamyl Acetate and Linalool on Off-Flavour Perception in Beer." *Brewing Science* 63(7–8): 94–99.

Hieronymus, Stan. 2005. *Brew Like a Monk: Trappist, Abbey, and Strong Belgian Ales and How to Brew Them*. Boulder: Brewers Publications.

———. 2012. *For the Love of Hops: The Practical Guide to Aroma, Bitterness and the Culture of Hops*. Boulder: Brewers Publications.

Hornsey, Ian S. 2003. *A History of Beer and Brewing*. Cambridge, UK: Royal Society of Chemistry.

Jackson, Michael. 1982a. *The Pocket Guide to Beer: A Discriminating Guide to the World's Finest Brews*. New York: Perigee Trade.

———. 1982b. *The World Guide to Beer*. London: New Burlington Books.

Klemp, K. Florian. 2007. "Belgian Witbier." *All About Beer Magazine*, vol. 28(3), July 1.

———. 2010. "Stylistically Speaking Schwarzbier." *All About Beer Magazine*, vol. 30(6), January 1.

Knudsen, Finn B. 1999. "Fermentation, Principles and Practices." In *The Practical Brewer: A Manual for the Brewing Industry*. 3rd ed. Edited by John T. McCabe, 235–61. Wauwatosa, Wisconsin: Master Brewers Association of the Americas.

Kunze, Wolfgang. 2004. *Technology Brewing and Malting*. Translated by Sue Pratt. 3rd int. ed. Berlin: VLB.

Lodahl, Martin. 1994. "Belgian, Trappists and Abbey Beers." *Brewing Techniques*, Brewing in Styles, vol. 2, no. 6 (November/December). Republished online at http://www.morebeer.com/brewingtechniques/library/styles/2_6style.html.

Mallett, John. 2014. *Malt: A Practical Guide from Field to Brewhouse*. Boulder: Brewers Publications.

Markowski, Phil, with contributions from Tomme Arthur and Yvan De Baets. 2004. *Farmhouse Ales: Culture and Craftsmanship in the Belgian Tradition*. Boulder: Brewers Publications.

Maye, John Paul, Robert Smith, and Jeremy Leker. 2016. "Humulinone Formation in Hops and Hop Pellets and Its Implications for Dry Hopped Beers." *Technical Quarterly of the Master Brewers Association of Americas* 53(1): 23–27. doi:10.1094/TQ-53-1-0227-01.

Miller, David G. 1990. *Continental Pilsener*. Boulder: Brewers Publications.

Moen, Alan. 2003. "Taxing the Pour." *All About Beer Magazine* vol. 24(2), May 1.

Mosher, Randy. 1994. "Parti-Gyle Brewing." *Brewing Techniques*, vol. 2, no. 2 (March/April). Republished online at http://www.morebeer.com /brewingtechniques/library/backissues/issue2.2/mosher.html.

Nagao, Yoko, Hozue Kodama, Toshihiko Yonezawa, Ayako Taguchi, Seiji Fujino, Koh Nakahara, Ken Haruma, and Tohru Fushiki. "Correlation between the Drinkability of Beer and Gastric Emptying." *Bioscience, Biotechnology, and Biochemistry* 62(5): 846–51. doi:10.1271/bbb.62.846.

Noonan, Gregory J. 1993. *Scotch Ale*. Boulder: Brewers Publications.

Ogle, Maureen. 2006. *Ambitious Brew*. Orlando: Harvest Books.

Oliver, Garrett. 2003. *The Brewmaster's Table*. New York: HarperCollins.

Oliver, Garrett, ed. 2012. *The Oxford Companion to Beer*. Oxford: Oxford University Press.

Palmer, John, and Colin Kaminski. 2013. *Water: A Comprehensive Guide for Brewers*. Boulder: Brewers Publications.

Palmer, John J. 2017. *How to Brew*. 4th ed. Boulder: Brewers Publications.

Patino, Hugo. 1999. "Overview of Cellar Operations." In *The Practical Brewer: A Manual for the Brewing Industry*. 3rd ed. Edited by John T. McCabe, 299–325. Wauwatosa, Wisconsin: Master Brewers Association of the Americas.

Peacock, Val. 2011. "Percent Co-Humulone in Hops: Effect on Bitterness, Utilization Rate, Foam Enhancement and Rate of Beer Staling." Proceedings of MBAA Annual Conference. http://www.mbaa.com/meetings/archive/2011/Proceedings/pages/O-31.aspx.

Pellettieri, Mary. 2015. *Quality Management: Essential Planning for Breweries*. Boulder: Brewers Publications.

Raines, Maribeth. 1993. "Methods of Sanitization and Sterilization." *Brewing Techniques*, vol. 1, no. 2 (July/August). Republished online at http://www.morebeer.com/brewingtechniques/library/backissues/issue1.2/raines.html.

Rehberger, Arthur J. and Gary E. Luther, 1999. "Wort Boiling." In *The Practical Brewer: A Manual for the Brewing Industry*. 3rd ed. Edited by John T. McCabe, 165–99. Wauwatosa, Wisconsin: Master Brewers Association of the Americas.

Rigby, F.L. 1972. "A Theory on the Flavor of Beer." *Journal of the American Society for Brewing Chemists*. 46–50.

Sanchez, Gil W. 1999. "Water." In *The Practical Brewer: A Manual For The Brewing Industry*. 3rd ed. Edited by John T. McCabe, 33–52. Wauwatosa, Wisconsin: Master Brewers Association of the Americas.

Smith, Gregg. 1998. *Beer in America*. Boulder: Siris Books.

Sparrow, Jeff. 2005. *Wild Brews: Beer Beyond the Influence of Brewer's Yeast*. Boulder: Brewers Publications.

Steele, Mitch. 2012. *IPA: Brewing Techniques, Recipes and the Evolution of India Pale Ale*. Boulder: Brewers Publications.

Takacs, Peter, and James J. Hackbarth. 2007. "Oxygen-Enhanced Fermentation." *Technical Quarterly of the Master Brewers Association of Americas* 44(2): 104–107.

Thausing, Julius, A.H. Bauer, and Anton Schwarz, eds. 1882. *Theory and Practice of the Preparation of Malt and the Fabrication of Beer: With Special Reference to the Vienna Process of Brewing*. Philadelphia: H.C. Baird & Co.

Vance, Del. 2006. *Beer in the Beehive*. Salt Lake City: Dream Garden Press.

Vaughan, Anne, Tadhg O'Sullivan, and Douwe van Sinderen. 2005. "Enhancing the Microbiological Stability of Malt and Beer: A Review." *Journal of the Institute of Brewing* 111(4): 355–71.

Vygotsky, L.S. 1978. *Mind in Society*. Edited by Michael Cole, Vera John-Steiner, Sylvia Scribner, and Ellen Souberman. Cambridge, MA: Harvard University Press.

Wackerbauer, K., and U. Balzer. 1992. "Der Einfluss des Cohumulons auf die Bierqualität." *Brauwelt* 122(10/11): 396–98.

Wahl, Robert, and Max Henius. 1908. *American Handy Book of the Brewing, Malting and Auxiliary Trades*. 3rd ed. Chicago: Wahl-Henius Institute.

Warner, Eric. 1992. *German Wheat Beer*. Boulder: Brewers Publications.

White, Chris, and Jamil Zainasheff. 2010. *Yeast: The Practical Guide to Beer Fermentation*. Boulder: Brewers Publications.

Yenne, Bill. 2003. *The American Brewer: From Colonial Evolution To Microbrew Revolution*. St. Paul: MBI Publishing Company.

Index

Entries in **boldface** refer to photos and illustrations.

Guinness Foreign Extra Stout, 16

Guinness Original (Extra Stout), 16

Hallertauer Brauerei, 172

Hansen, Emil Christian, 37

Harris, John, xv

Hart Brewing, 162

haze, 60, 76

hefeweizen, 30, 31

Heisel, Scott, 75

helles, 8, 32, 40, 78, 97, 171, 173;
    Bavarian, 33, 74; classic, 33; food
    with, 109; German, 54

Helmke, Jim, 78, 99

Herkimer Pub & Brewery, 93

Heron, Carl, 215-16

Herr, Grandfather, 1, 73

Hieronymus, Stan, 23, 24

Hilltop Brewery, 138

Hindy, Steve, 205-6

*History of the Brewing Industry and
    Brewing Science in America,* 74

Hoegaarden, witbier from, 27

Hoegaarden Wit, 27

Hollister Brewing Company, 93, 94,
    186-87

Hollister Tiny Bubbles, 93, 94, 186;
    recipes for, 187-88, 188-90

Homebrew Shop, The, 190

Hop Growers of America, 117

Hop Quality Group, 166

hopping, 47; dry, xiv, xv, 84, 88, 90,
    112; flavor, 87; rates, 14, 27, 117

hops, 3, 24, 34, 65, **86**, 109, 128-29;
    adding, 88; aroma, 89, 119;
    Belma, 79; bitterness from, 54,
    86, 119; Bravo, 79; Cascade,

79, 85; Centennial, 85, 120;
Chinook, 85, 119, 121; Citra,
79; compounds in, 62, 64, 89;
contracts for, 120; degradation
of, 90; desire for, 102; East Kent
Goldings, 84; experimenting
with, 91; forward, 79, 83, 92;
fresh, 116; high-alpha acid, 84;
market for, 117; Northwest,
84, 92; pricing of, 117; profile/
balanced, 58; rates, 28; selecting,
88; Simcoe, 121; using, 117, 120;
varieties, 83, 87, 88

*Hops: Their Cultivation, Composition,
    and Usage* (Peacock), 89

hot water extraction (HWE), 120

Humboldt Brewing Company, 218

humulinone, 88, 89, 90, 91

HWY 128 Session Series, 94

IBU. *See* international bitterness units

India pale ales (IPAs), xvi, 54, 85, 121,
    122, 141, 158, 202; ABV of, 91,
    92, 119; Belgian, 115; craze of,
    102; double, 77, 116, 142, 152;
    English, 83; evolution of, 83;
    guidelines for, 82; mock, 118;
    New England-style, 102; session-
    style, 82, 83, 84, 86, 87, 90, 91;
    triple, 77, 113

ingredients, cost of, 116-18

Institute of Brewing and Distilling, 215

intangibles, considering, 67-68

international bitterness units (IBUs), 3,
    14, 30, 33, 37, 54, 79, 84, 85, 86,
    88, 89, 90, 93, 95; low, 91; palate
    fatigue and, 62